—— THE ——
COMPLETE
WAR YEARS

LIFE IN BRITAIN DURING 1939 TO 1945

THE
COMPLETE
WAR YEARS

LIFE IN BRITAIN DURING 1939 TO 1945

JANICE ANDERSON

FUTURA

First published in Great Britain in 2010 by Futura

Copyright © Omnipress 2010

The moral right of the author has been asserted.

A CIP catalogue record for this book
is available from the British Library.

ISBN 978-0-7088-6546-0

Typeset in Great Britain by Omnipress Limited
Printed and bound in Great Britain

Futura
An imprint of
Little, Brown Book Group
100 Victoria Embankment
London EC4Y 0DY

An Hachette UK Company
www.hachette.co.uk

www.littlebrown.co.uk

Photo credits: Getty Images

The material in this book was previously used in:
The War Years
Women of the War Years
Children of the War Years

CONTENTS

INTRODUCTION

When the United Kingdom's prime minister, Neville Chamberlain announced on the wireless on 3 September 1939 that the country was at war with Germany, it was for the second time in the twentieth century – and with the same enemy. The difference this time, as Mother and Home *magazine put it in their November 1939 issue, was that 'the last was a soldier's war. This one is Everybody's'.*

TELLING THE COUNTRY
British prime minister Neville Chamberlain, 1869–1940, breaks the news in a BBC studio that Britain is at war.

It had been clear for much of the 1930s that Britain was likely to be caught up in a war again with the increasingly aggressive Germany of Adolf Hitler and the National Socialists. Sunday, 3 September 1939, was a beautiful day in England – 'a fine, sunny morning, apples shining', noted Virginia Woolf in her garden in Sussex. Like many others the length and breadth of the country, she had just heard Great Britain's prime minister, Neville Chamberlain, announce on the BBC wireless that, because Germany had made no undertaking to halt its invasion of Poland, a country with whom Britain had treaty obligations, the country was once again at war with Germany.

Most people were not surprised. Horrified, hugely distressed and sickened perhaps, but not surprised. As the 1930s progressed, the threatening activities in Europe of Germany's Fascist chancellor Adolf Hitler in his pursuit of *lebensraum* for Germany had made war look increasingly likely. And Italy's Fascist leader Benito Mussolini had also been flexing his muscles throughout the decade, invading Abyssinia (present-day Ethiopia) in 1936.

APPEASEMENT

'Appeasement' was the British government's answer to the actions of Germany for much of the 1930s. Exhausted and deeply in debt after the Great War of 1914–18, and battered again by the Depression of the early 1930s, Britain was in no state to fight another major war. Neville Chamberlain's last attempts at appeasement came during September 1938. After a flight to Munich to join the French prime minister, Edouard Daladier, in talks, the two leaders hoped to persuade Hitler not to invade Czechoslovakia and thus avert war. Chamberlain returned to England, waving a piece of paper in the air at Heston Airport and crying that he brought back 'peace with honour'. Later, he told a great crowd

ROYAL BROADCAST
On 3 September 1939, King George VI, who reigned from 1936–1952, made a broadcast to the nation after the outbreak of World War Two.

in Downing Street that he had brought 'peace for our time'. 'Our time' lasted less than a year.

AIR WARFARE

Britain had been bombed from zeppelins and twin-engined bombers during the 1914–18 war, and the government accepted that in any future conflict, air warfare would bring the country as much in the line of fire as its fighting forces overseas. In September 1939, Britain's people knew that they would soon be fighting on a 'home front' as dangerous and as full of death and destruction as any battle front.

THE KING BROADCASTS TO THE EMPIRE

'There may be dark days ahead, and war can no longer be confined to the battlefield. But we can only do the right as we see the right, and reverently commit our cause to God. If one and all we keep resolutely faithful to it ... then with God's help we will prevail. May he bless and keep us all.'

George VI addressing the nation via the BBC. 3 September 1939.

PEACE IN OUR TIME
30 September 1938. Neville Chamberlain making his 'peace in our time' address at Heston Airport on his return from Munich.

WOMEN AND WAR

The British government and its officials all agreed that such a war, if it were to be fought to a victorious end, would have to involve everyone, including women. Nazi Germany's ideal woman, tied to home, kitchen and children, did not play well in government war-planning offices in Britain.

This is not to say that Britain's male-dominated governing class was unsympathetic towards the German 'ideal woman', it was just that they knew it would not work in wartime. It was every British woman's patriotic duty to serve the country in any way she could in wartime, to respond to a national emergency. In no way did this imply that, once peace had returned, women should not also return to their pre-war lives.

This attitude was so ingrained that, well into the war, it allowed Prime Minister Winston Churchill to say that women who were asking for the same pay as their male colleagues in the teaching profession were being 'impertinent'. As late as 1944, an official government publication dealing with mobilisation in Britain and called, ironically enough, Man Power, said that 'the whole business of mobilising and employing women – wives, sweethearts and daughters – is new and tricky. It creates special and dangerous problems … over and above those encountered in the conscription and mobilisation of men.'

'Sweetheart' was an attractively romantic way to refer to young women, used most famously as the label for perhaps the best-known and most admired woman in wartime Britain,

FORCES' SWEETHEART
The popular British singer, Vera Lynn, became the Forces' sweetheart during World War Two. She was one of Britain's premier entertainers during the war, helping to keep up the spirits when times were difficult.

QUEUING FOR FOOD
This particular shopkeeper has posted a notice that only local people will be served and that identity cards will be inspected before any purchase can be made.

warm-voiced singer Vera Lynn, the 'Forces' Sweetheart'. But it was also a very old-fashioned word, harking back to Victorian and Edwardian days. It did not suggest the modern woman that 1930s feminists were trying to promote.

This inability to see women as simply potential workers – nobody thought there was anything 'tricky' about the fact that male workers were also 'husbands, lovers and sons' – would take more than six years of war to eradicate from male-dominated official thinking. It was, however, well buried during the war: the only country that was more effective than the United

Kingdom in mobilising women to help 'win the Peace' was the Soviet Union. And the USSR went a step further than even the British were prepared to go, sending their women to fight in their armed forces.

Thousands of British women joined the auxiliary army, navy and air force services or their nursing and medical units, during the war, and did essential, invaluable work at home and abroad. Thousands more worked in Civil Defence, courting danger and risking death day and night in London, and also in the country's industrial cities and dockyards – the destruction

PIG FOOD COLLECTION
Household waste was collected for pig feed during the war, a novel scheme set up in the London borough of Westminster.

of which was the Germany Luftwaffe's main aim. The number of women in the Women's Land Army and the Timber Corps had reached nearly 85,000 by mid-1943. Then there were the thousands of women who worked in industry and who were, especially if they worked in munitions factories, just as likely to be the targets of German bombers as were their sisters in Civil Defence.

Perhaps Britain's greatest asset in its fight against Hitler's Germany was its vast army of housewives. While remaining true to the 'women as homemakers' ideal, housewives took up the enormous challenges wartime threw at them without flinching. Most of them suddenly found themselves on their own, in sole charge of their households which might well include, as well as their own children, evacuees, billeted workers, and relatives bombed out of their homes. They quickly dealt with all the business of protecting their homes from damage, especially by incendiary bombs.

They queued for hours in all weathers outside shops, clutching the ration books for everyone in their household, and then, probably, queuing for hours more for a bus to get their shopping home. As the war went on, they learnt how to make nourishing meals with less and less – and thought nothing of serving them on top of the Morrison shelter which took up so much room that the dining table had had to make way for it. They became adept at growing their own vegetables, even on the roof of the Anderson shelter in the garden, and at keeping hens and pigs, carefully saving all their food waste either for their own pig or for the pig-swill bins that were put out on the pavements. They made do and mended so that they and their children were neatly and warmly, if not always fashionably, dressed.

As well as all this, most housewives found time to do their bit for the war effort outside the home, perhaps by joining the WVS, or working in Red

SIMPLE MESSAGE
The simplicity of the message on this World War Two poster says it all.

Cross shops or the new Citizen Advice Bureau information centres. They drove ambulances, worked in canteens, British Restaurants and emergency feeding centres. They joined savings groups and became part-time air raid wardens. There was very little that the ordinary housewife was not able to do if she put her mind to it.

The war over, most women left the services, the munitions factories, the hospitals and all their other wartime jobs to become housewives again: by 1951 the numbers of women in full-time employment had returned to 1939 levels, but now Britain was a welfare state, with good education and health systems available to all. There was also increasing prosperity for all, a prosperity that, to be enjoyed, had to be paid for. Women had learned how to hold down jobs while running a home during the war and they were prepared to do so again, to ensure that they and their families could enjoy the new prosperity that the new Elizabethan Age, and its female head of state, Elizabeth II, promised them.

CHILDREN AND WAR

For the children of Britain, the war years were an extraordinary experience. To take the bad statistics first: more than 7,700 children under the age of sixteen were killed as a result of enemy action and another near 7,700 were seriously wounded. Many thousands more were left fatherless, orphaned or without family altogether, as enemy bombing destroyed whole houses and everyone in them. For thousands of children and their families who escaped all this, there were many years of social upheaval, of being moved from one temporary kind of housing to another, of being evacuated, sometimes 'for the duration', to a part of the country many miles from home and family, where social customs were very different from anything they had experienced before.

GOING TO A NEW HOME
Some of the thousands of children who were evacuated to the countryside after the start of World War Two, wait for transport to their new reception areas.

CHAPTER ONE

WAR COMES TO THE HOME FRONT

WAR COMES TO THE HOME FRONT

The second great war of the twentieth century, which broke out in September 1939, engulfed the home populations of most of the countries that got caught up in it. In Europe, millions of men, women and children were killed or wounded and whole cities were devastated.

Because Britain escaped invasion – by a hairsbreadth, as later historians have come to believe – the country as a whole also escaped death and destruction to the horrifying scale that was experienced in Europe. But the country did not escape unscathed. There were many thousands of deaths, much injury, both physical and psychological, to men, women and children, as well as hardship and devastation.

PROTECTING THE HOME FRONT

Defence spending and planning for an integrated home defence and anti-air-raid system were stepped up, as was spending on bomber command so that Britain would be able to take the war to the enemy. The devastating effect of bombing from the air, demonstrated not only by the Italians in Abyssinia but also by German and Italian fascist forces in the Spanish Civil War, concentrated minds on how best to deal with the great number of casualties and widespread devastation from the all-out strike on the British mainland that officials had long thought would be the inevitable start to any war with Germany.

AIR RAID WARDENS' SERVICE

An Air Raid Wardens' Service, set up in April 1937, was an integral part of Britain's Civil Defence organisation. In January 1938, the first Air Raid Precautions Act, based on the findings of a secret air raid precautions subcommittee set up as far back as 1924, came into force. By September 1939, local authorities, empowered by the Act, had established a properly planned Air Raid Precautions (ARP) system involving ARP warden command posts (most of them very basic concrete boxes, surrounded by sandbags), as well as other Civil Defence services, such as emergency ambulance services (which in London included taxis, commandeered for

THE EMERGENCY POWERS (DEFENCE) ACT

The Emergency Powers (Defence) Act, passed in August 1939, was a stringent and wide-ranging Act that gave the government the power to make any regulation considered necessary or expedient to ensure public safety, defend the country, support all services essential to the life of the community and maintain public order – all without having to seek the approval of Parliament. In the coming years, the thousands of rules and regulations made under the terms of the Emergency Powers Act affected everyone in the country, covering everything from banks, munitions factories, wages and working hours to the internment of aliens and the 'enemy within'.

ME AND MY DOG
An ARP warden sits reading a book while on duty with his dog at his side.

the work and painted grey), first aid posts, a rescue, repair and demolition service, and local fire services expanded by the creation of an Auxiliary Fire Service.

During the anxious days of August and September 1938, local authorities had begun digging trenches in public parks and gardens. However, these were not to be filled in, and weeks before war was declared digging was increased so that by 3 September 1939, an estimated 500,000 people could have sheltered in trenches, guided to them by 'To the Trenches' notices in city streets – a dreadful reminder for many older men of the trench warfare they had experienced on the Western Front in the Great War.

Barrage balloons, or 'blimps', first seen in the sky over London in August 1938, also appeared again, at first mainly over London – tethered with metal cables to defend against low-level enemy air attack. Air raid sirens were sounded, so that people would recognise their meaning: 'enemy bombers approaching, take shelter'. And there were piles of sandbags everywhere, protecting doorways to important buildings, entrances to underground stations, first aid posts,

1939
POPULAR CULTURE

POPULAR SONGS

- *Over The Rainbow*, by Judy Garland
- *Moonlight Serenade*, by Glenn Miller
- *Strange Fruit*, by Billie Holliday
- *When The Saints Go Marching In*, by Louis Armstrong
- *Jeepers Creepers*, by Al Donohue
- *Begin The Beguine*, Chick Henderson with Joe Loss and his band
- *At The Woodchoppers' Ball*, by Woody Herman
- *Beer Barrel Polka*, by Will Glahe
- *There'll Always be an England*, by Ross Parker and Harry Par-Davies

POPULAR FILMS

- *Gone With The Wind*, starring Vivien Leigh and Clark Gable
- *The Wizard of Oz*, starring Judy Garland
- *Jesse James*, starring Tyrone Power, Henry Fonda, Nancy Kelly and Randolph Scott
- *Mr Smith Goes To Washington*, starring James Stewart, Jean Arthur and Claude Rains
- *The Hunchback Of Notre Dame*, starring Charles Laughten, Sir Cedric Hardwicke and Maureen O'Hara

shops and restaurants – and the statue of Eros in London's Piccadilly Circus. Few people, many believing either that diplomacy would avert a war that nobody, either British or German, wanted, or that if war came it would be quickly over, thought in 1939 that they would be living with barrage balloons, sandbags, air-raid sirens and officious ARP wardens for six long years.

It was that other great anti air raid innovation – the blackout – that helped make ARP wardens unpopular with the general public, especially householders. Since it was essential that no chink of light should show to guide enemy night-time bombers to populated areas, blackout rules were stringent, both inside houses and out in the street. Many was the householder ordered by an ARP warden or policeman to turn out his lights. ARP wardens were all local men and women familiar with the streets they patrolled, and with such important details as who lived in what house, who lived alone, and where fire hydrants, gas-main covers and electricity boxes were.

THE BLACKOUTS

At home, between the hours of sunset and sunrise, householders had to put up blackout material over all windows and other openings through which light might show. This meant that every night (beginning on 1 September 1939 at half an hour before sunset) Britain's homeowners had to spend some time going round their houses, pulling curtains so tightly that no ray of light showed and sealing doors, windows, fanlights and skylights with black fabric or paper, cardboard and thick paper. Since this could take some time in larger houses, many people left the black fabric or cardboard over non-essential windows, or even painted them with black paint. Blackout materials had to remain in place until half an hour after sunrise. Many also criss-crossed their windows with sticky tape, to prevent flying glass in the event of a bombing raid.

TRYING IT FOR SIZE
Two women in Islington, London, try out the height of their new air raid shelter, distributed by the government as protection against German bombing raids.

ILLUMINATED HELMETS
A policeman prepares illuminated helmets for wear when assisting pedestrians and traffic during the blackout hours of winter.

Not surprisingly, blackout fabrics, paint and cardboard soon disappeared from shops. Also not surprisingly, beams of light did show, and householders were often disturbed by the sound of their front-door bell or knocker (painted with luminous paint so that it would show up in the dark) being operated by the firm fingers of an irate ARP warden or policeman, quick to point out deficiencies.

Many householders also thought it prudent to take measures against a gas attack. Poison gas had been a terrible scourge on the Western Front in the Great War, and officials had to assume that the Germans would use it again. When things were looking very bleak for the future of Europe in the summer of 1938, the government had issued gas masks – thirty-eight million of them – to every man, woman and child in Britain (babies had to wait until the first months of the war to get their own, very awkward-to-wear, gas masks). As well as issuing gas masks, the government also directed that gas contamination stations and Local Gas Identification Squads, recruited from among qualified chemists, must be set up. Street cleaners were trained to deal with its effects and people were alerted to the types of gas they might encounter, including tear gases, lung irritants and blister gases, and how they might smell. At home, householders tried to keep one room sufficiently sealed with cellulose sheets and tape to make it gas-proof.

Outside in the street, the blackout regulations were so stringent that they caused more deaths and accidents than the enemy – who did not actually cause any on mainland Britain in the first months of the war – and had to be slackened somewhat. The government's first blackout order was to turn off all street lighting, all shop lighting and all neon advertising signs. Citizens could not carry torches, or even light a cigarette. Whether or not to go out after dark became a major decision for many; one housewife considered the night she 'came through the blackout for the first time on my own' so momentous that she recorded it in her diary.

The total night-time blackness was supposed to be alleviated for pedestrians and motorists by the white lines that were painted on kerbs, walls, trees and lamp posts. That they were far from successful was demonstrated by the fact that in the first month of the war, the number of people killed in road accidents nearly doubled. Then there were the many who were injured, often seriously, by tripping over unseen kerbs

TAKING PRECAUTIONS
Thirty-eight million gas masks were issued to every man, woman and child in Britain.

and sandbags, driving into walls and trees, stepping off railway station platforms, even walking into streams and canals.

Clearly, the country could not carry on having one citizen in every five injured in some way because of the blackout regulations, and within a few weeks they were relaxed. People were allowed to carry a torch at night, provided its light was covered with a double layer of tissue paper and it was switched off during air-raid alerts – and provided, too, that one could purchase both the torches and the batteries needed to keep them working.

DEALING WITH GAS MASKS

Gas masks were ugly, even grotesque objects. Adults' gas masks had an unattractive pig's snout shape and smelled of rubber and disinfectant; children's came in a Mickey Mouse shape, with red rubber face pieces and shiny eye-piece rims. As for babies, their strangely shaped masks were so designed that mothers had to pump air into them with a bellows. Naturally, everyone hoped that they would never have to wear theirs. As the threat of gas attacks receded – and there was no punishment for not carrying one's gas mask in its cardboard box – so they were either not carried at all or forgotten about and left behind in shops and cinemas, in the office, on buses and trains.

1939

JANUARY

- Hitler predicts in a speech to the Reichstag that a war in Europe would lead to 'the annihilation of the Jewish race in Europe'.
- 71 people die across Victoria in one of Australia's worst bushfires – it becomes known as 'Black Friday'.
- An earthquake kills 30,000 in Chile.
- In the Spanish Civil War, Spanish Nationlist troops, with the aid of Italy, take Barcelona.
- Hitler orders Plan Z – a five-year naval expansion programme with the aim of crushing the Royal Navy.

FEBRUARY

- British PM Neville Chamberlain announces that any German attack on France will be taken as an assault on Britain.
- The Golden Gate International Exposition opens in San Francisco.
- Sit-down strikes are outlawed by the Supreme Court of the United States.
- Japanese troops occupy Hainan Island.
- Borley Rectory – 'the most haunted house in England' – is badly damaged by fire.

ALTERNATIVE STREET LIGHTING
Workmen prepare for emergency blackouts in London by providing alternative street lighting.

Other rulings that were relaxed within a few weeks of the war's beginning were those that had closed all theatres and cinemas and stopped football matches and other events at which large numbers of people might come together. This was because the government was sure that the war would start with a massive air strike on the British mainland and that the best way of preventing unmanageable numbers of casualties was not to let people gather together in large numbers. When the expected air strike did not materialise, by which time it had been realised that keeping people marooned in their homes and away from social contact was extremely bad for morale, cinemas and theatres were opened again and the football programme swung into action.

FIGHTING THE WAR ON THE HOME FRONT

Nothing much of a warlike nature happened in Britain in the first weeks and months of the war. At sea, the merchant navy came under attack at once, the liner *Athenia* being torpedoed and sunk by a German U-boat (submarine) on 4 September with the loss of 112 civilian lives. It was not until November that the first bomb was dropped on Britain, in the Shetlands.

It was an isolated incident, far from the massive all-out attack that everyone had expected. Even over in France, the British Expeditionary Force (BEF) was not seeing any serious action.

At home, many of the inconveniences and difficulties experienced by people came as a result of Britain's own, long-thought-out plans for the defence of the country being put into operation. Petrol rationing was introduced three weeks after the start of the war, and food rationing, announced to no one's surprise in November (there had been rationing during the Great War, after all), finally came into force in January 1940.

AERIAL CAMERAS
WAAF instrument repairers with aerial cameras on which they work. On the left is an F24, which can take 5 x 5 exposures either manually or automatically. The other two are G28 gun cameras.

Conscription, which had been introduced for the first time in peacetime, by the Military Training Act of May 1939, when it applied only to young men of twenty and twenty-one, was extended to all men between eighteen and forty-one by the National Service (Armed Forces) Act, passed just two days before war was declared.

By this time well over a 250,000 men and women had already volunteered for the armed forces. Men in the uniforms of the Army, Royal Navy and Royal Air Force and women in their forces' uniforms – the Auxiliary Territorial Service (ATS), the Women's Royal Naval Service (WRNS) and the Women's Auxiliary Air Force (WAAF) – were becoming increasingly familiar sights in towns and cities the length and breadth of the country. And, as there had also been five times as many volunteers for the various Civil Defence services as for the armed forces, their identifying brassards (armbands) and uniforms,

WRNS
Women from the Royal Naval Service (WRNS) were becoming increasingly familiar sights in towns and cities the length and breadth of the country.

when they were given them, would soon also be just as familiar.

THE BORE WAR

People soon began to call this second great war of the twentieth century the 'Bore War', a play on words that recalled the Boer War at the end of Queen Victoria's reign. That war had been fought thousands of miles away; perhaps this one would also be fought away from home. Gas masks began to be left at home (though their cardboard cases were often used as lunch boxes by schoolchildren), children were brought back from the 'reception areas' to their urban homes and families, and shops and restaurants began reducing the size of the barricades of sandbags, many of which were already rotting, they had built around themselves.

In March 1940, the 'bore war' – by now being called, American-style, the 'phoney war' – began to turn into something much more menacing for the home front. Four days after Finland, which had been fighting the Soviet Union's Red Army for four months, finally surrendered, a bomb, dropped by a German plane apparently mistaking a village for an airfield, or perhaps the Scapa Flow naval base, killed a civilian in the Orkneys. A German U-boat had already had one spectacular success at Scapa Flow. When the battleship *Royal Oak* was torpedoed in October 1939, 800 sailors had lost their lives.

At much the same time, the German war machine, having seen Eastern Europe carved up into German and Russian spheres of influence, turned its full attention westwards. It looked first towards Scandinavia. Here there were rich mineral resources as well as bases for German U-boats, already apparently winning the battle of the Atlantic, where British merchant naval losses had been considerable.

On 8 April 1940, the British and French followed up an anti-German navy mine-laying exercise they had carried out along the coast of Norway by sending a small expeditionary force to Narvik in an attempt to stop the transport of Swedish iron ore to Germany. The next day, Germany, ignoring Norway's declaration of neutrality, attacked the country with combined air, sea and land forces so effectively that within half a day they had seized several important Norwegian ports and towns, including Narvik and Trondheim. The fightback from Norway and

NARVIK BURNS
The Norwegian town of Narvik burns after an Allied bombardment on 31 May 1940.

1939

MARCH

- Gandhi begins his fast in protest to the autocratic rule in India.
- Franco assumes control in Madrid.
- German troops move to occupy Czechoslovakia.
- The Spanish Civil War comes to an end as Madrid surrenders.

APRIL

- Faisal II becomes King of Iraq.
- Italy invades Albania.
- New York World Fair opens.
- Great Britain and France guarantee their support should Greece and Romania be attacked by Germany or Italy.
- Roosevelt pleads with Hitler and Mussolini to stop the violence.

MAY

- Lina Medina from Peru, is the youngest confirmed mother in medical history having given birth at the age of five.
- Germany and Italy sign the 'Pact of Steel' – a friendship alliance.
- US submarine USS *Squalus* sinks during a test dive, killing 26 sailors.
- DC Comics publishes its second popular superhero – *Batman*.

Denmark, also attacked, was undermanned and under-resourced, and British support was not backed up by air cover. The result was inevitable. Denmark and Norway were occupied; British forces could not be withdrawn from southern Norway until June.

The greatest change at home resulting from the embarrassing Norwegian debacle was the replacement of Prime Minister Neville Chamberlain, by Winston Churchill, as prime minister and minister of defence in a Coalition Government, on 10 May 1940.

On the day that Winston Churchill became prime minister, Britain heard the dreadful news that the Netherlands, Luxembourg and Belgium had been invaded. France's Maginot Line, which the BEF was helping to defend, looked very vulnerable. The 'phoney war' was over. On 13 May, a Royal Navy destroyer brought Queen Wilhelmina of the Netherlands to Britain, and Churchill, in his first address as prime minister to the House of Commons, told the British people that he had nothing to offer them 'but blood, toil, tears and sweat'. Two days later, Holland surrendered and Germany's blitzkrieg ('lightning war') tore through Belgium (which surrendered on 27 May) and broke through the French defences into France. French and British forces retreated before them.

The first the British people knew that the BEF – an army with nine divisions, more than 250,000 fighting men and thousands of vehicles – was in desperate need of rescue from beaches in northern France, in a pocket around the port of Dunkirk (Dunkerque), was on 29 May. On that day a call went out for all sea-going vessels that could be brought into use to cross the Channel to help the Royal Navy in an evacuation operation, called Operation Dynamo, that had begun on 26 May.

An armada of 'little ships' – pleasure steamers, lifeboats, rowing boats, fishing smacks, coal

A NEW PRIME MINISTER
Winston Churchill (1874–1965) leaving 10 Downing Street after his appointment as prime minister on 10 May 1940. He is accompanied by air minister Sir Kingsley Wood (left) and foreign secretary Anthony Eden (right).

WINSTON CHURCHILL

Winston Leonard Spencer Churchill, who became Britain's wartime leader on 10 May 1940, was descended from the great eighteenth-century military commander John Churchill, 1st Duke of Marlborough. Born in 1874, Churchill entered parliament as a Conservative in 1900, but switched to the Liberal Party six years later. He played a busy and energetic political part in the Great War, first as First Lord of the Admiralty (a post to which he was returned on 3 September 1939), then as Minister of Munitions. An outspoken and often critical politician after 1918, Churchill, back in the Conservative fold in 1924, spent much of the 1930s in the political wilderness, almost the only voice warning against the threat of Nazi Germany. In May 1940, Churchill, by then 65, believed he had begun 'a walk with destiny' for which his whole life up to then had been a preparation.

DUNKIRK RETREAT
Weary British soldiers waiting for evacuation from Dunkirk.

barges, yachts and tugs – went across the Channel and helped the Royal Navy. By 3 June, nearly 340,000 men, including many French troops, had been evacuated from the beaches of Dunkirk. Left behind in France were the BEF's heavy weaponry, ammunition and equipment, either abandoned or destroyed, and more than 68,000 men killed, wounded or missing. Dunkirk was a retreat and a defeat, but Winston Churchill, while reminding the House of Commons that 'wars are not won by retreats', still managed to turn it into a powerful morale-booster for the nation. The 'Dunkirk spirit' that Churchill invoked helped get Britain through the war.

The soldiers of the BEF, who returned to Britain to a heroes' welcome, with cheers, flag-waving and cups of tea, rather than the recriminations many of them had expected, found that they would not be alone in the defence of the nation. There was now a newly formed volunteer organisation, called 'Local Defence Volunteers' to help them.

On 14 May, people listening to the BBC's Home Service after that evening's nine o'clock news bulletin had heard Secretary of State for War, Anthony Eden, announcing that he was forming a new local defence organisation, which he called Local Defence Volunteers (LVD), that would give ordinary citizens, 'especially those not eligible to enrol in the armed forces', the chance to help in the defence of their country 'in its hour of peril'. He asked men who were British subjects and aged between seventeen and sixty-five to register at their local police station. They would not be paid, but they would be given uniforms (which they were – eventually), weapons (also eventually) and training.

THE HOME GUARD

By the next day some 250,000 men had already answered Eden's call – far more than the government had hoped or expected. By the end of June, the number of volunteers had reached one and a half million. From July, they were no longer called Local Defence Volunteers, Winston Churchill himself deciding that the name was uninspiring. Officially, the men were now members of the Home Guard; unofficially, because many of them were quite old and because in their first weeks they had no uniforms, no weapons (apart, perhaps, from a World War One rifle bayonet welded to a pole, or a pitchfork), and no training, they were soon dubbed 'Dad's Army'.

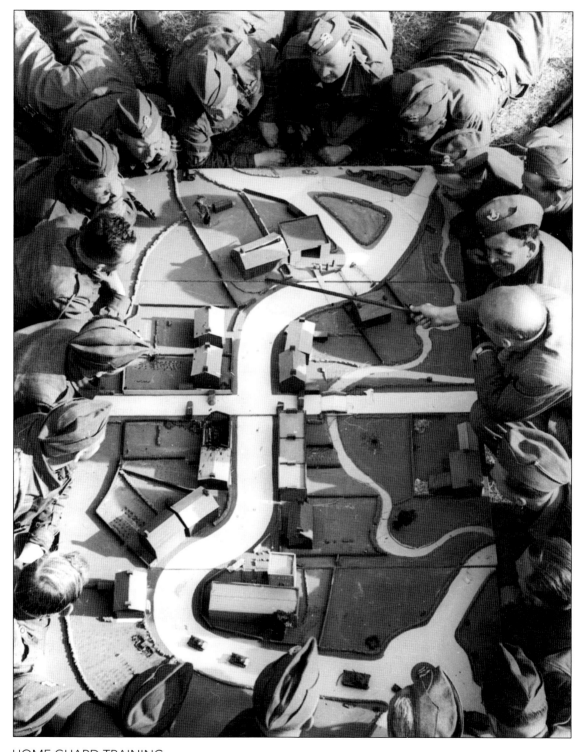

HOME GUARD TRAINING
Home guardsmen learn village defence at the War Office Training School in Osterley Park, which was situated west of London.

LOADING THE SPIGOT MORTAR
Members of the Post Office Home Guard get lessons on how to load a spigot mortar at a summer training camp in Hertfordshire.

The Home Guard, the largest civilian army ever formed in Britain, was, once trained and in uniform, a proficient and well-organised force, far from its 'Dad's Army' image. It knew all the basic army skills, from map-reading and reconnaissance to signalling in the field and carrying out night patrols, how to hunt, ambush and destroy tanks, how to make Molotov cocktails and how to carry out street fighting. . . While it was never called on to carry out the more extreme of these tasks, the Home Guard was kept busy until mid-1944, manning anti-aircraft batteries and coastal defences, guarding arms and fuel dumps, and helping in Civil Defence work, including teaching men and women how to use guns. Their existence meant that the regular armed forces were freed to fight overseas while the Home Guard's help in the preparations for the D-Day landings of 1944 was vital. France fell on 16 June 1940. 'I expect the Battle of Britain is about to begin,' Churchill told the House of Commons two days later. 'Let us therefore brace ourselves to our duties and so bear ourselves that, if the British Empire and its Commonwealth last for a thousand years, men will still say: "This was their finest hour".'

THE MEN OF DAD'S ARMY

Many Home Guard men were too old for active service, others were either not yet old enough to join up or were in reserved occupations. In the beginning, motley gatherings of the local bank manager and MP, butchers, bakers and farm labourers, as well as ex-brigadiers, colonels and naval captains, might have looked unlikely defenders of the nation. In November 1941, membership of the Home Guard became compulsory, on a part-time basis, for all men aged between eighteen and fifty-four who were not in the armed forces or some other form of Civil Defence. At its peak, the Home Guard numbered over 1,793,000 men, 1,206 of whom died on duty.

GUESS WHO?

A young gunner in the London Home Guard demonstrates camouflage techniques, using old pieces of sacking to disguise himself at his post.

The Battle of Britain did not have clear-cut start and finish dates. From about mid-June until mid-September, through a glorious English summer of fresh mornings and clear blue skies, Germany's air chief Hermann Goering launched his fighter planes against the RAF's bases. The destruction of the RAF and its airfields was essential to Hitler's invasion plan, Operation Sealion, which was timed to start on 15 September. Ironically, 15 September was the busiest day of the Battle of Britain, the Luftwaffe launching more than 1,700 sorties against southern England. After this date, the Germans, having failed to destroy Britain's airfields, changed tactics. Their invasion plan, postponed several times, was shelved. Britain's cities and industrial heartland would be bombed instead.

THE BLITZ

Now the Home Front really was in the front line. It would stay there for four long years, from the terrible Blitz of September 1940 to May 1941 to the V-1 flying bomb and V-2 long-range rocket attacks of 1944–45.

Hitler's attempt at an invasion of Britain

BATTLE OF BRITAIN

At the beginning of the battle, the RAF had about 470 serviceable aircraft, 330 of them Spitfires and Hurricanes. The Luftwaffe had 1,500 aircraft massed behind the French coast. During August, the RAF lost over 30 planes a day, at a time when Britain's aircraft production was running at about 95 fighter planes a week. By October 1940, the RAF has lost just over 1,000 aircraft, the Luftwaffe about 1,800.

In July 1940, the RAF had about 1,100 pilots, many just a year or two out of school. As well as British-born pilots, there were New Zealanders, Canadians, Americans, South Africans, Belgians, French, Poles and Czechs – and an Israeli and a Jamaican. A total of 307 of these men had been killed or listed as missing or captured by September. There were 300 wounded men. In all, Britain lost 537 airmen in the Battle of Britain, and Germany over 2,500.

did not come in the form of parachute troops landing out of the sky, as had happened in Europe and which Eden had anticipated in his BBC announcement of the formation of the Local Defence Volunteers in May. Instead, the air-raid sirens, last heard by many on the day that Neville Chamberlain told the British people they were at war, wailed over London again in the late afternoon of 7 September 1940. The Blitz, a long-drawn-out attack of Britain from the air, had begun.

The sound of the sirens was within minutes succeeded by a heavy, droning hum as hundreds of enemy bombers approached. Then came the thuds of thousands of bombs exploding, many of them incendiary bombs to start fires, and most of them in the East End docklands. The All Clear sounded at 6 p.m. But the fires burning in the East End acted as a marker for the Luftwaffe, who came back two hours later. This time, the All Clear did not sound until 4.30 the next morning.

Up until 7 September, nearly 4,000 British civilians had already been killed or wounded by the enemy. The attacks that started on 7 September were of a very different intensity. The numbers of enemy aircraft involved were huge, and their raids on London went on for fifty-seven nights without a break. There were also many daylight attacks. Nor did the Luftwaffe confine its attacks to the East End and the City. Within a week, the West End was being targeted, too.

In the coming weeks, many familiar West End buildings, from the John Lewis Oxford Street department store, which was completely burnt

DEVASTATION IN THE CITY
Damaged buildings in Cannon Street in the heart of the City of London during the Blitz.

1939

JUNE

- The last public execution takes place in France of convicted murderer Eugene Weidmann.
- Benny Goodman's radio series, *Song School*, comes to an end.
- A cargo ship, *St Louis*, is turned away from Florida carrying a cargo of 907 Jewish refugees.
- The government of Siam changes its name to Thailand ('Free Land').

JULY

- The last Jewish enterprises in Germany are closed down.
- The First World Science Fiction Convention opens in New York.
- Gandhi writes to Hitler addressing him as 'my friend', asking him to stop any possible conflict.

AUGUST

- Germany and the Soviet Union sign a non-aggression pact.
- The very first jet aircraft takes to the skies.
- The musical *The Wizard of Oz* premieres in Hollywood.
- Hitler and Stalin agree to divide Europe between themselves.
- IRA bomb explodes in Coventry, killing five people.

out, to Buckingham Palace, hit twice within four days, were bombed. 'Now we can look the East End in the face,' remarked Queen Elizabeth, before putting on her best coat, her pearls, her most spritely hat and a pair of high heels to visit the people and the bomb sites of the East End. The king and queen and the prime minister all grasped early on their importance as morale-boosters.

In the front line of the defence of local neighbourhoods during the Blitz was the ARP warden. The warden, usually a part-time volunteer, with one in six of them a woman, often worked for two and even three nights in a row. The normal ARP warden count was six to a post, with one post for every five hundred people. It was the ARP warden's job to report each bomb fall to the local control centre, which in turn allocated the emergency services (fire, ambulance and heavy rescue). When the emergency services arrived, the warden had to be on hand to direct them to fire hydrants, gas mains and those damaged buildings that were most likely to have people still inside.

Also of huge importance during the Blitz were volunteer fire watchers (later turned into an official arm of Civil Defence called the Fire Guard). Armed with just a bucket of sand and a stirrup pump, the men and women who acted as fire watchers for the long months of the Blitz saved many a building. They put incendiary bombs out of action by dumping sand on them, while the fine spray from a stirrup pump dealt with firebombs more safely than the heavy douse of water from a hose, which could cause bombs to fragment. It was fire watchers on the roof of St Paul's Cathedral, drawn from the cathedral's own staff, who saved Wren's masterpiece from destruction, allowing its dome to rise defiantly and triumphantly above the smoke and flames of the burning city.

On the last really heavy bombing day of the

Blitz in London, 10 May 1941, the Mansion House and fourteen hospitals were hit, 2,000 fires raged across London, and the chamber of the House of Commons was destroyed. Winston Churchill made sure he was photographed for the newspapers and magazines, his familiar hat, overcoat and walking stick all in place, standing indomitably amidst the ruins of the House of Commons.

German bombers soon extended the range of their attacks beyond London, attacking major ports from Liverpool to Plymouth, the Midlands' industrial heartland and transport and communication links between Britain's big cities. Two of the most devastating raids outside London took place in Birmingham and Coventry, already the targets of dozens of attacks, in November. In Coventry on 14–15 November, nearly five hundred and seventy people were killed, the city's great medieval cathedral was destroyed and many factories were severely damaged; within days, most of the factories were patched up and working again. It was much the same in Birmingham, where a raid lasting eleven hours on 22–23 November started nearly six hundred fires and killed almost eight hundred people.

TAKING SHELTER

From now on, the British people, exhorted by

BUILDING A SHELTER
Two ARP members construct a dug-out in the garden of Mrs Sant of Mytton Street, Manchester, which is to be used for shelter during air raids.

Public Information posters and leaflets to 'KEEP CALM and CARRY ON' stifled their terrors as best they could and did just that. People got on with their daily lives, sheltering at home from night-time bombing raids under the kitchen table, in the cupboard under the stairs, in the cellar, in the Morrison shelter in the living room or the Anderson shelter in the garden. Caught outside, people took shelter where they could, often under bridges or railway arches, in road tunnels and even in natural shelters such as caves; by October 1940, the Chislehurst Caves in Kent were sheltering 15,000 local residents.

There were supposed to be in all towns and cities good numbers of public shelters, suitable for people to stay in during bombing raids which, it was wrongly assumed by planners, would be short and intense. Such shelters might be in civic building basements or office buildings, in which space was requisitioned for the purpose, or they might be purpose-built. The latter were mostly brick boxes with concrete roofs, too small, without the facilities necessary to shelter large crowds for long periods, and liable to collapse if a bomb went off near them. There were never enough of these deeply unpopular public shelters, partly because of arguments between government and local authorities over who should pay for them.

Londoners had the Underground. At the start of the war, the Home Secretary, fearful of allowing large numbers of people to gather together and wanting to keep the Underground fully operational, refused to allow its stations to be used as shelters. Londoners had other ideas, and poured down into the Tube when the sirens wailed in September 1940. At first conditions below ground were pretty squalid, but gradually improved as better lighting and sanitary facilities were installed, canteens and some 22,000 bunk

CHRISTMAS UNDERGROUND
ARP members hang Christmas decorations in a cubicle of a shelter beneath a cinema in South London.

IN THE UNDERGROUND

At the height of the Blitz in London, around 177,000 people were spending their nights in a Tube station, regulars being given bed tickets. Those without bunks slept on the escalators, along the platforms and even in hammocks slung over the rails – once the power had been cut off for the night. Sheltering in the Underground did not guarantee safety. Sixty-four people died when Balham Station was bombed in October 1940, and 111 died at Bank Station in January 1941.

ROCKET DAMAGE
Rescue workers at the scene of a V-2 rocket attack on Farringdon Market in London.

beds were made available and regular cleaning was carried out. Some stations even laid on entertainment; in others, people made their own, with sing-songs being the order of the night in many. (Some people took earplugs below ground with them, along with books, knitting and other essentials, in order to get some sleep.)

IN THE CHANNEL ISLANDS

While the people of mainland Britain were enduring the Blitz, the people of the Channel Islands were having to come to terms with German occupation. The British Government had decided, albeit reluctantly, that in the event of war there was nothing they could do to protect these strategically unimportant islands, which had been British territory since the Norman Conquest. When war came, some 30,000 Channel Islanders were evacuated, leaving about 60,000 to sit out the war, hopefully too far from its main theatre to be of interest to the Germans.

But the Germans were interested, and on 28 June 1940, they bombed the two main islands, Jersey and Guernsey, killing forty-four people. Occupying forces began arriving on 30 June and by 3 July they had taken all four Channel Islands. They were the only part of British soil to be occupied by the Nazis during World War Two. Their harsh treatment, which included internment, rigorous ordering of all civilian social life, severe reprisals for any acts of disobedience or resistance and, after a year or two, little fuel, no electricity and considerable hunger, was a good indication of how the mainland would have suffered if Hitler's Operation Sealion, planned to start on 15 September 1940, had not been thwarted by the RAF and the Battle of Britain.

GERMAN OCCUPATION
A captured British flag about to be flown to Germany to be exhibited. Germany occupied the Channel Islands for much of the war.

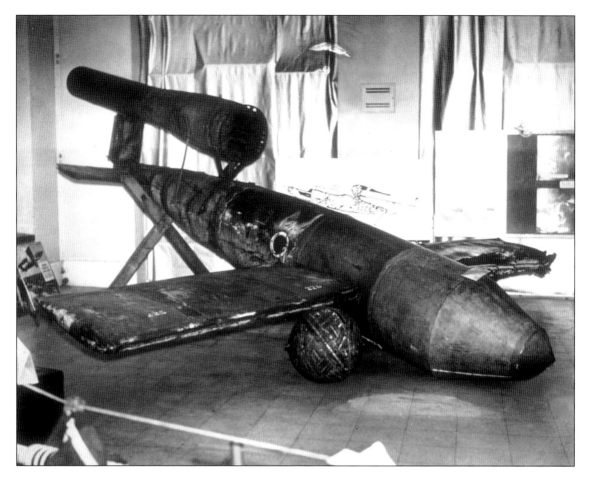

V-1 FLYING BOMB
In June 1942, Germany began working on a new secret weapon – the V-1 flying bomb.

THE DOODLEBUG

The worst of the war on the mainland seemed to everyone to be over by June 1944. The Allies had already landed in Europe, having sent over to Normandy on 6 June 1944 the largest seaborne invasion force the world had ever seen. Then came the V-1 and V-2 attacks, which were of a very different order from the bombings of 1940–41.

To start with, they were unexpected. And the weapons had been developed in great secrecy. Hitler believed that his new secret weapons would change the course of the war; they came too late for that, but they did cause considerable damage, both in terms of the destruction and death they wrought and in terms of the morale-depleting dread they caused.

The V-1 (short for Vergeltunsgwaffe Eins, or Retaliation Weapon One), was a jet-propelled unmanned aircraft carrying an explosive warhead. Launched from sites in Germany, 2,450 of them came over London and south-east England in the second half of June 1944. Their approach was heralded by a puttering whining sound that gave them the names 'buzz-bomb' or 'doodlebug'. Far worse than the puttering sound was the silence that succeeded it when the engine cut out. This meant that the V-1 was coming to earth, to explode on whatever, or whoever, was under it. As the blast effect of the V-1 was much greater than that of conventional bombs, so the devastation it caused was much more horrific and widespread. By September 1944, over a million Londoners had been evacuated from the city; many more left of their own accord.

By early September the V-1 attacks had petered out. Then came the V-2s. Between 8 September 1944 and 27 March 1945, when the last one landed on Orpington in Kent, some 1,050 V-2s fell on England. They were rockets, moving too fast to be intercepted – or even heard – and came down almost vertically. The first anyone knew they were there was the sound of an enormous explosion. Fortunately, Germany's use of the V-2, the world's first true ballistic missile, was halted when advancing Allied forces knocked out their launch bases in France.

At last the Home Guard could be stood down. As 1945 progressed, Britain could begin seriously to believe that victory – and peace – would soon come.

BLITZ CRICKET
A group of men playing cricket on a blitzed site during their lunch hour.

CHILDREN ON THE HOME FRONT

The surprising thing is the very positive view of the war taken, years later, by the majority of the children who lived through it. Among the positive changes that came out of the war, several radically affected the lives of future generations of children.

The war jerked Britain's political leaders out of their complacent acceptance of the living conditions endured by thousands, even millions of poor, working-class people. The great evacuation schemes of the war brought Britain's middle classes face to face with the reality of life in the inner cities, where so many children knew nothing of indoor plumbing, or of having regular baths, regular changes of clothes, or hair free of nits and parasites…. The result was the Welfare State, developed from the Beveridge Report that was accepted by Parliament at a time when the country was fighting grimly for its very survival.

The war also brought about a great breaking down of class barriers. While parents became aware of the great divide existing between the classes in Britain, their children found that their horizons were considerably widened. For children from the inner cities, there was the amazing discovery that beyond the city streets was a different world, one with many open, green spaces and farms where men and women worked to produce food. If a boy or girl evacuated from an inner city was reasonably lucky, they might find foster parents who would take them roller skating, let them join the Boy Scouts or Girl Guides, and spend their summer holidays on one of the country's beaches still free of barbed wire. No wonder many children returned only reluctantly to their families at the war's end.

And there was plenty of horizon-widening for middle-class children, too. When schoolgirl Joan Elliott's father was moved to Scottish

1939

SEPTEMBER
- The German battleship *Schleswig-Holstein* opens fire on a Polish military base outside Danzig – the first shots of World War Two.
- Norway, Finland, Sweden, Switzerland, Spain, Ireland and the USA declare neutrality.
- The UK, France, New Zealand, Australia, South Africa, Canada and Nepal declare war on Germany.
- Soviet Union joins Germany's invasion of Poland.
- Warsaw surrenders to the Nazis.

OCTOBER
- The last Polish army is defeated.
- Roosevelt receives a letter from Einstein urging him to rapidly develop an atomic bomb programme.
- Germany annexes western Poland.
- German U-boat *U-47* sinks British battleship HMS *Royal Oak*.
- Nylon stockings go on sale for the first time in the USA.

NOVEMBER
- The first rabbit is born using artificial insemination.
- Columnist Hedda Hopper debuts on radio with Hedda Hopper's Hollywood.

BOMBED INN

Boys help to clear rubble on the bombed site of the Hopscotch Inn, near Euston Station, London.
The site is to be turned into a junior club for children by the Save The Children Fund.

SOME GRIM STATISTICS

While the numbers of children killed and wounded in Britain during World War Two make very sad reading, they are, thankfully, small in comparison with the dreadful figures from other countries. The number of Jewish children who perished in the Holocaust exceeded one million, while 400,000 Russian children died in the siege of Leningrad (St Petersburg). Several million children died in Germany, where 6 million under-16-year-olds were caught up in the fighting as combatants and civilians; 5,500 children were killed in Hamburg in 1943 in devastating Allied raids. The world still does not know how many Japanese children were killed instantly, died later or were born malformed in mind and body when the Allies dropped Atom bombs on Hiroshima and Nagasaki in 1945.

GIRL GUIDES
Girl Guides of the 7th and 8th Putney Companies at work on their hospital allotment producing much needed vegetables.

1939

NOVEMBER

- The Winter War begins with Soviet forces invading Finland.
- Two British SIS agents are captured by the Germans.
- Roosevelt lays the cornerstone of the Jefferson Memorial in Washington DC.
- The gangster Al Capone is released from Alcatraz.
- In retaliation to protests against the Nazis in Czechoslovakia, Hitler orders the murder of nine students, sends over 1,200 to concentration camps and closes all Czech universities.

DECEMBER

- La Guardia airport opens in New York City.
- HMS *Nelson* is struck by a mine off the Scottish coast.
- HMS *Duchess* sinks after a collision with HMS *Barham* with the loss of 124 men.
- Start of the Battle of the River Plate.
- The film *Gone With The Wind* premieres in Atlanta, Georgia.
- A massive earthquake in Anatolia, Turkey, kills 30,000 people.
- USSR is expelled from the United Nations.
- Finland defeats the Soviet forces in the Battle of Tolvajärvi.

Command, the whole family went, including their maid, their grandmother and her maid, to stay in a small village outside Edinburgh. Joan and her siblings discovered a new freedom playing on various pieces of green land where their special play friends were a family of boys from 'the wrong side of the tracks'. The boys taught her many scurrilous rhymes that played a considerable part in her education.

Education was, in fact, another part of children's lives that underwent many changes during the war. It was not just that school life was turned upside down by the upheavals of evacuation and the calling up of so many young teachers. The war also accelerated changes in the education system that had been begun in the 1930s. The great Education Act of 1944 was the result of many years planning, which did not let up because 'there was a war on' – the great wartime excuse for not allowing things to happen.

But it must not be forgotten that there was, indeed, a war on, and one in which children were involved from the beginning. Children were brought into all the great wartime campaigns, such as 'Dig For Victory' and 'Make Do and Mend'. As the war progressed and the children were old enough – as young as twelve, in many cases, they were also brought into civil defence work and even into the junior corps of the armed services.

Children were also the government's major target of one of its greatest wartime concerns: keeping the nation well-fed and healthy. Throughout the war, babies and children were ensured a good supply of fresh milk and eggs, cod liver oil and orange juice, and the Ministry of Food kept up a steady barrage of information, including its own BBC radio programme, aimed at ensuring that Britain's children enjoyed – perhaps not the right word, given some of the not very palatable recipes dreamed up by the Ministry – a sound, nutritious diet.

On the whole, the nation did pretty well by its children during World War Two. It is noticeable in wartime photographs that most children look healthy, well-fed and warmly clothed. As for the children of the war years themselves, the memories may be mixed, but the overwhelming memory is of a time when everyone did their bit, and did it with their neighbours and their friends in a remarkably cheerful spirit. School lessons and examinations went on more or less as usual, although a few war drills were added to the curriculum. Perhaps toys were at a shortage, but children are children and they make do with what they have.

KNITTING FOR THE TROOPS
A young boy makes his contribution to the war effort by knitting for the troops, while his younger brother gives him a helping hand.

CHAPTER TWO

THE ARMED SERVICES AT HOME

THE ARMED SERVICES AT HOME

Britain's military manpower was far from being at full strength in September 1939. During the 1930s, the government had concentrated its military spending on home protection and on deterrence, building up the country's defensive air shield and bomber command at the expense of the Army, in terms of both manpower and equipment.

At the same time, Neville Chamberlain, after he became prime minister in 1937, had said that he would not consider bringing in conscription in peacetime.

Events during the signing of the 1938 Munich Agreement had given a boost to recruitment, not only to the ARP services but also to the military services, especially the Territorial Army and the RAF Volunteer Reserve. However, the government, remembering the rush to volunteer in 1914, which had badly depleted manpower in several essential industries, tried to check this spate of volunteering by publishing a Schedule of Reserved Occupations in November 1938.

With war soon looking more and more likely, it was clear that manpower in the armed forces, especially the Army, was well below strength and must be increased. Chamberlain changed his

COMPULSORY MILITARY SERVICE

Conscription was brought into Britain for the first time in peacetime by the Military Training Act, signed into law in May 1939. The Act made all men liable for call-up when they reached their twentieth year. If accepted, they would be trained and would serve full-time for six months, then would serve part time for three-and-a-half years in Territorial units.

The day war was declared, the conscription age was widened to cover men aged between eighteen and forty-one. In December 1941, the age limit was extended to fifty-one.

ARP POSTER
A British government recruitment poster for the Air Raid Precautions (ARP).

SCHEDULE OF RESERVED OCCUPATIONS

NOVEMBER 1938

At the outbreak of war, all men between the ages of eighteen and forty-one were liable for conscription into the armed forces. However, in November 1938, a Schedule of Reserved Occupations was drawn up which meant that certain key skilled workers were exempt from conscription. It was a complicated scheme which covered a wide range of jobs including:

- railway workers
- dockyard workers
- miners
- farmers
- agricultural workers
- schoolteachers
- doctors
- engineers

As the war advanced, the need for men to join the armed forces grew. The scheme was frequently reviewed and women played their part by filling many of the vacancies left by the conscripted men. Many of the men who were required to work in the necessary trades were frustrated at not being able to fight for their country and joined civil defence units such as the Home Guard or the ARP.

mind about conscription and, in April 1939, in the teeth of stiff opposition in the Commons and out in the country from the Labour Party and the trade union movement, the government drove a conscription bill through Parliament.

Conscription did not give a man any choice about which of the services he went into, and the Military Training Act, combined with the scare Munich had given the nation, gave a boost to voluntary recruitment. This is because, in theory, volunteers could choose which service they wished to enter. In fact, because the Army was most in need of recruits, the majority of volunteers were directed into it anyway.

By December 1939, more than one-and-a-half million men were experiencing the rigours of military training and discipline, which meant, if they were in the Army, about three months of basic training in barracks. More than two-thirds of them were in the Army, with the remainder being almost equally divided between the Royal Navy and the RAF. In addition to the men, 143,000 women, all of them volunteers, were serving in the women's auxiliary services – the Auxiliary Territorial Services, ATS the Women's Royal Naval Service (WRNS), where they were called 'Wrens', and the Women's Auxiliary Air Force (WAAF) – and in various nursing services attached to the armed forces.

For most of the war, about one-and-a-half million British service men and women were stationed at home, working in home defence,

NURSING AUXILIARIES

Nursing auxiliaries are receiving instruction on anatomy at the Booth Hall Hospital in Manchester. Their role was to supplement hospital staff and man first aid posts, as well as carrying on with their civil jobs as far as possible.

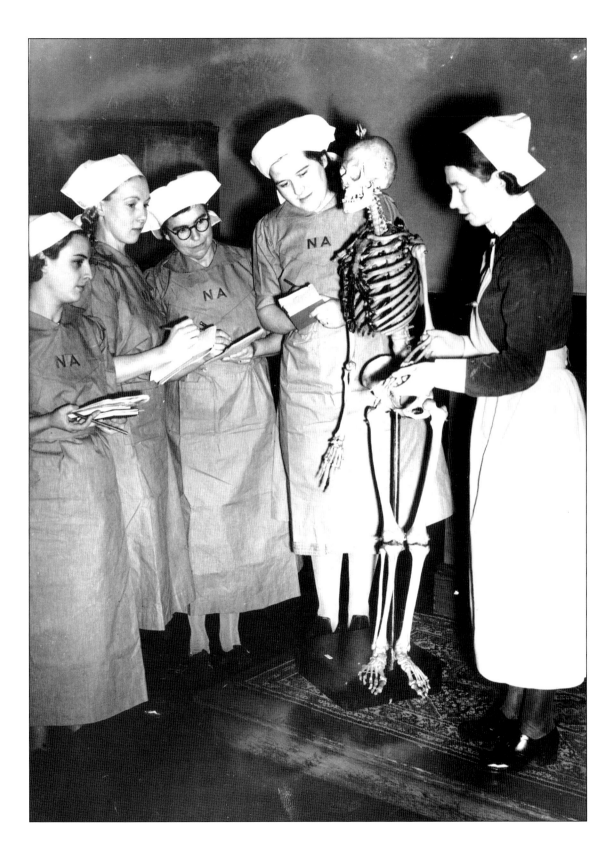

anti-aircraft, logistical training and administrative units. After Dunkirk, there were few theatres of war abroad that British troops were well enough equipped to be sent to. The armed services concentrated on re-grouping and re-equipping in preparation for the time when they could move on to the attack – if not in Europe then certainly in the Middle East and North Africa, where British and Dominion forces began enjoying some notable successes in 1941.

As well as the British forces, there was, among the servicemen sent from the countries of the Empire and Commonwealth, a large contingent of Canadians, which arrived in Scotland in December 1939. They had been intended for fighting in Norway and France, alongside the BEF, but events prevented either deployment. For two long years the Canadians helped in the defence of Britain and saw no action in Europe until the disastrous Dieppe Raid of August 1942. They next saw action in the Mediterranean in 1943 before joining Montgomery's 8th Army in Italy.

APPLYING FOR 'CO' STATUS

For those men who, for reasons of moral, religious or political conscience, felt they could not fight, life became difficult when conscription was brought in. The National Service (Armed Forces) Act, which had widened the ages at which men were liable for conscription, had also set up a Military Services Register, on which were put the names of all men liable for military service. A man objecting to his name's being put on the Register could apply to be put on a Register of Conscientious Objectors instead. He would have to argue his case before a local tribunal.

CANADIAN SOLDIERS
A Canadian soldier gives the thumbs-up sign as he arrives on British soil.

POPULAR CULTURE
1940

POPULAR SONGS
- *In The Mood*, Glenn Miller
- *Frenesi*, Artie Shaw
- *Only Forever*, Bing Crosby
- *I'll Never Smile Again*, Tommy Dorsey
- *When You Wish Upon A Star*, Cliff Edwards (Ukulele Ike)
- *A Nightingale Sang In Berkeley Square*, Glenn Miller
- *Blueberry Hill*, Gene Autry
- *Run Rabbit Run*, Flanagan & Allen
- *We're Gonna Hang Out The Washing On The Siegfried Line*, Flanagan & Allen
- *Lili Marlene*, Anne Shelton
- *The Blackout Stroll*, Joe Loss and his band

POPULAR FILMS
- *Pinocchio*, Disney animation
- *Fantasia*, Disney animation
- *Boom Town*, starring Clark Gable and Spencer Tracy
- *Rebecca*, starring Laurence Olivier and Joan Fontaine
- *Sante Fe Trail*, starring Errol Flynn
- *All This, and Heaven Too*, starring Bette Davis and Charles Boyer
- *Foreign Correspondent* by Alfred Hitchcock, starring Joel McCrea, Herbert Marshall and Laraine Day
- *The Great Dictator*, starring Charlie Chaplin
- *The Mark of Zorro*, starring Tyrone Power and Basil Rathbone

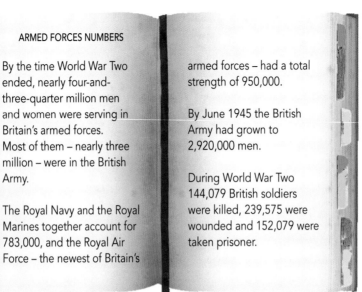

ARMED FORCES NUMBERS

By the time World War Two ended, nearly four-and-three-quarter million men and women were serving in Britain's armed forces. Most of them – nearly three million – were in the British Army.

The Royal Navy and the Royal Marines together account for 783,000, and the Royal Air Force – the newest of Britain's armed forces – had a total strength of 950,000.

By June 1945 the British Army had grown to 2,920,000 men.

During World War Two 144,079 British soldiers were killed, 239,575 were wounded and 152,079 were taken prisoner.

At the start of the war, some twenty-two out of every thousand men from the first age group liable for service applied to be registered as conscientious objectors. A minority of these Conscientious Objectors (or COs, as they came to be called) were given unconditional exemption from call-up; others were exempted on condition that they registered for other, non-military work, usually in Civil Defence or on the land; many requests for exemption were rejected entirely. Exemptions were granted in widely varying numbers from local authority to local authority. It could have become something of a post-code lottery but for the fact that conscientious objection dwindled as the war progressed; by mid-1940, only about six men in every thousand were applying for CO status.

THE RAF AND WAAF

When the war turned from 'phoney' to the real thing and the main battle zone was in the skies over southern England, especially during the Battle of Britain and the Blitz that followed it, the most hard-worked of Britain's military services were the RAF and the WAAF. The RAF provided the fighter pilots in the air and the technical crews on the ground. The WAAF provided many members of the staff in the operations rooms, where incoming enemy planes were tracked, their courses plotted and intercept directions were sent to the pilots in the air.

The RAF was greatly helped by being able to use the still top-secret radar. A chain of what looked like radio masts but which were, in fact, radar stations, had been built along the coast to give advance warning of incoming Luftwaffe planes. Radar meant that the RAF did not have to waste manpower and fuel patrols in the air, but could get them airborne from their bases in time to meet the incoming bombers and their fighter escorts. The huge value of radar was demonstrated when the Luftwaffe knocked out the radar station at Ventnor on the Isle of Wight, punching a large hole in the protective shield offered by radar that took ten days to fill.

The whole pattern of the armed forces'

BOMBER PILOTS
A crew of British bomber pilots walking in front of their aircraft – from left to right Observer,
Wireless Operator, Rear Gunner, Second Pilot, Pilot Captain.

AN AMERICAN SOLDIER AND HIS ENGLISH GIRLFRIEND
A favourite spot for GIs to meet their girlfriends was London's Hyde Park.

presence in Britain changed dramatically after the Japanese bombing of Pearl Harbor in December 1941 brought the United States of America into the war on the Allied side. Hitherto, the Americans had hoped to keep out of the war, which was seen as a European thing, and their help for Britain after the fall of France had been in the very practical form of the Lend-Lease programme, which brought Britain much needed replacement armour and ships.

United States forces began arriving in Britain in January 1942. By 1943, American GIs were 'over here' in such large numbers that they formed by far the largest single block of non-British servicemen in the country. The GIs were in Britain to help develop the great invasion plan that went into action in June 1944. American airmen were here to strengthen the air attack on Germany. With the arrival of the Americans, the war against Germany went on to the offensive.

GI BRIDES

When American servicemen began arriving in Britain in increasingly large numbers from mid-1942, embittered British men, especially Tommies, were soon muttering that GIs were 'overpaid, oversexed and over here'. The Tommies were right about the 'overpaid' bit: GIs had nearly seven times the pay of British servicemen, as well as seemingly unlimited supplies of chocolates, nylon stockings and other things sure to attract British girls. GIs were relaxed, generous and eager to give British girls a good time at army camp dances and in dance halls where American bands played music to jive, boogie-woogie and jitterbug to. It is not surprising that, with so many British men away overseas, thousands of British girls should have relationships with GIs. While many of these resulted in illegitimate babies who grew up never to know their fathers, nearly eighty thousand British women married American servicemen. Thousands of GI brides went to the United States after VE Day, many of them gathering with their children at reception camps, prior to boarding ships for the journey to their new lives.

CHAPTER THREE

THE CHANGING ROLE OF WOMEN

THE CHANGING ROLE OF WOMEN

The major contribution of women to the war effort during World War One, which did more than the activities of the suffragettes to gain them the vote in general elections in 1918, also speeded up the process of making women more acceptable in the workplace.

This process was hugely accelerated during World War Two. Whether at home, at work, in Civil Defence, or in the armed forces, women played a big part in helping Britain win the war.

WOMEN AT WAR

At the beginning of the war, women could choose for themselves what their contribution to the war effort would be. At home, the women of the household found the necessary blackout materials and bought the tape that criss-crossed their windows even before war was declared. While it might be the menfolk of the family who erected in the garden the corrugated metal Anderson shelter, it was the women who made sure that it, or the understairs cupboard or the cellar, if their house had one, was stocked with emergency rations, blankets and torches or candles. It was also women who had the greatest say in whether or not to evacuate their children and sometimes themselves, from the danger zones.

As the war progressed and more and more men were called up, even from reserved occupations, many women got jobs in what had hitherto been pretty much male preserves, such as the railways, bus driving and captaining the transport barges that moved many essential materials along canals and waterways. Some of them moved into the air, ferrying aircraft, from fighters and bombers to transport planes, from the factories where they had been built or repaired to airfields and RAF stations. Women eventually overcame early male prejudice to man anti-aircraft ('ack ack') posts and to maintain and hoist the unwieldy barrage balloons, filled with 20,000 cubic feet (570 cubic metres) of hydrogen, that so effectively deterred low-flying enemy aircraft. Thousands more, while carrying on with their day jobs, also volunteered for one of the Civil Defence organisations, working as ARP wardens, auxiliary policewomen, ambulance drivers, first-aid workers, fire watchers or in the Women's Auxiliary Fire Service.

OPPOSITE: ANDERSON ALLOTMENT
A resident in Clapham, south London, waters the vegetables she has planted on the roof of her Anderson shelter built in her garden.

FIRST 'DUSTWOMAN'
A female dustman carries a tub full of old cans back to her dustcart. Women in Ilford became the first to work as dustwomen during the war.

One of the most valuable contributions to the war effort a housewife could make was to join or help the Women's Voluntary Service (WVS). The WVS, founded in 1938 by Stella Isaacs, Marchioness of Reading, was an almost entirely voluntary service. Of the hundreds of thousands of women – their exact numbers were never officially counted – who worked in its name during the war, only about 200 key workers were ever given more money than what covered their out-of-pocket expenses.

As the war went on, the women of the WVS, familiar figures in their uniform green-grey tweed suits, beetroot-red jumpers and felt hats, found work for themselves everywhere. Among the exhausted servicemen brought home from Dunkirk, it was the WVS who provided essential foot-washing facilities, washed and darned socks and served thousands of meals and cups of tea. During the Blitz, they kept up local censuses for the ARP services, organised convoys to get people out of heavily bombed neighbourhoods, drove canteens to the centre of clearing-up operations after a bombing raid, provided food and clothing for those who had been bombed out of their homes, and helped with the evacuation and care of children orphaned or separated from their families.

For women who preferred to work in the country, or who had liked gardening in peace time, the recruiting posters for the Women's Land Army, formed to provide essential agricultural workers to replace male farm workers now in the forces, sounded enticing. Women quickly joined the Women's Land Army in their thousands (80,000 of them by the end of the war), leaving behind jobs in shops and restaurants, offices and hairdressers to work on the land and grow and harvest the foods that the nation would need. Life was back-breakingly hard for most Land Girls, with the usual fifty-hour week extending

1940
INTERESTING FACTS

MARCH
- Édouard Daladier resigns as the prime minister of France and is replaced by Paul Reynaud.

APRIL
- Booker T. Washington is the first African American to appear on a postage stamp.
- Germany invades Denmark and Norway in Operation Weserübung.
- After the Nazis take over Denmark, the British occupy the Faroe Islands to prevent possible German occupation.
- The Jamaica Racetrack, New York, makes history by introducing the pari-mutuel betting equipment.
- A fire at the Rhythm Night Club in Natchez, Mississippi kills 198 people.

MAY
- The Battle of France begins.
- The UK invade Iceland.
- Neville Chamberlain resigns as British prime minister and is replaced by Winston Churchill.
- Churchill makes his first speech to the House of Commons and says, 'I have nothing to offer you but blood, toil, tears and sweat'.
- Queen Wilhelmina of the Netherlands flees to London along with her government.

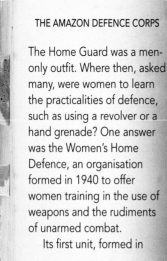

THE AMAZON DEFENCE CORPS

The Home Guard was a men-only outfit. Where then, asked many, were women to learn the practicalities of defence, such as using a revolver or a hand grenade? One answer was the Women's Home Defence, an organisation formed in 1940 to offer women training in the use of weapons and the rudiments of unarmed combat.

Its first unit, formed in June 1940, called itself the Amazon Defence Corps, and by the end of 1942 there were said to be 250 Women's Home Defence units in the country.

Technically, because they wore uniforms and provided weapons training (often given by Home Guard members), the units were private armies and therefore illegal. The War Office chose to turn a blind eye to their activities.

to twice that in harvest time, and with wages low, billeting arrangements often spartan and holidays few and far between.

Another out-of-doors wartime job that attracted some women was the Forestry Service. Here, women workers found themselves called 'Lumber Jills' or − perhaps less of a compliment − 'Polecats'.

For many women with jobs when war was declared, it was a matter of just carrying on with them. Although World War One had shown that women could step into many skilled jobs in male dominated industries, in 1939 the government was slow to consider suggesting that women should volunteer for work in factories and on heavy industry sites, both to replace men and to work along-side them.

It was not until January 1941, that the Ministry of Labour, abandoning 'voluntaryism', began directing workers to the industries where they were most needed. For the first time, Britain's women, instead of being asked to volunteer for work, were directed to jobs. At the beginning of the year, only women of twenty and twenty-one were directed to put their names on registers of employment; by the end of 1941 registration of women had been extended up to those aged thirty. In fact, the majority of women accepted suggested jobs, and few had compulsory direc-tions issued against them. In May 1943, part-time work (which could mean up to thirty hours a week) became compulsory for all women aged between eighteen and forty-five. In all, some ten million women were registered for work, either full-time or part-time, by early 1943.

There was no great outcry against the conscription of women. Indeed, women − and the nation as a whole − had long foreseen that voluntary appeals to women were not working

OPPOSITE: SALVAGE DEPOT
The WVS unloading salvage at a depot before going to be sorted.

and that the country was desperately in need of workers and armed forces personnel, of both sexes. This was particularly so in the women's services. Many young women had enthusiastically volunteered for the ATS, the WRNS and the WAAF in 1939, and were soon being seen out and about in their smart uniforms. But a great many of them had since thought better of it and had drifted away.

In April 1941, the government had attempted to halt the loss of female service personnel by making the women's auxiliary services officially part of the Armed Forces of the Crown. From July 1941, women enjoyed full military status – but were also now subject to full military discipline. The National Service (No. 2) Act did not force women to undertake 'combatant duties' if they chose to join one of the women's services.

While most women in the armed forces found themselves in clerical or culinary jobs, there were jobs, such as those that took members of the WAAF into jobs at RAF stations, that put them very much in the front line. There were many interesting jobs available for women in the services, of course. Princess Elizabeth, the king's eldest daughter, opted for service in the ATS

BALING HAY
Members of the Women's Land Army using a baling machine on a farm in West Suffolk.

SAY 'CHEESE'
A group of WAAFs prepare to have their photographs taken after the announcement that the RAF was looking for the smartest WAAF to pose for a recruitment poster.

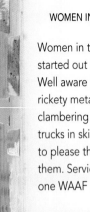

WOMEN IN A MAN'S WORLD

Women in the armed forces started out the war in skirts. Well aware that climbing rickety metal ladders or clambering into jeeps and trucks in skirts was likely only to please the men around them. Servicewomen, recalled one WAAF member, 'were all delighted to read one day that we could wear trousers'. Most military camps made few, if any, concessions to servicewomen, and women found themselves washing in the same kind of concrete shed equipped only with cold water as men.

GETTING DOWN AND DIRTY
A member of the Mechanised Transport Training Corps changes a wheel at an ARP post in Lambeth, south London.

MUNITIONS FACTORY
Women munition workers finishing shell cases during World War Two.

when she was old enough. As well as learning to drive 'almost any kind of vehicle', as the recruiting posters put it, she, like many other women in the services, became adept at stripping truck engines and maintaining army vehicles.

By 1943, ninety per cent of single women in Britain and eighty per cent of married women were doing war work of some kind. Many of the seven million women in full-time civilian work were putting in long hours in engineering and munitions factories, turning out the machines and weapons that, within a year, would be helping in the great work of defeating the Axis powers. At the same time, the services were benefiting from the work of one-and-half million women now serving in Britain's armed forces.

1940
INTERESTING FACTS

MAY
- Rotterdam is heavily bombed by the Luftwaffe – 980 people are killed and 20,000 buildings erased.
- Recruitment begins in the UK of the Home Guard.
- The first McDonald's restaurant opens in California.
- Brussels falls to German forces.
- Belgian government flees to Ostend.
- Philippe Pétain is named vice-premier of France.
- Auschwitz concentration camp opens in Poland.
- Dunkirk evacuation of British Expeditionary Forces starts.
- Churchill warns House of Commons to 'prepare itself for hard and heavy tidings'.

JUNE
- Paris is bombed by the Luftwaffe for the first time.
- The evacuation of 300,000 troops from Dunkirk ends.
- Churchill tells the House of Commons 'We shall never surrender'.
- Canada declares war on Italy.
- Norway surrenders to Germany.
- French government flees to Bordeaux as Paris falls under German occupation.

INTO IN THE ARMED FORCES

The Military Training Act that came into force in Britain in May 1939 introduced conscription – but only for young men aged twenty and twenty-one. It did not apply to women. Nor did the National Service (Armed Forces) Act, which Parliament passed on the first day of war.

Even before the start of World War Two young women had volunteered with enthusiasm for the auxiliary services, many of them because they wanted to emulate fathers and brothers in the way they served their country in its hour of need in World War One. Others simply fancied the idea of getting away from home, travelling, finding adventure and wearing a smart uniform. It was probably from among the latter that the drift away from the auxiliary services gathered pace during the Phoney War. At this time in the ATS, for instance, there were only five 'trades' offered to women, none of which were exciting or adventurous.

As their skills and confidence grew, women's roles in World War Two became more extensive and, by 1945, there were more than two million women working for the war effort. Women contributed to the war effort in many ways, earning the respect of society and laying the foundation for the women's movement.

As the war advanced, women became more involved in combat, especially in anti-aircraft units due to the very nature of World War Two. World War One was mainly fought in France, whereas this second conflict was a global conflict on an unprecedented scale. Great Britain was aware that they would need as many hands as possible if they were to win the war, so the urgency of expanding the role of women was inevitable. Women's roles were not, of course, isolated to Great Britain, many women overseas served in the resistances of France, Italy and Poland, although the USA was not keen to use

HANDLING A RIFLE
A WRNS officer learns how to handle a rifle during her training as an armourer.

females in combat. Canada and Australia did not allow women to fly military planes, but Great Britain used women to ferry planes as part of the Air Transport Auxiliary. Women were also enrolled in the Special Operations Executive (SOE) which used their skills in highly dangerous roles as secret agents and underground radio operations in Nazi-operated Europe.

The Third Reich, like Great Britain, had similar roles for their women. In occupied Poland, women played a major role in the resistance movement, which meant they were frequently on the front line. They were mainly used as couriers to carry messages between cells of the resistance movement and clandestine printing establishments.

Despite their important role in the military, many women felt they were not treated equally

WRNS MECHANICS
Although initially recruited to release men to serve at sea, the women of the WRNS soon took on a diverse range of work that had been previously considered beyond their capabilities. Here two members can be seen servicing a plane.

to their male counterparts. Many commanding officers kept women out of combat, and even falsely accused some of promiscuity.

When writer, broadcaster and actor Anne Valery joined the ATS at seventeen, she found basic training 'a doddle' compared with the austere and regimented life of a girls' public school. 'And', she wrote in *Talking About the War,* 'it had the added bonus of no compulsory cold baths, evenings off in the fleshpots of wherever I was stationed, plus the heady freedom of unsupervised leaves.... For girls from poor families, army life was an undreamt luxury because of its three meals a day, a change of underclothes, new shoes, and nightwear instead of a vest. Many had never been to the dentist

THE ATS SECRETARY AND THE END OF THE WAR

The last posting of the war for ATS sergeant secretary Susan Heald was at the Supreme Headquarters Allied Expeditionary Force in Rheims. For five days in May 1945 she and other typists typed surrender documents to be signed by Germany from early in the morning until late at night. Working on old Imperial typewriters, Sergeant Heald typed up the English and German versions of the Act of Military Surrender and its many attachments, while other typists prepared Russian and French versions. Sergeant Heald witnessed the signing of the surrender documents by Germany's chief of staff, General Alfred Jodl, on 7 May. She then typed out the signal to the War Office in London that said 'The mission of this Allied Force was fulfilled at 0241, local time, May 7th, 1945'. She and the other typists celebrated by drinking champagne out of mess tins – and then went to bed, as they had been working non-stop for twenty hours. Sergeant Heald was mentioned in despatches for her work.

1940

INTERESTING FACTS

JANUARY

- Luftwaffe General Hermann Göring assumes control of all war industries in Germany.
- In the Winter War, the Russian 44th Assault Division is destroyed by Finnish forces.
- Food rationing begins in Great Britain.
- Brisbane, Australia, records its hottest day in history – 43.2°C (109.7°F).
- Three trains crash and explode in Osaka, Japan, killing 181 people.

FEBRUARY

- Walt Disney release their second full-length animation – *Pinocchio*.
- Tom and Jerry make their debut appearance in *Puss Gets The Boot*.
- In Tibet, four-year-old Tenzin Gyatso is proclaimed as the next Dalai Lama.

MARCH

- Elmer Fudd makes his debut in *Elmer's Candid Camera*.
- A time bomb destroys the offices of a Swedish communist newspaper killing five people.
- Soviet Union and Finland sign a peace treaty ending the Winter War.
- Hitler and Mussolini meet at Brenner Pass in the Alps to form an alliance against France and the UK.

and their teeth were in such a bad state that our camp dentist told me that sometimes he had to spend an entire session cleaning them, before he could see what needed to be done.… Grouped round a smelly stove in the barrack room, ex-debs, orphans and secretaries swapped their life stories.… by the end of Basic Training, class had all but disappeared.'

For many ATS women, including George VI's daughter, Princess Elizabeth, their work took them into the engine, under the chassis and into the driving seat of a vast array of army vehicles, from staff cars, military ambulances and three-ton trucks to gun limbers and tanks. They were trained in essential vehicle maintenance at ATS Motor Transport Training Centres. In 1943 it was estimated that 80 per cent of Army driving was done by women. By this time ATS members were also serving with regular army units in anti-aircraft batteries, usually acting as spotters for the men who manned the guns, and working with the Home Guard as well.

When the ATS was first established it provided support to the RAF, but in 1939 the WAAF was formed and took over the ATS's role. Like the ATS, the WAAF grew rapidly after the war began, counting more than sixty-four thousand officers and other ranks by 1940, to 182,000 at the end of the war. Their duties remained firmly on the ground, however, where the majority of them eventually replaced airmen working in over eighty different trades, including aircraft maintenance and instrument and flight mechanics. WAAF women became skilled electricians, fitters and armourers. Other airwomen worked as drivers, clerks or cooks, and a few ran classes instructing the Home Guard in aircraft recognition.

Particularly vital roles played by airwomen in wartime were the interpretation of photographs of enemy targets, including: airfields, industrial

WHEELING A TORPEDO
Members of the WRNS wheel a torpedo for loading onto a Swordfish warplane.

sites and supply stores, the plotting of incoming waves of enemy aircraft, and meteorological observation. w

By 1944 most of the Service Meteorological Officers in the Flying Training Command were women; their work was very important, given the way in which weather conditions could affect the success or failure of bombing missions. A WAAF meteorological observer had to make hourly observations of the weather, sending her findings by teleprinter to group headquarters, and drawing up weather maps. She often found

EMERGENCY FIELD KITCHEN
ATS recruits were taught how to set up and run an emergency field kitchen. The kitchen could be built from dustbins, milk churns and other items of everyday life.

herself working at night when the rest of her station's Met Office staff were quietly sleeping, waiting for that night's mission to return home.

As WAAF personnel were not permitted to fly planes, any woman wanting to do so had to forget about the WAAF and try for a place in the civilian Air Transport Auxiliary (ATA). The ATA was founded in September 1939 to provide an aircraft ferrying service, generally from factory to airfield, that would not use valuable RAF pilots. It began by recruiting men only – of course – who had a pilot's licence and at least 250 hours' flying experience. As in all other areas of the war, however, recruitment policy soon changed and

KEEPING THE BALLOONS FLYING

Barrage balloons, or 'blimps' as they came to be called, were flown from open spaces over cities, ports and harbours, airfields, industrial sites and other places to discourage low-level attacks and dive-bombing. They were initially operated by ten-man crews of the RAF's Balloon Command, but in early 1941 were gradually handed over to the WAAF (*below*), with sixteen airwomen doing the job of ten RAF men. Eventually, the WAAF operated 1,029 barrage balloon sites throughout Britain. It was hard, physically demanding and dangerous work, especially when there were strong winds blowing. The important things about the balloons was not the balloons themselves so much as the steel cables – lethal to aircraft – that the balloons held upright in the air.

from January 1940 women with more than 600 hours flying experience were recruited by an initially reluctant ATA.

At first they were not allowed to fly operational aircraft or to fly outside Britain, nor were they ever attached to RAF units, remaining in their own civilian pools. Eventually 164 women, including the near-legendary Amy Johnson and Diana Barnato, daughter of the motor-racing champion Woolf Barnato, as well as Americans, Australians, South Africans and others from a total of twenty-eight nations, were recruited into the ATA, 108 of them as pilots.

Once they were permitted to fly operational aircraft – mostly Hurricanes, Mosquitoes and, their favourite, Spitfires – they spent the war ferrying combat planes from the factories to RAF squadrons, Fleet Air Arm bases and the maintenance depots. As Diana Barnato recalled later, they flew every day in all weathers, without radio and unarmed, avoiding barrage balloons and occasionally being shot at by the enemy and, 'now and then, by our own side.' Later in the war they flew aircraft to squadrons in Europe, including France and the Netherlands. They were the only women of the war's Western partners who flew in a war zone. Even the women of the US Women's Air Service Pilots (WASPs) were kept at least three thousand miles from a war zone.

An organisation which attracted women who wished to be drivers, to bear arms and to be connected to the Army, although not in it, was the First Aid Nursing Yeomanry, or FANY, an organisation set up in World War One, during

1940
INTERESTING FACTS

JUNE
- A group of 728 Polish prisoners become the first inmates of Auschwitz.
- Pétain becomes prime minister of France and asks Germany for peace terms.
- Allied troops start to evacuate France in Operation Ariel.
- Luftwaffe sink RMS *Lancastria* killing over 2,500 people.
- Churchill announces that 'The Battle of Britain is about to begin'.
- German forces land in Guernsey, marking the start of a five-year occupation of the Channel Islands.

JULY
- Ringo Starr (Richard Starkey) the drummer with the Beatles is born.

AUGUST
- Churchill pays tribute to the Royal Air Force – 'Never in the field of human conflict was so much owed by so many to so few'.
- Leon Trotsky is assassinated in Mexico by a Soviet agent with an ice axe.

WOMEN MECHANICS
As the need for trained men increased, members of the Women's Division could be found carrying out everything from aircraft and car mechanics, to packing parachutes and ferrying aircraft between airfields. These women are rivetting inside an aircraft fusilage.

AMY JOHNSON
English aviator Amy Johnson (1903–1941) standing in front of her Gipsy Moth just before she undertook a nineteen day solo flight to Australia on 5 May 1930. She later went on to join the ATA to help in the war effort.

which FANYs soon stopped being mounted on horses and took to driving vehicles. During World War Two the FANY developed a strong link with the Special Operations Executive (SOE), the secret intelligence organisation founded on a direct order from Churchill in 1940. The women agents working for the SOE were drawn from the ranks of the FANY and the WAAF, and FANYs provided drivers, despatch riders, coders, wireless operators – their most essential function – and even parachute packers for the SOE.

The third important women's auxiliary force was the Women's Royal Navy Service (WRNS), whose members were invariably called 'Wrens'. The closest that Wrens got to sea was manning harbour craft in all weathers in naval bases all round Britain's coast. They were never allowed to go to sea in a ship of the Royal Navy; as a wartime recruiting poster put it, 'Join the Wrens and free a man for the Fleet'.

The Wrens' greatest task during the war was plotting the progress, day and night, of the Battle of the Atlantic from the Operations Room of Western Approaches Command. Often their most dangerous task was serving as coastal mine-spotters. If a Wren was a Visual Signaller, she spent much of her time outside in all weathers keeping contact with ships at anchor, outside the harbour where she was based. She would communicate by means of Morse code, semaphore, flag signals and Aldis signalling lamps, all of which she had to use competently and efficiently.

By 1944 two-thirds of WRNS officers were doing the work of naval officers who had been sent to sea, replacing many of them as cypher decoders and in technical and secretarial work. As in the other women's auxiliary services, there were also many 'trades' undertaken by the WRNS, from welders, carpenters, armourers, ship repair and maintenance workers.

For the women who served in the auxiliary services, the war was a time for gaining confidence in their abilities to do a man's job, and to experience an ever-widening world of

SECRETIVE WOMEN

While British Intelligence was not a branch of the armed forces, its work brought it into very close contact with them. No one knows exactly how many men and women were involved in the work of the Special Operations Executive (SOE), but there are thought to have been some 10,000 men and 3,200 women working for the SOE in 1944, when it was at its greatest operational strength. Of the more than 400 agents sent to France by the SOE, thirty-nine were women, thirteen of whom never made it back to Britain and safety. Three SOE women agents – Noor Inayat Khan, Odette Hallowes and Violette Szabo – were awarded the George Cross. As for that other arm of British Intelligence, Bletchley Park, as Winston Church remarked, they were 'the geese that laid golden eggs, but never cackled', so the numbers of women working there have not been confirmed. A few women were at Bletchley Park from the time the Secret Intelligence Service moved in briefly during the Munich Crisis and then permanently in autumn 1939.

PILOTS ADJUST CHUTES
Women pilots of the Air Transport Auxiliary (ATA) adjust their parachutes. From 1941, the ATA took on the role of Royal Air Force ferry pools transporting aircraft between factories, airfields and maintenance units.

opportunities amidst the comradeship of other women. However, it should not be forgotten that for many other women, connected to the services by marriage as opposed to vocation, the war was a much less happy experience. Apart from the distress of having to wave their husbands goodbye when their call-up papers came through, the wives of servicemen who were not officers were often left in a very difficult financial situation.

If they had small children, they could not work themselves and therefore had to try to make-do on the low allowance the Government allotted to the wives and dependants of servicemen. An army private's wife was paid seventeen shillings a week for herself, five shillings for her first child, three shillings for the second, two for the third, and just one shilling each for every child after that. Her husband contributed seven shillings out of his own wages, leaving him with a just a bit

WOMEN ON WATCH
Women members of the ATS operate a searchlight during a period of surveillance.

CABINET EXCHANGE
The telephone exchange in the Cabinet War Rooms were situated under Whitehall. The exchange was housed in a reinforced bunker to protect it from attack during the Blitz.

more than a shilling a day – in sharp contrast, the allowance given to the carers of each evacuated child in Britain was eight shillings and sixpence. The pension paid to the widows of servicemen who did not return home was also small.

There is no doubt without the contribution of women during World War Two, our efforts would have been severely weakened. Their strength and determination contributed immenselty to Great Britain's overall might during the conflict.

SEMAPHORE

One of the more common methods of communication by signalmen and women during World War Two was the use of semaphore. Semaphore was the communication between ships using a flag alphabet. It was based on the positioning and patterning of the flags, and it meant that messages could be sent when other methods were not practical or available. The signalman or woman on a ship used hand-held flags to send messages to nearby ships. They held a flag in each hand and then rotated the flags into certain positions, each one representing a different letter of the alphabet.

The semaphore signalling system was designed by the Chappe brothers in France in the late 18th century. It was originally used to carry despatches between French army units, including those commanded by Napoleon.

Today the flags used are usually square and divided diagonally into a red and a yellow section, with the red in the uppermost triangle.

JOBS FOR WOMEN
A woman learns how to use an LNER telegraph machine during World War Two. The machine is used for transmitting and receiving messages over long distances.

SELF-SUFFICIENT
Women no longer relied on men to get them out of a sticky situation, as this ATS driver proves by righting her own vehicle.

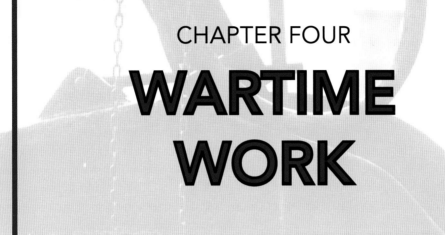

CHAPTER FOUR

WARTIME WORK

WARTIME WORK

'Getting on with the job' took on a whole new meaning on the home front during the war. For those who stayed in their pre-war jobs, working conditions for bank managers and milkmen, shopkeepers and bus drivers alike, became increasingly difficult.

People got used to walking to work past damaged buildings and across rubble and broken glass, perhaps after a night spent fire-watching or on ARP duty, or sleeping in an Anderson shelter or down in the Underground.

Once at their place of work, they might sweep up the glass and stick a notice saying 'More open than usual' on the door, or dust down their desks and write letters that might have to be delivered by hand by a member of staff assigned to the job or by teams of special Post Office workers. For other workers, jobs and working conditions changed radically. Factories switched from their peace-time manufacturing to war production, making silk parachutes instead of Viyella shirts perhaps, or wooden aeroplanes, such as the wood-fuselage Mosquito fighter-bomber instead of wooden furniture.

Many factories kept working seven days a week, their labour forces working 10–12 hour shifts. Wages were controlled and strikes banned. Tea breaks, at first limited because they interrupted production, were quickly recognised as being essential for workers' morale and health. From quite early in the war it became compulsory for factories to set up workers' canteens (in many

of which the availability of cigarettes became as important a matter as getting a cup of tea). By the end of 1944, there were some 30,500 workers' canteens in factories in all parts of Britain.

War put an extraordinary strain on Britain's workforce, which soon found itself in a tug of war between the requirements of the armed services and those of the industries that supplied them while also supplying the nation. In the early months of 1940, when unemployment was high in Britain, the government did not think that there would be a problem finding men to volunteer for all the new jobs that a wartime economy created, despite the increased demand for fighting men. Ernest Bevin, the energetic minister of labour, was sure that following a policy of 'voluntaryism' would get the men needed to do the jobs.

The government had also considerably depleted the potential armed forces recruitment pool in the British workforce with its Reserved Occupations scheme of January 1939. Under the scheme, some five million men over a certain age, which differed from one occupation to another, in a wide range of occupations, from boiler-making, skilled engineering and lighthouse

OPPOSITE: DELIVERY AFTER RAID
A milkman delivering milk in a London street that has been devastated by a German bombing raid. Firemen are dampening down the ruins behind him.

SHIPBUILDING

Two ship builders at work, their work vital for the continuation of waging war against the enemy.

WINNING THE BATTLE OF BRITAIN IN THE FACTORIES

Fighter aircraft production, unable to produce aircraft fast enough to replace those lost in operations over Europe, was turned into a Battle of Britain-winning operation by the Canadian-born newspaper magnate Lord Beaverbrook, who was made minister of aircraft production by Churchill in May 1940. Following his personal motto – 'Work without Stopping' – he drove the workers on Britain's aircraft production assembly lines through a punishing (and ultimately unsustainable) regime from early June to early November 1940 that produced an average of 62 Hurricanes and 33 Spitfires every week. Where Britain's aircraft industry produced some 4,280 fighter planes in 1940, Germany's managed less than half that number.

keeping to doctors and teachers, were exempted from military service.

While the government had made one step towards controlling the movement of labour in June 1940 by bringing in a Dockers Registration Order, under which dock workers had to register so that they could be moved to wherever in the country they were most needed, it was still seriously underestimating the effect of the Army's manpower requirements on industry. In August 1940, at the height of the Battle of Britain, the Army said that it would need 357,000 recruits by March 1941, followed by another 100,000 a month thereafter. A leading civil servant, Sir William Beveridge was appointed to head a new Manpower Requirements Committee, the purpose of which was to create a detailed numerical and statistical survey of Britain's manpower requirements so that future demand could be assessed and fulfilled.

Beveridge's report, available in December 1940, shook the government severely. In essence, the report said that there were not nearly enough workers in Britain to supply the Army with the numbers of recruits it was demanding while

1940
INTERESTING FACTS

SEPTEMBER
- An agreement between the USA and Great Britain is announced.
- Germany starts to bomb London (the first of 57 consecutive nights).
- 17,000-year-old cave paintings are discovered in Lascaux, France.
- The Hercules Munitions plant in New Jersey explodes killing 55 people.
- Germany, Italy and Japan sign the Tripartite Pact.

OCTOBER
- John Lennon is born during a German air raid.
- Draft registration begins in the USA.
- Italy invades Greece, signalling the start of the Balkans Campaign.

HELPING 'UNCLE JOE'

An extra burden was put on British manufacturing output in 1941 when the Soviet Union was invaded by its former ally, Germany. The Russians, far from buckling under the German onslaught, stood firm. Now one of Britain's allies, Russia had to be helped. Lord Beaverbrook orchestrated a 'Tanks for Russia' week in September, during which every tank that came off the assembly lines, often produced in factories working double time, would be shipped to Russia and the Eastern Front. The first tank for Russia off the assembly line was named 'Stalin';. Others had slogans like 'One for Joe' or 'Greetings to our allies in USSR' chalked on them. Most of the tanks, aircraft, raw materials and food supplies, (which was largely paid for by an Aid to Russia fund set up by Mrs Clementine Churchill) were sent to Russia's ice-free port of Murmansk in merchant navy Arctic Convoys.

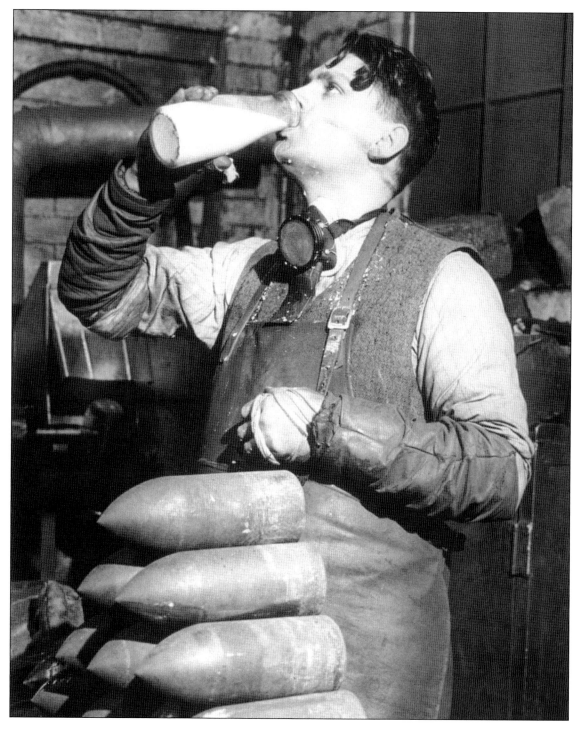

TAKING A BREAK
A factory worker takes a break to drink his daily quota of milk in between grinding bomb shells. In factories where the atmosphere contained a high percentage of lead, workers were advised to drink milk twice a day to counteract the quality of the air they breathed.

leaving enough men working in the munitions industry to produce the amount of arms and armaments this greatly expanded military force would need.

During 1941, largely as a result of the Manpower Requirements Committee's report, Britain's workforce was radically reorganised by the Ministry of Labour, Ernest Bevin having accepted that 'voluntaryism' would have to be replaced by compulsion.

The Reserved Occupations scheme was revised so that distinctions could be made within the reserved occupations between those firms doing essential war work and those whose output was inessential to the war effort. In the former, the ages at which workers could be reserved was lowered, while scheduled ages were revised upwards in the latter. By the end of 1941, there were some 100,000 firms on the Ministry of Labour's Protected Establishments Register.

Bevin also brought in a scheme, by way of a Registration of Employment Order published in March 1941, that allowed the government

to direct people to essential work. The scheme began with the registration of men aged over forty-five and – with great reluctance, for the government did not like the idea of ordering women into work – women of twenty and twenty-one (extended upwards to thirty by the end of the year).

Another law introduced in March 1941, was an Essential Work Order. This covered some four-and-a-half million workers in privately-owned factories in engineering, aircraft production, shipbuilding, building industries, railways and mining, that the Ministry of Labour had decided were doing work of national importance in wartime. Unless they conducted themselves very badly indeed in the workplace, these workers could not be sacked nor could they take leave from work without the permission of the local National Service Office.

Well aware of the importance of having good relations with the workforce and their trade unions in wartime, Bevin and the Ministry of Labour tried to design labour policies that would

BEVIN BOYS

Labour shortages were serious in coal mining, an essential war industry. By 1943, the workforce was an ageing one with few volunteers coming forward. Ernest Bevin's 'Bevin Boys Scheme' of 1943 was another exercise in compulsion. Under the scheme, the names of all men of twenty-five years and under who had not yet enlisted were entered in a lottery from which ten per cent were selected by ballot to go down the mines. The scheme was very unpopular, and forty per cent of those selected objected. Very few objections were upheld and 147 men were eventually sent to prison for refusing to obey their direction to the mines. The Scheme could only be a short-term one, but it brought 21,800 young 'Bevin Boys' to join the 16,000 'optants' (men who had opted for coal mining when they were called up) into the mines and solved a wartime manpower crisis.

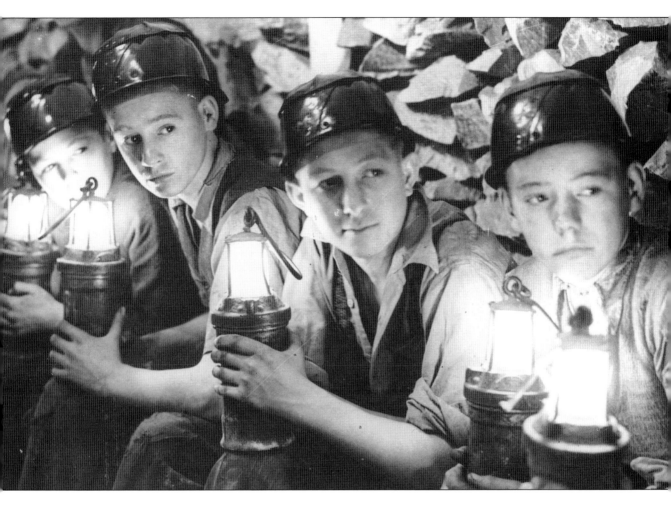

MINE BOYS
Boys from a mining village help to increase Britain's coal output during the war. Their faces show the fear of their first trip underground.

avoid confrontation as much as possible – while also doing something to increase job security and improve working conditions. Even so, and despite strikes having been declared illegal in 1940, over a million working days were lost in 1941 because of strikes and other industrial action, often backed by the trade unions.

It was the sheer, grinding hard work for very long hours, often in pursuit of impossible-to-reach production targets, and often in factories just patched up after the latest bombing raid, that caused many of the strikes. On the whole, the authorities were careful not to go the full length the law allowed by imprisoning striking workers.

Overall, working life in Britain changedradically – and forever – during World War Two. Compulsion, while it allowed the government to move workers to where they were most needed, also meant that people experienced a new mobility. Class and cultural differences became unimportant as people from different backgrounds and different parts of the country worked together, not just to defeat the evil of Nazism, but also to 'build a better Britain'.

1940
INTERESTING FACTS

NOVEMBER
- Roosevelt becomes the US's first and only third-term president.
- Author Agatha Christie publishes *And Then There Were None*.
- The Tacoma Narrows Bridge in Washington collapses during a storm.
- An earthquake in Bucharest, Romania, kills 1000 people.
- An unexpected blizzard kills 144 people in Midwest USA.
- Walt Disney's *Fantasia* is released.
- The city of Coventry is destroyed by 500 Luftwaffe bombers. 75,000 buildings are destroyed and 568 people are killed.
- Hungary, Romania and Slovakia join the Axis powers.

DECEMBER
- Operation Compass – British forces in North Africa begin their first major offensive.
- The city of Sheffield is blitzed by German air raids.
- Roosevelt reveals his Lend-Lease scheme to send aid to Great Britain.
- Gandhi writes his second personal letter to Hitler.
- Second Great Fire of London as bombs start 1,500 fires.

DOING MEN'S WORK

During World War Two, workers in the armaments factories and dockyards of Britain and her allies from the Empire – Australia, Canada, New Zealand and South Africa – provided the Allied cause with 700 warships, thousands of merchant ships, 135,000 aircraft, 160,000 tanks and other armoured vehicles. Nearly seven million of the twenty million or so workers involved were women.

The call-up of men of suitable age not in reserved occupations meant that it was in-evitable, as it had been in World War One, that women would have to be employed to work in the men's places. About five million women in Britain had paid jobs in September 1939. Many of them would have stayed at home but for the fact that the depression of the 1930s put many men and breadwinners out of work. When the war started in 1939, the government made cut-backs in non-essential industries, closing many factories or else making them re-tool to produce essential war-time goods. While many women found themselves making munitions, rather than furniture or fabrics, for instance, nearly 175,000 women found themselves without a job of any kind.

Thus, many women, especially among those who had left school at fourteen to work in factories, were in a position to volunteer for work that would really help the war effort: if your work as a fifteen-year-old involved cutting out the satin linings that went into cutlery boxes, then work in a factory producing things important to the war effort sounded interesting, even attractive – and, of course, it could be work that might involve more money than you had earned in your old job.

OPPOSITE: WOMAN'S WORK
This woman is grinding a 6-pounder tank gun barrel at a British factory where over 650 women were employed in order to release the men for the services during wartime.

MORALE-BOOSTER FROM THE RAF

Attempts to sap the morale of Britain's munitions workers played a major part in the broadcasts from Germany made by Lord Haw Haw (*below*) (the notorious traitor, William Joyce, who fled to Germany in 1939), but his taunts were seldom left unanswered. Phyllis Pearson, an artist and map-maker, was given a pass allowing her to draw the workers in a munitions factory in Blackburn – 'absolutely superb women [whose] morale was high even though they were working under unbelievable pressure'. She recalled nearly fifty years later, for the broadcaster and journalist Mavis Nicholson, how one particular broadcast by Lord Haw Haw was swiftly countered. Lord Haw Haw had said, after the Battle of El Alamein, that the shells from British munitions factories could not pierce the armour of German tanks being chased across the Western Desert. Just two days after Lord Haw Haw's broadcast, photographs taken by the RAF in North Africa clearly showing German tanks wrecked by British shells were put up in the factory.

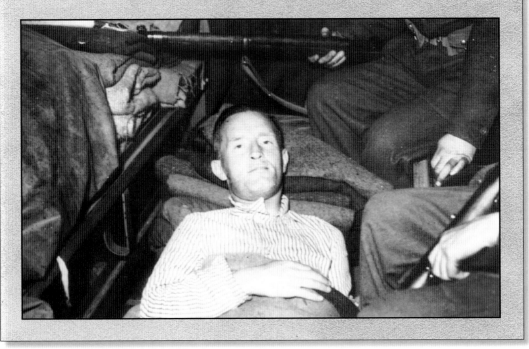

MUNITIONS WORK

Women were called up for war work from March 1941 and, although there were many different types of jobs, many went to work in the munitions factories. Above is a woman at work in a London munitions factory producing Bren guns and other small arms.

WARTIME HARVEST

A group of land girls bring in sheaves of wheat from a field reclaimed for the war effort from four hundred acres of unused land on the Sussex Downs. The field is thought to have been the largest of its kind in Britain. Opposite – a pair of Women's Land Army volunteers take a welcome break to drink from Lady Well in Sticklepath, England.

WOMEN WELDERS

The British government created this slogan to reassure women that they could do factory work as easily as housework: 'If you've sewed on buttons, or made buttonholes on a machine, you can learn to do spot welding'.

At the start of the war, women's readiness to take on jobs previously done by men was not matched by the Government's eagerness to employ them. The Government was well aware of the trade unions' antipathy towards allowing women to take over men's jobs. Among male workers, few of whom felt the jingoistic patriotism that had swept young men into the recruiting offices in August 1914, there was a similar reluctance to see women on the machines or the assembly lines next to them. Then there was the wide-spread belief that women, being physically inferior, would not be able to do men's work well or efficiently. An extension of this argument was the feeling that women would never deserve to be paid the same as men. Even more serious was the fear that putting women to work would be a real danger to home and family life. When would houses be cleaned, food bought, and meals provided for children and husbands returning from their reserved occupation work?

As the war went on and the great contribution that women were making to the civilian war effort was recognised, much of the sting went out of such arguments. As the popular song of 1942 put it: 'it's the girl that makes the thing that holds the oil that oils the ring, that works the thingumebob that's going to win the war'. With men disappearing into the armed forces in increasing numbers, the need for women to replace them became increasingly urgent, especially in armaments and munitions factories. At the beginning of the war, women already with jobs were expected to simply carry on with them.

In the early months of the war women beginning work in engineering, munitions and armaments factories found that, in many cases, the men they would eventually replace were still on the job, resentful at having to go to war

A MAN'S WAGE FOR A MAN'S JOB

Some women doing men's work during the war did achieve wage parity with men. One such was Edith Kent, the first woman to work as a welder in Devonport dockyard in Plymouth, where she began work in 1941. Kent was a skilled worker and short enough, at 4 ft 11 in, to crawl inside the torpedo tubes she worked on. In 1943 she was given a pay rise from £5 6s (five pounds six shillings) to £6 6s, which meant she was earning the same as the men, and more than some of them. At this time, the average male manual worker in Britain was earning about £5 8s 6d a week. The hard work did Edith Kent no harm. She celebrated her hundredth birthday with a tea dance in 2008.

anyway, and even more resentful of the women waiting to take their jobs. Again and again, women reported how difficult their first weeks and months were, trying to understand the work and machines that were never fully explained to them, in factories that were cold, unfriendly and uncomfortable places, and, more often than not, with insufficient lavatories and wash places for a suddenly greatly increased female workforce.

Working away from home became a major issue for women during the war, and whether a woman was 'mobile' or 'immobile' became an important employment exchange distinction.

Their home commitments meant that many women had to stay within daily travelling distance of their work, while others, mostly young and with no family commitments, could find themselves sent almost anywhere in the country that had been designated a Demand Region for workers. (Britain was divided into eleven regions, designated either 'Supply' or 'Demand', by the Ministry of Labour.) If the woman was directed to a factory far from home, she could very likely find herself living in a hostel, a school or hall, which had been commandeered as living accommodation for workers 'for the duration'.

THE NERVE CENTRE
Women from the Auxiliary Fire Service work in the London Fire Regional Control Room where the mobilising of fire appliances was carried out by means of detailed maps.

Eventually, many women factory workers found themselves working up to sixty or eighty hours a week, and in aircraft factories when the very survival of the nation depended on having enough planes to fight the enemy, an exhausting 112 hours a week. In fact, forty-five hours was more usual, in eight-hour shifts if the factory was on a twenty-four-hour production schedule, and up to twelve-hour shifts – say, from 6 a.m. to 6 p.m. – if the factory or works did not carry on through the night. If a woman was married and had a husband at home, she might not see him for days on end, if one or other of them was on the night shift (from 10 p.m. until 6 a.m.). A lot of young married women chose pregnancy as the way out of full-time factory work.

When piece-work was brought in, replacing an earlier system which provided bonuses for those who worked well or exceeded targets, it was very easy for a woman not to earn her full wage, perhaps by having to wait for a broken machine to be repaired. During the war, equal pay for equal work did not become a target for women as it was to do in the decades after it. On the whole, most women were happy to be getting money regularly, which could be used to help with household bills. Even when they were in better paid jobs – generally to be found in munitions work or in transport, especially the railways or buses – women expected to be paid less than men.

WOMEN'S LAND ARMY

Another group of women doing men's work during the war were the members of the Women's Land Army. Armies of female land workers were set up in Scotland and in England and Wales during World War One, but were rather too late on the scene to be really effective. With war obviously looming again, the lesson was learnt and the Women's Land Army (WLA) was reconvened in June 1939, with an official

POPULAR CULTURE
1941

POPULAR SONGS
- *Chattanooga Choo Choo*, Glenn Miller
- *A String Of Pearls*, Glenn Miller
- *Green Eyes*, Jimmy Dorsey
- *Amapola* (Pretty Little Poppy), Jimmy Dorsey
- *God Bless The Child*, Billie Holiday
- *Boogie Woogie Bugle Boy*, The Andrew Sisters
- *Tonight We Love*, Nelson Eddy
- *Oh! Look At Me Now*, Tommy Dorsey with Frank Sinatra

1941 saw the height of the Big Band era and the dance halls ruled. Ballroom tickets were affordable to most and the Depression was quickly becoming a distant memory. Frank Sinatra was Tommy Dorsey's lead vocalist, backed by the Pied Pipers.

POPULAR FILMS
- *Sergeant York*, starring Gary Cooper
- *Buck Privates*, starring Abbott and Costello
- *Tobacco Road*, starring Charley Grapewin
- *Dumbo*, Walt Disney animation
- *How Green Was My Valley*, starring Walter Pidgeon and Maureen O'Hara
- *Citizen Kane*, starring Orson Welles
- *The Maltese Falcon*, starring Humphrey Bogart
- *Here Comes Mr Jordan*, Robert Montgomery

FIREFIGHTERS
It wasn't just in Britain that women were called into the fire service. This picture shows women directing a hose after the Japanese attack on the US naval base at Pearl Harbor.

minimum recruitment age of seventeen – which was often ignored or lied about by girls eager to join. By 1944, the WLA was a force of eighty thousand women, a third of whom came from Britain's cities and had no previous experience of farm work. A sister organisation, the Women's Timber Corps, one of whose more vital wartime jobs was cutting pit props for coal mines, was started in 1942 and eventually numbered six thousand women.

Although Land Girls, and the Lumberjills of the Timber Corps, were issued with a uniform, including a green jersey, cream shirt, brown breeches, brown felt hat and khaki overcoat, the term 'Army' was something of a misnomer – even though the WLA was definitely in the front line of the 'Dig for Victory' campaign. A Land Girl could modify her uniform to suit her personal taste – the breeches, although at first seen as quite daring style-wise, were often

LUMBERJILLS

A group of young women working in the lumber industry, fell and strip young trees while war rages on around them.

LEAPING LANDGIRLS
Even after a hard day's work, land girls still knew how to have fun.

replaced by dungarees or standard trousers – and the only discipline she was subjected to was the threat of dismissal if her work was not up to standard. Since dismissal from the WLA simply meant redirection into the auxiliary services or war industry, deliberately trying to get the sack was not much of an option for exhausted Land Girls or Lumberjills.

Many young women chose to join the WLA because they thought working out-of-doors was preferable to being cooped up in a factory and also, since they would be in the country, they would be far away from the bombing. On the whole, the Women's Land Army met both these criteria – although not always: the artist Mary Fedden found herself, after just six weeks at an agricultural college in Devon, working on a farm in Gloucestershire next to the Filton aircraft works which was subjected to very regular bombings for a year. And it was often exhausting work with very basic accommodation that had no hot water or electricity to look forward to at the end of the working day. Nor was the pay very good: about 17s 6d (about 82p) a week, plus keep.

In fact, being a Land Girl was far more arduous than working in a factory. The work had to be done every day, and sometimes far into the night, summer and winter, in good weather and bad. On many farms, there might be one or two older male farm workers to advise and help with really heavy work, like building hay ricks or pig pens, but many Land Girls found themselves on an all-female farm, where they were the farmer's only help, with perhaps some help from schoolboys and schoolgirls at harvest time and also some help, later in the war, from German and Italian prisoners of war. Many Land Girls found that German POWs worked harder than the Italians, but that the latter were much more light-hearted, and sang a lot – beautifully.

More than sixty years after World War Two

1941
INTERESTING FACTS

JANUARY
- Bugs Bunny makes his second appearance in *Elmer's Pet Rabbit*.
- Lend-Lease is introduced into the US Congress.
- British troops attack Italian-held Eritrea.
- British and Australian forces attack and capture Tobruk, Libya.
- Aviator Charles Lindbergh suggests to US Congress that they negotiate a neutrality pact with Hitler.

FEBRUARY
- The Air Training Corps was formed.
- Benghazi falls to the Western Desert Force and Rommel is appointed commander of Afrika Korps.
- Three nights of intensive bombing raids over Swansea, South Wales. A total number of 397 casualties and 230 deaths.
- Glenn T. Seaborg discovers plutonium.

MARCH
- *Captain America and Bucky* comic first published.
- Bulgaria joins the Axis powers.
- Roosevelt signs the Lend-Lease Act.
- Roosevelt opens National Gallery of Art in Washington DC.

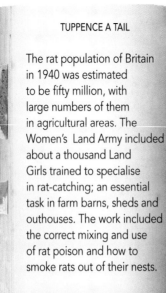

TUPPENCE A TAIL

The rat population of Britain in 1940 was estimated to be fifty million, with large numbers of them in agricultural areas. The Women's Land Army included about a thousand Land Girls trained to specialise in rat-catching; an essential task in farm barns, sheds and outhouses. The work included the correct mixing and use of rat poison and how to smoke rats out of their nests.

Because the Land Girls' wages were not large, many girls, specialised in the job or not, joined rat-catching sessions with the farmer and his dogs in order to earn a little extra cash. The standard price for rat skins was 2d a tail. Another source of income was moleskins. The moles, when killed, would be skinned and the pelts mounted on boards to dry before being sold.

ended, Britain officially honoured the work of the Women's Land Army, which was disbanded in 1950. There were still some thirty thousand surviving Land Girls and Lumberjills in 2008, all of them eligible to receive a special commemorative badge, to be worn on Remembrance Sundays and other official occasions, recognising their 'tireless work for the benefit of their nation' in wartime.

WARTIME NURSES

Nursing provided a third alternative for women choosing to do civilian work during the war. War made huge demands on Britain's civilian nursing systems, severely aggravated by the fact that World War Two, unlike the first, was fought as much on the Home Front as on the battlefield. Trained nurses were needed in Britain as much at ARP first-aid posts, in ambulances and in air-raid shelters as they were in hospitals, which themselves had thousands more patients to deal with than in peace-time. While teaching hospitals could train their own nurses, organisations

including the British Red Cross, the Order of St John of Jerusalem, the First Aid Nursing Yeomanry and the Voluntary Aid Detachments (VADs), were called on to provide nurses both at home and overseas, many of them in the auxiliary services, where they worked as volunteers rather than service personnel.

The Ministry of Health set up an Emergency Medical Service before the war started and also began recalling trained nurses who had retired or who had left nursing when they married. There was also the Civil Nursing reserve, which young women could join on a part-time basis; the advent of war turned Civil Nursing reservists into auxiliary nurses, liable to be called up to help with the various evacuation schemes that were quickly put into action.

By the end of September 1939, the Ministry had enrolled fifteen thousand trained nurses and twenty thousand auxiliary nurses and accepted

VOLUNTARY AID DETACHMENT
Nurses demonstrate how to fit an infant's gas helmet at the VAD annual training camp in
Fleetwood. It was fitted with a hand-operated pump underneath for supplying air to the child.

1940
INTERESTING FACTS

MARCH
- Ernest Bevin calls for women to fill vital jobs.
- Rommel launches first offence in Cyrenaica.
- Yugoslavia joins the Axis powers.
- British naval forces defeat Italy at the Battle of Cape Matapan, sinking five warships.
- A German Lorenz code machine operator accidentally sent a message twice, giving the British mathematician Bill Tutte time to decipher it.

APRIL
- Axis forces capture Benghazi.
- Germany invades Yugoslavia and Greece.
- German troops enter Belgrade.
- Soviet Union and Japan sign a neutrality act.
- Alexandros Koryzis, the Greek prime minister, commits suicide as German troops approach Athens.

MAY
- The breakfast cereal, Cheerios, is introduced by General Mills under the name CheeriOats.
- Orson Welles' film *Citizen Kane* premieres in New York.
- Bob Hope performs his first USO show at California's March Field.
- House of Commons is damaged following an air raid.

for training another seventy-six thousand people, most of them women. By the end of the war, so great was the need for trained nurses, that the training time for State Registered Nurses had been reduced by 1945 from four years to three. Since the minimum age for training was eighteen, many girls younger than this did part-time training, joining organisations such as the Red Cross and working in emergency centres for the homeless or first aid posts as well as in hospitals.

The biggest provider of nurse aides during the war was the Voluntary Aid Detachment (VAD). Formed in 1910, the VAD, most of whose members were women and all of whom were volunteers, did invaluable work, both at home, on the Western Front and even further afield during World War One. Before World War Two broke out, VADs were reorganised so that they could give additional support to the general medical services in the event of war.

About fifteen thousand women became VADs during the war, many of them by joining the Red Cross, which gave them some initial nurse-aid training. VADs were civilian volunteers, although they did wear a smart uniform, and were not counted as part of the auxiliary services, even when working in services hospitals or medical centres. As untrained volunteers, VADs tended to get all the dirty work but also found themselves doing the work of qualified nurses, such as giving injections and helping in operations.

CHILDREN HELP THE WAR EFFORT
World War Two was like no other war that Britain had been involved in. Because it was fought on the Home Front as well as in many far away countries, there was no way that children could be kept sheltered in happy ignorance of the fact that there was a war on. From the beginning, the government reached out to children old enough to help in war work.

Once the great evacuation of mothers and children from the perceived war zones had been completed – and the planning for this had closely involved the children for months before it actually took place – various ministries quickly swung into action with such famous schemes as the 'Dig for Victory' and 'Make do and mend' campaigns.

The DIG FOR VICTORY campaign – to use the capital letters in which the government

GROW YOUR OWN FOOD
A young Duke of Norfolk demonstrates the correct way to hold a rabbit during an exhibition designed to educate people about growing their own food.

GARDENING ON THE CURRICULUM
Children from Surrey elementary school are taught gardening during the holidays to keep them occupied and also to help them contribute to the war effort.

launched its great scheme at the outbreak of war – was essential to the country's survival because much agricultural land had been given over to pasture or taken out of use as the country's reliance on foreign food imports increased in the 1930s. German U-boats in the Atlantic greatly diminished the amount of food Britain could expect to receive from the countries of the Empire. The Dig for Victory campaign was therefore conducted on a very large scale indeed, with millions of propaganda posters and instructional leaflets being distributed the length and breadth of the country.

When he launched the Dig for Victory scheme in a BBC broadcast in October 1939, the Agriculture Minister, Sir Reginald Dorman-Smith called only on men and women to dig an allotment in their spare time. However, his words won an enthusiastic response from children too, which the government was not slow to respond to. Among the hundreds of brightly coloured Dig for Victory posters that began pouring out of the Ministry of Food, many actually showed children doing the digging and the Ministry reinforced the message by distributing posters and leaflets to schools in every part of the country to be pinned up in classrooms, canteens and corridors.

Parks and botanical gardens, back yards and front gardens, school playgrounds, wasteland and, as the war went on, thousands of bomb sites were turned into allotments – about 1,400,000 of them by 1943 – for the growing of vegetables to feed the people. Many householders also managed to fit a hen house into their gardens which, by mid-war were producing something like twenty-five per cent of the country's officially acknowledged supplies of fresh eggs.

Another form of live-stock which many people kept was the pig. A pig-keeping craze swept Britain, with thousands of Pig Clubs keeping pigs in back gardens, on allotments and behind pubs. The pigs were fed on kitchen waste, much of which was collected in special pig food bins set up on street corners. At the same time, thousands of acres of agricultural land were

VEGETABLES AS PROPAGANDA

Potato Pete and Doctor Carrot were two figures created by the Ministry of Food as part of its propaganda campaign to boost wartime growth and consumption of vegetables. Both potatoes and carrots, which were widely grown on allotments and in gardens, featured in perhaps the Ministry's most notorious dish, Woolton Pie, named after Lord Woolton, the Minister of Food. Propaganda of another kind helped fuel the popularity of carrots among children. In order to keep secret their use of radar to warn them of incoming planes, the Air Ministry prepared some spoof research in 1941 purporting to show that British fighter pilots had extra-good night vision because they ate lots of carrots. While the story may not have taken-in the enemy for long, it was probably much more successful than any of the Ministry of Food's recipes in boosting the eating of carrots among British children.

THE GRIM REALITY OF KEEPING HENS

Although she was just a very little girl in wartime Chingford, Mary Murphy remembers well how her mother dealt with the family's hens.

'My mother, who was a butcher's daughter from Kent, kept chickens at the bottom of our long, narrow garden among the fruit trees and blackcurrant bushes. She used to buy day-old chicks from Hoe Street market – Rhode Island Reds and White Leghorns – and we kept them warm with a light bulb in a cardboard box until they were old enough to go outside. I had to collect the eggs from the nest box in the chicken coop, still warm and smelling of the sweet straw. My father was too sentimental to kill them, but my mother had no qualms. I still have the axe. She would give the chicken to me by its feet with its head hanging off and blood still dripping to carry back to the house. I would hold it at arm's length because sure enough half way down the garden its wings would start flapping.'

brought back into use throughout Britain.

Children played a big part in all these different ways of providing food in wartime. 'Digging for Victory' became not only a usefully patriotic activity for children, but also something that, as well as being interesting and exciting, was surprisingly life-enhancing. Even eating boiled cabbage in the school canteen at lunchtime could have something pleasurable about it when you knew that the cabbage came from the allotment outside on the playing fields and that it had been grown by your schoolmates.

Home-produced foods could have their drawbacks for children. Schoolgirl Joan Elliott, at home in Sheffield during the school holidays, remembers the awful smell of the hen food, which had to be boiled every day to stop it going off. She also remembers a particular Sunday lunch when the family had roast chicken. 'Is this Dora?' asked one of Joan's siblings, naming the family's favourite, rather elderly hen. There was a dreadful silence before the family went on eating.

Among the children who benefited most from 'Digging for Victory' were the thousands

HARVESTING POTATOES
Boys from Five Ways Grammar School in Birmingham harvest potatoes on a farm in Wales during World War Two.

PIG AND POULTRY CLUB
Schoolchildren in Harrogate, with the help of their headmaster, started their own pig and poultry club. Here, one of the young farmers is holding one of the farm's geese.

THE TIMBER CORPS
Miss Daphne Hubbard, a member of the Timber Corps, fells a tree at a timber camp in Bury St. Edmunds, England.

of children evacuated from big cities into the countryside. Not only did they discover that – in the often-quoted remark of a boy writing home to his mother – 'they have something called spring here', but they also learnt where food came from – milk from cows, not bottles, for instance – and how it was produced. Many of them enjoyed helping on the farm so much that when they grew up they left city life behind and returned to work in agriculture.

As more and more agricultural workers were called up, so thousands of young people had to be brought in to work on farms. While the well-known Women's Land Army worked on the land all year round, at harvest time many thousands on children, including whole classes from city schools, joined in helping bring the harvest home. If these children were billeted on farms, then they might also spend much time feeding hens, looking after goats and even learning to milk cows and help – with supervision – in cleaning the milking parlour and looking after the cow shed.

For children living in towns and cities other splendid ways of helping with the war effort soon presented themselves. It was the newspaper magnate Lord Beaverbrook, appointed Minister of Aircraft Production in 1940, who made the word 'salvage' into a weapon of war that could be wielded by children as much as adults.

In a newspaper article published in July 1940, Beaverbrook asked the British public for aluminium to help make fighter planes. He had

POTS AND PANS
Housewives turned out their cupboards to find old aluminium pots and pans for use in the war effort. The aluminium was smelted into pure ingots, which in turn were made into essential parts for Royal Airforce planes.

seen how the desperate need for fighter planes in the summer of 1940 had led to every crashed plane being taken to the ministry's vast Metal and Produce Recovery Depot in Oxfordshire so that every reusable spare part could be salvaged. But, said Lord Beaverbrook, the planemakers were still not getting enough aluminium. Could the people help? Indeed, they could. Housewives up and down the land began searching their cupboards for pots and pans to take to their nearest WVS depot.

In the end the government got an embarrassment of aluminium, much of it of little use in aircraft production. But Lord Beaverbrook's 'stunt', as it came to be called, had touched a chord with men, women and children. 'Salvage' became as important a word in the war on the Home Front as the phrases 'Dig for Victory' and 'Make do and mend'. Schools, children's comics, newspapers and magazines all encouraged children in their salvage-collecting efforts. *Good Housekeeping*, for instance, ran a Children's Salvage Competition in 1943 which required children to enter designs for posters with a salvage theme, the prizes for which were Savings Certificates and Savings Stamps – and the chance for the prize-winning children to see their posters reproduced in the magazine.

Among the salvage schemes entered into with enthusiasm by children were schemes to collect metal, glass, including jam jars (provided they weren't being used as beer glasses in country pubs), paper, books (used to re-stock Blitzed libraries and for keeping the Services supplied with reading material), tins, rags and scraps of material (especially wool for battle dress) and silver paper, all of which could be reprocessed or re-used in some way. Even meat bones were useful, for they could be turned into aircraft glue.

The metal that children could gather included old bicycles, tricycles and pedal cars,

1941
INTERESTING FACTS

MAY
- British Royal Navy capture a German submarine U-110. On board is the latest Enigma cryptography machine which the Allies later use to break coded German messages.
- Rudolf Hess parachutes into Scotland, supposedly on a peace mission.
- The Z3 – the first working fully automatic computer – is presented in Berlin by Konrad Zuse.
- First British jet aircraft takes to the air.
- Battle of Crete begins.
- The German *Bismarck* is damaged in an aerial torpedo attack. The following day it sinks in the North Atlantic, killing 2,300 people.

JUNE
- 4,000 residents of Chongqing are asphyxiated in a bomb shelter during a bombing raid.
- British and Free French forces invade Syria.
- An ammunition plant explodes on the outskirts of Belgrade killing 1,500 people.
- Walt Disney's *The Reluctant Dragon* is released.
- Operation Barbarossa – Germany invades the Soviet Union.
- Hungary, Slovakia and Albania

prams – both real and toy, the metal tops of their mother's scouring powder packs and many battered and rusty tin toys. The last, given the drastically reduced toy production during the war, could be a real sacrifice on the part of the child handing over the toy car or train.

Hundreds of thousands of children joined 'Cogs' corps, a nationwide scheme that turned children into 'cogs' in the great salvage-collecting machine. As *The Times* newspaper noted in 1941, the Cogs scheme was based 'on the knowledge that all children like responsible, worthwhile work to do. Schools were asked to co-operate and most did'. There was a Cog battle song, written by a WVS member, with a first line of 'There'll always be a dustbin', Cogs could win badges for collecting scrap and, for some corps, there were lapel badges, like the one in the shape of a cogwheel designed by a local woman for a corps in Kent.

Apart from the great salvage business, there was another unexpected result of Lord Beaverbrook's call for aluminium for fighter planes. Spitfire Funds, in which people gathered together to raise money to pay for the building of new aircraft, with Spitfires (estimated by the Ministry of Aircraft Production to cost £5000 each) the most popular, were a spontaneous reaction of the public to the call for pots and pans. Again, children were in the forefront of collecting money, often through their schools which ran Spitfire Funds of their own. And, according to the historian Angus Calder, in *The People's War*, it was a schoolboy who started the practice of paying for parts of aircraft when he sent a guinea (£1 5p) to Lord Beaverbrook to pay for a Spitfire's thermometer. Beaverbrook immediately published a list of what it would cost people to pay for aircraft parts, from sixpence (two and a half new pence) for a rivet to £2000 for a wing.

While Beaverbrook's price list, if not actually plucked from the empty air, bore little relation to economic reality in the aircraft building business, it was a portent of the savings boom that became such a feature of life in wartime Britain. In fact,

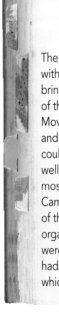

CHILDREN'S WARTIME SAVINGS SCHEMES

The War Savings Campaign, with its great theme of saving to bring victory, was an extension of the 1930s' National Savings Movement. Savings Certificates and Savings Stamps, which could be bought by children as well as adults, were two of the most important elements in the Campaign. Among the hundreds of thousands of savings groups organised during the War, many were in schools. Head teachers had a supply of savings stamps which pupils could buy with money raised outside school in a myriad different ways, sticking the stamps into their own savings stamps booklets. Larger schools might collect several thousand pounds a year in National Savings. In addition, children were alerted, like their parents, to the value of saving for the war effort by the BBC's regular Sunday evening updates on saving schemes throughout the country. Special savings 'drives' such as War Weapons Week, Warships Week and Wings for Victory Weeks encouraged the public, too.

saving money to help the war effort became an even bigger obsession with everyone, including children, than collecting salvage.

Many thousands of older children learnt the discipline of working together to help their country in its hour of need by way of such voluntary youth organisations as the Boy Scouts, Girl Guides, Boys Brigade and the junior wing of the Red Cross. Other young people, who if the war had not intervened, would still have been schoolchildren until they reached fifteen, found themselves doing paid adult work at fourteen.

SALVAGE SCHEME
A housewife puts household items in marked sacks during a salvage scheme in Hornsey, north London.

PULL WITH ALL YOUR MIGHT
A man and a boy use all their strength to try and salvage a bicycle from the rubble of a bombed house in London.

Although they could not legally join such organisations as ARP until they were sixteen, there was nothing to prevent fourteen-year-olds taking on other great responsibilities, filling the vacancies left by older men called up into the services.

The Post Office was an important employer of fourteen-year-olds. Although Post Office managers tried to ensure that their youngest employees got at least half a day's schooling a week, for very many children, the day they left school at fourteen was the last day of their formal education. Many of them were employed as telegram delivery boys, riding on their bicycles through war-damaged streets to deliver messages. As there was really only one kind of telegram that got priority delivery during the War – the one from the War Office that contained the news that a husband or son was missing or had been killed – delivering telegrams became a truly terrible job for any fourteen-year-old.

In early 1941, with the Blitz at its height and invasion all too likely, the Ministry of Information

CHARITY BICK, G.M.

The George Medal, awarded in recognition of acts of outstanding gallantry on the Home Front, was established by King George VI in 1940, the same year that the George Cross (the civilian equivalent of the Victoria Cross) was established. The youngest person to be awarded a George Medal during the Second World War was 14-years-old Charity Bick. Charity chose to lie about her age, saying she was 16 in order to get a job as an ARP Services Despatch Rider. She was awarded the George Medal for her extraordinary bravery during a very heavy air-raid on Birmingham in February 1941. During the raid she not only helped her ARP warden father put out an incendiary bomb but also rode a bicycle a mile and a quarter through a heavy bombing raid to get a message to the ARP control post about another serious incident that had knocked out telephone lines.

in co-operation with the War Office issued fourteen million copies of a leaflet called 'Beating the INVADER' the main part of which was a message signed by Prime Minister, Winston Churchill, in which he told the nation to 'STAND FIRM' and 'CARRY ON'. A few months later, with the war situation looking no better, young people were brought officially into the war effort, with all sixteen- to eighteen-year-olds being required to register for war service, whether in a youth organisation or a junior service.

The Air Ministry had already (in January 1941) formed the Air Training Corps (ATC), for boys aged between sixteen and eighteen. This was the first state-directed, properly regimented youth movement ever organised in Britain. Thousands of boys learned to identify aeroplanes with the aid of illustrations on cigarette cards and outlines published in comics and newspapers. They were thrilled by the exploits of the RAF fighter pilots who had saved the nation in the Battle of Britain, and were greatly attracted by the thought of wearing a proper RAF uniform. Within six months some two hundred thousand boys, all proudly wearing smart uniforms, were sitting at desks happy to study the mathematics and related subjects that most of them had found pretty boring at school.

The ATC example was quickly followed by the Army and the Royal Navy, who founded the Army Cadet Force and the Sea Cadets as their youth training corps. The War Office also scrapped the old Officers' Training Corps and replaced them with Junior Training Corps (JTC), or school cadet units. The boys could officially sign up for the Cadets at fourteen, although many did so at twelve. The Cadets operated in schools under the auspices of the Army Cadet Force. One of the attractions of joining a school JTC was attending an annual camp at which the boys learned to use rifles, Sten guns and even Thompson sub-machine guns.

Fourteen-year-old boys could also join a Sea Cadets corps, which they could stay in until they reached eighteen, learning the skills needed to become a trained seaman in the Royal Navy or the Merchant Navy.

Not surprisingly, girls were not offered the same sort of national service opportunities as boys in 1939, and it was not until 1942 that the Girls' Training Corps (GTC), the Girls' Naval Training Corps (GNTC) and the Women's Junior Air Corps (WJAC) were formed to give girls pre-service entry training. Inevitably, perhaps, many girls,

NOT ENOUGH PRAMS
Workers at a Market pram factory in Letchworth, Hertfordshire, do their best to solve the shortage of baby carriages in Britain.

THE SEA CADETS
Boys as young as fourteen years of age could join the British Sea Cadets. Here one of the cadets can be seen training for semaphore signalling.

despite their smart uniforms, found themselves doing much more tea-making, cooking and office work than fighting training, although they were introduced to the complexities of Morse Code, radio communications, signalling and electronic engineering.

DEFENDING THE PEOPLE

British towns were bombed from aeroplanes during World War One – not extensively and with less than fifteen thousand people killed – but enough to bring anti-aircraft guns, air-raid warnings and searchlights into use as part of the nation's regular home defence equipment. It was clear that should there be another war, the British population would be in the front line. Clear, too, was the fact that Britain's citizens would have to be involved in a radically improved civil defence operation, expanded to include defending the nation from air attack.

Although the British government began thinking about air raid precautions in 1924, during the meetings of a sub-committee of the Committee for Imperial Defence, not a lot in the way of serious planning was done for another decade. A committee set up in 1931 to look into the provision of Air Raid Precautions (ARP) services in London reported that, in the face of some truly appalling estimates of the number of bombs that could be expected to drop on Britain from the first day of any war, plans should be made to evacuate about 3.5 million people from London.

In 1934-35 ARP planning was extended beyond London to cover the country as a whole, as part of the nation's overall civil defence planning. At the same time, an Air Raid

1941
INTERESTING FACTS

JULY
- Japan calls up one million men for military service.
- Germans massacre Polish scientists and writers in the captured city of Lwów.
- A BBC broadcast by 'Colonel Britton' calls on the people of occupied Europe to resist the Nazis under the slogan of 'V for Victory'.
- General Douglas MacArthur is named commander of all US forces in the Philipinnes.

AUGUST
- The first American Jeep is produced.
- Roosevelt and Winston create the Atlantic Charter.
- UK and Soviet forces invade Iran.
- The Soviets announce the destruction of the Dnieper Dam to prevent its capture by the Germans.

SEPTEMBER
- Jews over the age of six forced to wear the Star of David in all German-occupied areas.
- The Siege of Leningrad begins.

WOMEN'S JUNIOR AIR CORPS
These two young women from the Women's Junior Air Corps are attending a rally at Belle Vue, Manchester. Before attending the funfair they are making sure their hair is in place.

EVACUATION REHEARSAL
A group of children set off on an evacuation rehearsal in London.

Precautions department was formed within the Home Office. ARP planners were jerked into more serious action by the part played by planes in the Spanish Civil War from 1936, especially the hugely destructive bombing in April 1937 of the Basque town of Guernica by the German Condor Legion supporting the Fascists. In France, the government had already issued a handbook explaining its evacuation plans to all French people. At first, the action in Britain was still moderate – not much more than a radio appeal in January 1937 for volunteers for ARP work and a request to local authorities to beef up their civil defence planning, in which ARP would play a major role. The response was poor, and at the beginning of 1938 the government used force in the form of the Air Raid Precautions Act, to get local authorities to do detailed planning on civil defence, including how the ARP, first aid and ambulance, fire services and bomb disposal units would be organised and used in the event of war. Interestingly, civil defence did not become an organisation with capital letters – Civil Defence – until September 1941, when Air Raid Precautions and the new National Fire Service (NFS) were amalgamated.

Each local authority was directed to have a Civil Defence headquarters building, from which the various services would be directed to where their services were needed most. The London Regional Civil Defence Headquarters, which oversaw the work of the nine civil defence areas into which the capital was divided, was set up in a hastily reinforced basement in the Geological Museum in South Kensington. When the first workers – all of them young women aged nineteen or twenty – arrived, there was still plenty of evidence of the presence of rats and mice amid the cement dust left behind by the reinforcing work. The women worked in shifts – ten or twelve women in each of three eight-hour shifts every day, with the first shift starting at 7 a.m. and the last at 11 p.m.

Volunteering for ARP remained slow until Hitler invaded Czechoslovakia in September 1938. Now volunteer numbers soared, with the new members finding themselves helping with ARP blackout trials and practice responses to 'incidents' – ARP volunteers always responded to 'incidents', never to fires, gas-main explosions, burst water-mains or bombs. They were responsible for making sure that people responded to the blackout regulations and that no chink of light could be seen through the windows. Also, if families became separated during an air raid, they were responsible for reuniting them if at all possible.

The ARP jobs that men and women could

1941
INTERESTING FACTS

SEPTEMBER
- The first Liberty ship, SS *Patrick Henry*, is launched at Baltimore, Maryland.
- The Moscow Conference begins to arrange urgent assistance for Russia.
- Babi Yar massacre – German troops kill 33,771 Jews from Kiev.

OCTOBER
- Operation Typhoon – a German offensive against Moscow.
- General Hideki Tojo becomes the fortieth prime minister of Japan.
- Thousands of civilians are killed by the Germans as they rampage Yugoslavia.
- Walt Disney releases his animated film, *Dumbo*.
- Roosevelt approves US$1 billion Lend-Lease aid to the Soviet Union.
- Destroyer USS *Reuben James* is torpedoed by the Germans killing more than 100 sailors.

NOVEMBER
- Soviet hospital ship, *Armenia*, is sunk by German planes while evacuating refugees. Approximately 5,000 lives are lost.
- Ski troops are launched for the first time as the temperatures start to drop drastically in the Soviet Union.

A RAIN OF DEATH

The 1931 committee looking into ARP services in Britain was given a terrifying series of estimates by experts. The committee was told that in a future war, the country could expect to receive an opening assault from the enemy's air force (aka Germany's Luftwaffe) of up to 3,500 tons of bombs in the first twenty-four hours, and as many as 600 tons of bombs dropped on it every day thereafter. In the opening assault, there could be 60,000 people killed and 120,000 wounded; in every week after that, the ARP services could be dealing with 66,000 dead and 130,000 wounded. In the face of such figures, the committee was forced to the conclusion that evacuation would be an essential part of wartime defence. No one seemed to have doubted the ability of Germany to produce bombers in such huge numbers and of a size necessary to deliver such attacks. In the event, such cataclysmic figures were never realised. Over the seventy-six nights of bombing during the Blitz in London there were nearly 10,000 deaths and at the end of the devastating eleven-hour raid on Coventry on 14 November 1940, 554 people were dead and a thousand houses had been destroyed, along with many factories and Coventry's medieval cathedral.

volunteer for included wardens and messengers, casualty and first aid workers, stretcher bearers, ambulance drivers and people trained to provide an anti-gas service. From the first, women volunteered in greater numbers than men, perhaps because men knew that in the event of war they would either be in reserved occupations at home or called-up into the forces. It was not until May 1940 that men were given their own civil defence organisation, the Local Defence Volunteers, later re-named the Home Guard and soon known to all as 'Dad's Army'.

Women who volunteered early for the ARP services were mostly directed into the ambulance services, either as drivers or as first aid assistants. As civilian volunteers, they had no ranks or officer titles, but there was an ARP uniform. At first, this simply amounted to the ARP volunteer wearing a metal helmet, an armband, a metal badge and carrying a whistle. By the end of 1939, ARP women were wearing mackintosh-style coats made of a thin, dark-blue denim-like material. A much more practical heavier battle-dress style uniform, including trousers,

COVENTRY CATHEDRAL
The ruins of Coventry Cathedral after bombing by Germans in November 1940.

BOMB DAMAGE
An air raid warden clambers through the ruins of a building after a night of bombing by the
Luftwaffe.

greatcoat and beret was introduced in 1941. Eventually, ARP people who had completed their training were given a fine sterling silver badge, designed by Eric Gill, the sculptor and type designer produced by the Royal Mint and issued by the Government. As local authorities issued their own Civil Defence badges, there was soon a great number of Civil Defence and ARP badges to be seen on the lapels and caps of ARP workers throughout the country.

Women who had volunteered to be air raid wardens when war was declared, found themselves with little to do in the first months of the war except avoid accidents in blacked-out streets. As Helen Brook, who founded the Brook Advisory Centres in the 1960s, recalled, she would often have to get out of bed at 2 a.m., 'dressed up in all this gear', which included trousers so long they had to be rolled up, a whistle, a rattle and a tin hat, and walk about the pitch-black streets of her beat, north of Oxford Street in London, for two hours. Her refuge, should bombs drop, was the area steps down to a cellar. Her 'boss' was a retired naval commander who made his wardens keep naval hours and have dog watches.

With the Phoney War finished, it was time for the girls in the London Regional Civil Defence headquarters to put away their knitting, reading and table tennis. Now, in properly bombproof quarters, the headquarters staff were fully occupied manning its telephone exchange, message room and control room, from where they coordinated the ARP, ambulance, fire and rescue services in London.

As the reality of the war sunk in, so did the reality of being a volunteer ARP worker, which had suddenly become a much more serious and dangerous role. Over the subsequent months more and more men were called up for service, so women played an increasingly vital part in ARP. They worked as wardens, ambulance drivers

A stirling silver ARP badge.

(with knowledge of elementary mechanics), fire-watchers, auxiliary nurses, gas decontamination experts (for which they had to have a certificate confirming that they had completed a special training course), motorcycle messengers, and directing the responses to 'incidents'.

At the height of the Blitz in London in 1940, one in every six ARP Wardens, the key to calm, efficient local civil defence, was a woman. Their posts were concrete boxes, measuring 10 feet x 8 feet, and protected by sandbags piled up round them and on their roofs.

Another important Civil Defence service was the Auxiliary Fire Service (AFS). This was a voluntary organisation, founded in 1938 and originally aimed at men only, which was intended to supplement the work of the London Fire Brigade and the country's local fire service organisations, of which there were 1600 in 1939. By the time the war started, some twenty-three

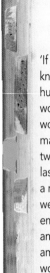

CALLING FOR A MILLION VOLUNTEERS

'If the emergency arose, I know you would come in your hundreds of thousands. But you would be untrained. For the work we may have to do, one man trained beforehand is worth two or three who come at the last moment. We want at least a million men and women, and we want them for work that in an emergency would be exacting and dangerous. The job is not an amusement in peace time, nor would it be a soft job in time of war. It is a serious job for free men and women who care for their fellows and their Country.' With these words, reprinted in a recruitment leaflet issued by the Home Office and the Scottish Office, the Home Secretary, in a wireless broadcast concerning the Air Raid Precautions Act in March 1938, launched the recruitment drive for British citizens to take their part 'in the voluntary organisation of the Air Raid Precautions Services'.

thousand men and women had volunteered for the AFS, the women getting in by virtue of a rather vague clause in the Government's 'National Service' booklet that said that women 'between the ages of twenty and fifty' would be wanted for 'appropriate services'.

At first, 'appropriate services' for women in the AFS meant mainly administrative work in fire stations and civil defence control centres, where they did such typical women's work as operating telephone switchboards, doing clerical work and running mobile canteens. But before long, as elsewhere in wartime Britain, women were doing men's work, driving fire tenders and messengers' motorbikes (which they repaired and maintained) and working as pump teams and fire-hose operators.

Soon there were so many all-women pump teams in the AFS that women-only competitions were held. When Mrs Marjorie Meath's team from D Division HQ in Birmingham won the cup in the Midlands women's teams competition, the cup was taken round the eleven stations in the division – and was filled with an appropriately celebratory liquid at each one. There was at least one fire station in Britain – Holcombe Fire Station in Chatham, Kent – that was operated entirely by women. Twenty-five women members of the AFS were killed on duty during the war, and many more were hurt.

The AFS played a major part in fighting the fires of the Blitz in London and other cities in 1940–41. Often, relations between the auxiliaries and the fire-fighting professionals were strained,

ARP POSTER
One of a series of British government recruitment posters for the ARP encouraging women to do their part for the war effort.

SALT OF THE EARTH
Nurses waiting on dock for wounded soldiers to be unloaded from a British hospital ship.

FIRE TRAINING
Chorus girls who responded to the call for volunteer fire watchers are trained by Newcastle fire brigade to deal with incendiary devices on the roof of Newcastle Theatre Royal.

not just over fire-fighting matters but also over questions of pay and working conditions, with the auxiliaries, 'doing their bit for the war effort', being ready to accept low wages, no overtime, no holiday pay and, often, no uniform; also problems arose because of the widely varying sizes of equipment, especially hoses, used in different local fire services, so sending reinforcements across county boundaries was often a waste of manpower. In August 1941, the National Fire Service was formed by merging the country's professional fire-fighting bodies and the AFS.

Women were given their own ranking structure within the fire service. By 1943, the most senior female rank was Chief Woman Fire Officer, epaulettes with three silver stripes alternating with red and topped by a small impeller signifying her rank. Below her came Regional Woman Fire Officer, then Area Officer, Assistant Area Officer, Group Officer, Assistant Group Officer and Leading Firewoman.

It should not be forgotten that during the war, fire-fighting, particularly dealing with incendiary bombs, became a civil defence job that many people did in addition to their daily work. From September 1940, when the first Fire Watchers

Order was issued, it was compulsory for men to do a minimum of forty-eight hours fire-watching duty every month; as with most things in wartime, women also found themselves doing fire-watching duty, usually in their own work places. All work places in the danger areas, from banks, offices, department stores, shops, factories, churches and cinemas instituted rotas for their staff and other helpers to do fire-watching duty at night. Fire-watchers were usually given some instruction in dealing with incendiary bombs and operating stirrup pumps. It was the men and women who worked in St Paul's Cathedral in London who did most of the work of dealing with the incendiary bombs on the building's roof, so that its great dome was able to rise unscathed and apparently invincible above the flames and smoke of the Blitz.

While ARP and the AFS/NFS could count large numbers of women in their volunteer forces, there were other, smaller all-women volunteer organisations that did invaluable work during the war. One was the Women's Auxiliary Police Force. Never numbering more than ten thousand, the force did mostly administrative and driving work and was attached to county and city police forces. Although it never became a national force, the WAPF did have its own insignia and uniform.

Officially, women were not allowed in the Home Guard – it was felt there were already sufficient voluntary organisations that women could join. Some units, however, decided to allow women to do certain administrative duties and it soon became obvious that there help was very beneficial to the war effort. In 1942, the Women's Home Guard Auxiliaries were formed, which gave women the right to officially work alongside members of the Home Guard. They were not issued with a uniform like their male counterparts, but a bakelite badge bearing the initials H.G.

While Britain's governing powers may have been slow to come round to the idea that women could do men's work in wartime, they never, unlike their counterparts in the Soviet Union,

WOMEN'S WAGES IN CIVIL DEFENCE

In all areas of working life in Britain in the 1940s, women were generally paid less than men, even when doing the same work. When women teachers asked for pay parity with men during the war, Prime Minister Winston Churchill snorted that their demand was 'impertinent'.

As in all work in wartime Britain, so in Civil Defence work, women were generally paid considerably less than men. In autumn 1940, in the early days of the Blitz, full-time ARP and AFS male workers were being paid a wage of £3 5s a week; women were getting £2 3s 6d – a third less. Some part-time male workers, who might be losing money because of working fewer hours in their day job, got compensation of a few shillings a day.

Women did not.

AT THE DOUBLE
Members of the First Aid Nursing Yeomanry (FANYS) running to their ambulances during a 'stand to' in the Southern Command.

came to terms with the idea that women could shoulder arms like their fathers and brothers in the defence of their country. The suggestion from women that they might be allowed to join the Home Guard was rejected by the government in 1940, and the increasingly vocal demand from such feminist women Members of Parliament as Lady Astor, Dr Irene Ward and Dr Edith Summerskill that women should be allowed to serve their country fully in the armed services was never considered.

In response to this, the redoubtable Dr Summerskill, MP for Fulham West in London, thinking that it was wrong that in wartime with

1941
INTERESTING FACTS

NOVEMBER
- The aircraft carrier HMS *Ark Royal* is hit by a German U-boat and sinks.
- Operation Crusader in North Africa begins.
- Australian cruiser HMAS *Sydney* sinks killing 645 sailors.

DECEMBER
- The UK declares war on Finland.
- Soviets begin counter-attacks against the Germans closing in on Moscow.
- The Japanese navy launch a surprise attack on the US fleet at Pearl Harbor forcing the US into the war.
- The US, UK, China and the Netherlands officially declare war on Japan.
- Japan invades Hong Kong, Malaya, Manila and Singapore.
- Two British battleships, HMS *Prince of Wales* and HMS *Repulse* are both sunk by Japanese aircraft.
- Germany, Italy, Hungary and Romania declare war on the US.
- India declares war on Japan.
- The US seizes the French ship SS *Normandie*.
- Hitler becomes Supreme Commander-in-Chief of the German army.
- US garrison surrenders as Japanese land on Wake Island.
- British forces capture Benghazi.

LADY ASTOR
American-born Nancy Langhorne Astor (1879–1964) became the first woman to serve as a member of the British parliament, a position she held from 1919 to 1945.

POLICE DRIVER
A member of the Women's Auxiliary Police Corps helps the war effort by driving an ambulance.

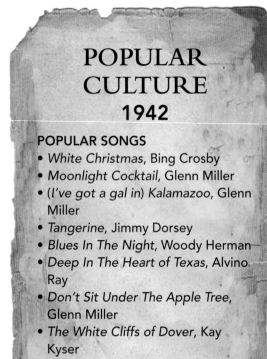

POPULAR CULTURE
1942

POPULAR SONGS
- *White Christmas*, Bing Crosby
- *Moonlight Cocktail*, Glenn Miller
- *(I've got a gal in) Kalamazoo*, Glenn Miller
- *Tangerine*, Jimmy Dorsey
- *Blues In The Night*, Woody Herman
- *Deep In The Heart of Texas*, Alvino Ray
- *Don't Sit Under The Apple Tree*, Glenn Miller
- *The White Cliffs of Dover*, Kay Kyser
- *Jersey Bounce*, Benny Goodman

Brunch chocolate bars and bars of Plain York chocolate all sold at 2½d (1p) and were two points each. The famous fruit gums were no longer sold in tubes or packets but were sold loose at 7d (3p) and were four points per 4 ounces.

POPULAR FILMS
- *In Which We Serve*, starring Noel Coward and Celia Johnson
- *Mrs Miniver*, starring Greer Garson and Walter Pidgeon.
- *Yankee Doodle Dandy*, starring James Cagney and Joan Leslie
- *Road to Morocco*, starring Bing Crosby, Bob Hope and Dorothy Lamour
- *Casablanca*, starring Humphrey Bogart and Ingrid Bergman

invasion threatening, half the adult population did not know at least how to use a rifle, started the Women's Home Defence League (WHDL) in 1941. Dr Summerskill did not see the members of the WHDL replacing the men of the Home Guard; rather, they could be of great help to them, doing less physically demanding work that would free the men for active anti-enemy work.

Within a year, some two hundred local units of the WHDL had been set up in all parts of the country. Members, who wore a badge but not a uniform, learned such suitably womanly things as first aid, field cooking and Morse code. They were also given training in unarmed combat and the use of a .22 rifle. The cash to fund such training was raised through a wide range of social activities. By April 1943 the government had backed down sufficiently to permit the members of the WHDL to join the Home Guard as 'nominated women'; in July 1944, the 'nominated women' were renamed Home Guard Auxiliaries. By the end of the war there were thirty thousand of them.

HOME GUARDS
Two women participate in a civilian defence drill after being allowed to join the Home Guard as
'nominated women' in July 1944.

CHAPTER FIVE

EVACUATION AND REFUGE

EVACUATION

Children were deeply affected by World War Two. It is estimated that as many as two million children were evacuated from their homes at the start of the war and the operation which became known as 'Operation Pied Piper' was a massive undertaking.

ID CHECK
A little girl examines her friend's identity tag as they and other children get ready to be evacuated from London to the safety of the countryside.

Even as the peace treaty that settled affairs after World War One was being signed, Europe's governments and politicians were considering how best to save their civilian populations in the all too likely event of another war. Plans to evacuate civilians from major cities and industrial areas were first officially discussed in Britain in the early 1920s, when a special Air Raid Precautions (ARP) committee began investigating the pros and cons of air raid defence.

Two essential points were obvious from the outset. First, it would be very bad for national morale if thousands of people were killed or seriously injured in the first days of the war, as most experts expected. Evacuation would have to be done swiftly and, if possible, before war broke out. Second, in a parliamentary democracy people could not be ordered to move away from their homes and neighbourhoods to places that might be safer in the event of war. They would have to be persuaded. Since any worthwhile war effort would grind to a halt if major cities and important industrial areas were to be deprived of their working populations, total evacuation was not possible. This meant that evacuation would have to be selective as well as voluntary.

Britain was slower than other countries in Europe to make serious plans for evacuating their populations in the event of war. The early work of the ARP committee was desultory and lacking in in-depth planning; very little thought was given at this stage to what should happen to people once they had been evacuated. But as the 1930s progressed, people began to concentrate much more seriously on the matter. National Socialist Germany, lead by Adolf Hitler, was becoming increasingly belligerent and militaristic. Then came the Spanish Civil War with its terrible devastation and loss of life.

In July 1938, two years after France had issued evacuation guidance to its citizens, the British

1942

JANUARY
- Manila is captured by Japanese forces.
- The Siege of the Bataan Peninsula begins.
- William Hitler's (Adolf Hitler's nephew) house is destroyed in an air raid on Liverpool. He then joins the US navy to fight against his uncle.
- Actress Carole Lombard and her mother are killed in a plane crash near Las Vegas.
- Thailand declares war on the UK and the USA.

FEBRUARY
- Daylight saving goes into effect in the US.
- SS *Normandie* capsizes after catching fire the previous day in New York.
- Singapore surrenders to Japan.
- Japanese warplanes attack Darwin, Australia.
- Roosevelt orders MacArthur to evacuate the Philippines as US defence of the nation collapses.
- A major coal dust explosion in Honkeiko, China, claims 1,549 lives.
- *How Green Was My Valley* wins Best Picture at the 14th Academy Awards.
- Battle of the Java Sea – a victory for the Japanese.

government delivered to all households *The Householders' Handbook*, in which it was suggested that in the event of war, such members of the household as children, elderly people, invalids and pets should be sent, if possible, to stay with friends and relatives in the country. Much more serious planning was taking place behind the scenes. A Committee on Evacuation, chaired by Sir John Anderson, the Lord Privy Seal, was set up in May 1938, by which time it was clear that, even though any evacuation scheme would be voluntary, the government must be in control of evacuation plans in order to avoid the panic and chaos seen in Spain. It was also clear by now that the emphasis should be on evacuating children, with their mothers in the case of very young children, from the danger areas.

By this time, non-government organisations were also swinging into action. wProminent among these was the Women's Voluntary Service (WVS), formed by the redoubtable Stella Isaacs, Marchioness of Reading, in June 1938. Although its founding purpose was the recruitment of women into the civil defence services, the WVS turned out to be one of the nation's greatest civilian wartime assets. Within a few weeks of its founding, the WVS had set up an Evacuation Committee with members including representatives of the Girls Guides and the Women's Institutes (WI). This committee appointed WVS Evacuation Officers to work with local authorities to coordinate the billeting of evacuees in every county in the land that was likely to receive evacuees. The inclusion of the Girl Guides in the WVS evacuation scheme meant that children were able to help other children, for many of the Girl Guides meeting the great columns of schoolchildren evacuated from the danger areas in September 1939 were themselves 'teenagers' (a term not yet invented) and therefore still legally children.

War suddenly seemed very close indeed in September 1938, when Germany laid claim to the Sudetenland, which lay on the border with Czechoslovakia, a country with which Britain had treaty obligations. At the height of the Munich Crisis, as this incident came to be called, the government was ready to assist with the evacuation, on a voluntary basis, of two million people, a quarter of them school-children, from London alone. By the end of September, many parents of school-age children in London were receiving from head teachers letters that, so far from dealing with matters of education, were asking them to send their children to school with neatly packed and clearly labelled luggage, and with sufficient food (listed in the letter) to last them for a couple of days. They were to be evacuated, mostly by train, bus, or coach, but also by steamer and ferry boat, with fellow pupils and their teachers, for an unspecified time – and, in many cases, to an unspecified place.

PACKED AND READY TO GO
A group of evacuee children carrying their belongings in suitcases and bags as they stand at the station, ready to start their new lives away from the dangers of London.

A WAITING GAME
A group of evacuees wait patiently for the train to take them to Blackpool. This was to be a trial run, if war started during the week they were away, the children would stay, if not, they would return home and start school as normal.

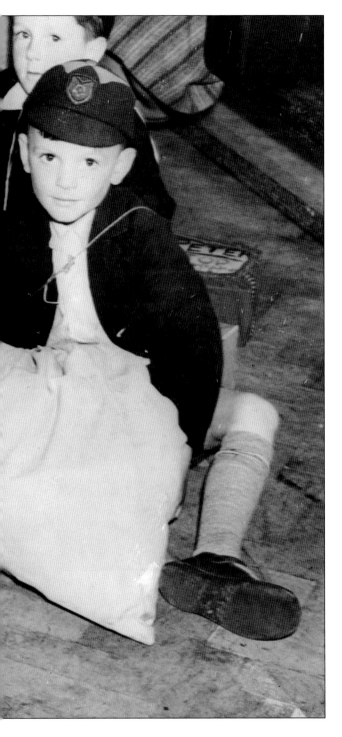

Fortunately, the crisis was resolved without war, the prime minister, Neville Chamberlain coming back from Germany at the end of September with a 'piece of paper' that promised 'peace for our time'. Although few believed that the 'time' available for peace was very long, at least the Munich Crisis gave the country a chance to rehearse an admittedly rudimentary evacuation scheme and to iron out the worst of the flaws – one of the greatest of which was the identification of suitable billets – the rehearsal had thrown up.

The British Government's evacuation scheme, passed on to local authorities at the beginning of 1939, was based on dividing the country into three areas. The danger zones, called 'Evacuation Areas', were those parts of the country, including the capital, large urban areas, industrial regions including Birmingham, Salford, Newcastle and Gateshead and the important dockyards of the Clyde around Glasgow. And such important major military installations as the Medway towns in Kent and Rosyth in Scotland, thought most at risk from a major aerial attack in the first days of the war. The decision to omit the major Devon naval base of Plymouth from this list was taken because Plymouth was thought to be too far away to come within range of German 'first strike' attacks. This serious miscalculation was not put right until after the heavy raids on Plymouth in March and April 1941.

'Reception Areas' were the parts of the country, mostly rural and coastal areas thought to be out of range of attack, to which evacuees would be sent. Once these areas were decided upon, the first task of local authorities, aided by such voluntary organisations as the WVS and the WI was to assess the amount of 'surplus accommodation' available for evacuees. 'Neutral Areas' were those that neither sent nor received evacuees.

The government's evacuation scheme identified four groups likely to be caught up in evacuation. One of the four groups included those individuals and families able to afford to make their own, private arrangements for leaving the Evacuation Areas. It is thought that

TIME TO GO
Children from the English Martyrs Roman Catholic School board a train at Waterloo Station before being evacuated to the safety of the countryside.

about two million people quietly left the danger areas for the peace of western coastal resorts and rural Britain, staying with relatives or in hotels and guest houses, in the months before war was declared. Thousands more left the country altogether, many of them taking ships to the United States. In both these groups were many children. The evacuation of children by ship to the United States came to an abrupt end in 1940, with the sinking of a ship carrying a large group of children to America.

This left three groups where some form of government assistance would be necessary: businesses and private companies, the government and civil service, and – probably needing the most financial assistance – children, their mothers and invalids. This last group, estimated to total about four million, would come largely from working class areas, such as the East End of London, and the inner, more crowded parts of the great industrial cities of the north of England and of Scotland.

Evacuating the children of Britain from the Evacuation Areas depended on the meshing together of a great network of individuals and organisations. From the schools and their teaching staff who would be evacuated with their pupils, and the railway companies who would provide the trains – and the timetables – to shift hundreds of thousands of bewildered children, to organisations like the WVS and local authorities who sought out the 'surplus accommodation' in the Reception Areas. People

offering accommodation to evacuees were paid an amount sufficient to cover their costs. Well before war was declared in September 1939, local authorities in the Reception Areas were able to tell the government that they could make available accommodation for not far short of five million people. Evacuation was fast becoming an experiment in social reorganisation on an unprecedented scale.

One of the government's major tasks was to persuade parents to send their children out of the Evacuation Areas. Women, because there were so many more of them at home, were the main target of government propaganda. In the Reception Areas posters began appearing in the spring of 1939 asking for women to help with the evacuation service: 'Offer your services to your local council', exhorted the posters. In the Evacuation Areas, the posters were aimed at

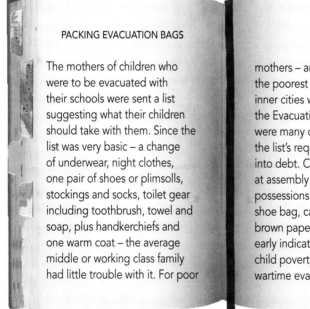

PACKING EVACUATION BAGS

The mothers of children who were to be evacuated with their schools were sent a list suggesting what their children should take with them. Since the list was very basic – a change of underwear, night clothes, one pair of shoes or plimsolls, stockings and socks, toilet gear including toothbrush, towel and soap, plus handkerchiefs and one warm coat – the average middle or working class family had little trouble with it. For poor mothers – and, since some of the poorest parts of Britain's inner cities were to the fore in the Evacuation Areas, there were many of them – fulfilling the list's requirements put them into debt. Children turning up at assembly points with their possessions in a pillow case, shoe bag, cardboard box or brown paper parcel was an early indication of the depth of child poverty in Britain that the wartime evacuations revealed.

1942

MARCH
- Construction begins on the largest ammunition factory in the US at Badger Army Ammunition Plant.
- British commandoes raid St Nazaire on the coast of France.

APRIL
- Japanese navy attacks Colombo in Ceylon. HMS *Cornwall* and HMS *Dorsetshire* are both sunk.
- The 'Death March' begins from the Bataan Peninsula.
- King George VI awards the George Cross to Malta to honour their bravery.
- All Jews in the Netherlands are required to wear the Star of David.
- Explosion at a chemical factory in Belgium kills 200 and injures 1,000.

MAY
- The very first undersea pipeline for carrying oil is tested in Operation Pluto.
- Allied victory at the Battle of the Coral Sea.
- Soviets capture the city of Kharkov from the Germans in the Second Battle of Kharkov.
- First African–American seamen are admitted in the US Navy.
- Czech paratroopers attempt an assassination on Reinhard Heydrich in Prague.

mothers. By early 1939, the 1938 *Householders' Handbook*'s mild suggestion that evacuation would be a good idea had turned into something much more direct: '*MOTHERS Send Them Out of London, Give them a chance of greater safety and health*', the wording of posters used in London, was typical of those with a similar message being displayed in Britain's major cities.

Most mothers did not need posters to force them into thinking about whether evacuation was a good idea or not. For months, everyday family life was being moved on to a war footing. As far back as September 1938, all adults and children (but not babies, for whom gas masks were not provided until the outbreak of war), had been practising using the smelly and unattractive gas masks that had been delivered to every adult and child in the country during the Munich Crisis. By May 1939, every mother who wished to be evacuated with her small children should have registered at her local maternity or child welfare centre, making it clear at the time if she wished her older children to be taken out of school to go with her.

The 'evacuate or not' decision was very difficult for those mothers all of whose children were of school age. Such children were expected to be evacuated with their schools and teachers, so that their mothers would have to wave them goodbye from the school gate. There was a major evacuation rehearsal in most evacuation areas in the country on 28 August 1939. From 6 a.m. children began arriving at their schools dressed ready to go, labels on their coats and on the single

---

TEARS OF CONFUSION
Young Freddie Somer of Winton Street School arrives at King's Cross Station in London, but is distressed at the thought of being relocated and having to leave his mother.

ON THEIR WAY
A group of London children look out of a railway carriage window en route to a place of safety.

suitcases or bags, packed with the suggested list of clothes, just one toy per child, and a parcel of food, and with the boxes containing their gas masks hanging round their necks.

On 31 August, while desperate negotiations with Hitler were still going on in a last-ditch effort to prevent war, the Ministry of Health announced that, 'as a precautionary measure,' the evacuation of school children and other priority classes would start the next day, 1 September 1939. On paper, the evacuation, code-named Operation Pied Piper, looked well organised. In reality, there were such crowds of children milling about at railway stations – both mainline and suburban stations had to be brought into use to cope with the numbers – over the three days

TIME TO READ
Carol Griffin, wounded in an air raid on a school in Lewisham, reads a book with her friend Diana Knight, as they prepare to be evacuated from London.

1942

JUNE

- Mexico declares war on Germany, Italy and Japan.
- Reinhard Heydrich succumbs to his injuries sustained in the assassination attack.
- Japan invades the Aleutian Islands – first invasion of US soil for 128 years.
- Australian cities of Sydney and Newcastle are shelled by Japanese submarines.
- Nazis burn the village of Lidice in Czechoslovakia in reprisal for the killing of Heydrich and massacres 173 male residents.
- On her 13th birthday, Anne Frank makes the first entry in her diary.
- Axis forces capture Tobruk.

JULY

- First Battle of El Alamein.
- Anne Frank's family goes into hiding.
- Vichy government headed by Pierre Laval, rounds up around 20,000 Jews and imprisons them in the Winter Velodrome.
- Germans perform test flights of the Messerschmitt Me-262 for the first time.
- The deportation of Jews from the Warsaw Ghetto begins.
- Women accepted for Volunteer Emergency Services.
- OXFAM is founded.

the evacuation lasted that the carefully worked out timetables went by the board. Operation Pied Piper intended that whole schools would be evacuated en masse, but in the chaotic conditions, classes got separated and groups of children were loaded onto the first available train and sent off to what, in many cases, was an unknown destination; arriving tired, hungry, dirty and frightened, many hours later.

In the event, total evacuation of children to safe Reception Areas was never achieved in 1939 and most Reception Areas received far fewer children than they had been led to expect. Where some 80 per cent of mothers interviewed during the Munich Crisis had said that they planned to evacuate their children in the event of war, a year later a much calmer – or perhaps more fatalistic – view seemed the norm. Just over a third of the children expected to be evacuated from London were sent away from the metropolis in 1939, 377,000 of them with their teachers.

In the Birmingham industrial area, Rotherham, Sheffield and other large cities, even fewer children were sent away to escape enemy action than in London. These low figures may have been a result of indifferent publicity for the evacuation scheme by some local authorities. It could also have been because local people did not like the government's arrangements for them. The city of Sheffield, for instance, had wanted to send their children into Derbyshire, but the government had insisted on Lincolnshire – further away from Sheffield and a lot nearer to Hitler's Luftwaffe. A lack of simple, joined-up thinking resulted in many ill-conceived evacuations, such as the dispatching of a large group of Catholic and Irish children from the poorest parts of Liverpool into Calvinist north Wales.

Things were less than ideal in the Reception Areas, too. For many children, the memory of their arrival in the place where they were perhaps to remain for a long time, was confused and frightening. So far from being assigned directly to suitable billets, children found themselves lined up in school halls, village halls and even on railway station platforms with those offering billets free to choose those children they liked the look of, perhaps, if it was a rural community, because they were boys who could be useful labour on the farms. Recalling such scenes in later life, people used terms like 'cattle market' to describe the business. Many people offering billets could take only one or two children, so families with several brothers and sisters could find themselves separated from each other.

'GRANNY' NORRIS

'Granny' Norris pours tea for some of the evacuees she looked after during World War Two. She received the British Empire Medal for her 'unremitting care' of a large number of London evacuee children.

IMPROVISATION
For those children who had not been evacuated, it was important to find safe places for them during an air raid. This day nursery in the East End of London used a linen cupboard.

TEMPORARY SCHOOL
An inn in Camberley, Surrey, was converted into a nursery school and billeting centre for 3,000 of the mothers and children evacuated from London.

A ROYAL EXAMPLE

The daughters of King George VI and Queen Elizabeth were aged thirteen and nine in September 1939. Setting an example to the nation, the queen refused to send her daughters to Canada, as the Dutch royal family had done, at the outbreak of war. She did, however, keep them out of London. The princesses spent much of the war at Windsor Castle, where the dungeons provided a safe refuge from the Blitz. During her radio broadcast to 'the children of the Empire' during the BBC's Children's Hour in October 1940, Princess Elizabeth spoke of the sadness of being separated from her parents. Although the king and queen spent much of their daytime in London at Buckingham Palace, which was bombed several times during the war, they spent most of their nights at Windsor Castle. The royal princesses saw much more of their parents than many children during the war.

DROXFORD VILLAGE
The village of Droxford in Hampshire became the Allied Invasion headquarters for two days in June 1944. The inhabitants were excited about meeting Churchill and young Christopher McIntosh pictured here once encountered Jan Smuts the prime minister of South Africa who worked closely with Churchill in World War Two.

Of course, very many children were happy with their new foster parents, often calling them 'Auntie' and 'Uncle', perhaps staying with them for the duration of the war and keeping up regular contact for years after. For many inner city children, life in the country, where the changing seasons were noticeable in a way hardly seen in inner city areas, was a revelation. As well as those British children caught up in evacuation, the government and local authorities also had to deal with British nationals coming into the country from outside the mainland. Foremost among these were the people of the Channel Islands. In fact, although the Channel Islands had been included in general evacuation discussions, no serious plans were laid for evacuation to Britain. In June 1940, when the dreadful day came on which the British government had to inform the Channel Islands that they could not be defended from the Germans, the people of the Channel Islands were given less than two days to organise the evacuation of their children and the mothers of children under school age. In ten days at the end of June some 29,000 islanders

WARTIME REUNION

Parents from London are reunited with their children in Saffron Walden, Essex. Nearly 1,000 parents attended the reunion party hosted by the mayor of the town.

CHILDREN
are safer in the country
. . . leave them there

were able to cram on to the small fleet of ships that took them to safety in England. Many of the children were sent away with their schools, and did not see their parents again for five long years. In the single pieces of luggage each child was allowed to carry, they could pack only one toy.

The Channel Islands' evacuees landed first at Weymouth and were then dispersed to various places in west and north England and in Scotland. Eventually, some 36,000 Channel Islanders reached Britain as evacuees. They were cut off from any meaningful contact with their families still on the islands, apart from a few, heavily censored letters, sent via the Red Cross. In England, a Channel Islands Committee helped maintain the islanders as a community.

The first great World War Two evacuation in Britain, in September 1939, began to fall apart when the expected air assaults from Germany did not come. In the months of the Phoney War, as

1942

AUGUST
- Battle of Guadalcanal in the Solomon Islands.
- Six German would-be saboteurs are executed.
- Gandhi is arrest in Bombay by British forces.
- Allied forces raid Dieppe, France.
- Brazil declares war on Germany and Italy.

SEPTEMBER
- Battle of Milne Bay – Japan suffers their first defeat on land.
- Andrée Borrel and Lise de Baissac became the first female SOE agents to be parachuted into occupied France.

OCTOBER
- British cruiser *Curaçao* collides with the *Queen Mary* and sinks killing 338 people.
- The first man-made rocket to reach space is launched from Test Stand VII at Peenemünde, Germany.
- German U-boat sinks the ferry SS *Caribou*, killing 137.
- Bombay suffers a major hurricane and flood which kills 40,000 people.
- British forces begin a major offensive against Axis forces at El Alamein in Egypt.

the strangely quiet opening months of the War came to be called, mothers and children began to drift back home. Many children were very unhappy in the alien environments of their billets, and begged their parents to take them home, and expectant mothers and those with babies were bored and lonely. Despite a change of tone in the government's poster-based propaganda campaign, which now called on mothers to 'Leave Them Where They Are', parents were soon taking their children home in ever-increasing numbers. A second attempt at another wave of evacuation in December 1939 met with a poor response.

After the major evacuation of September 1939, there were other, rather smaller waves of evacuation in Britain during the war, most notably after the start of the Blitz in 1940 and then again during the V1 flying bomb (or 'doodlebugs') and V2 rocket attacks in 1944–45. The V weapon attacks began just a week after the D-Day landings in France in June 1944. They were so serious and caused such damage and loss of life that an evacuation scheme for children from southern England was very quickly put into effect.

Mary Murphy, who was just five in 1944, was evacuated from Chingford in Essex to Weston-super-Mare, right on the other side of England. Here, she and her friends joined up with evacuee children from London's East End to have mud fights under the pier with local gangs of children. The mud was thick and smelly, and they all had to be hosed down when they got back to their billets.

'After two weeks, our landlady had had enough of us and we were sent back to London in disgrace. We didn't mind because she was grumpy and the food was awful.'

While evacuation undoubtedly saved lives, its long-term effect was unexpected – no less than the creation in Britain of the Welfare State, with its associated National Health Service and other state benefits schemes.

Many of the children evacuated to mainly middle-class homes in quiet towns and country villages came from the poorest slums of Britain's inner cities. Comfortably housed, well-fed and warmly clothed middle-class people were suddenly confronted by children from a world of poverty and deprivation that they thought had vanished with the Victorian age. There were many children who had never encountered an indoor lavatory, never held a fork and knife and seldom, if ever, had a bath. Some of them were still being sewn into heavy (or even paper) underwear at the beginning of winter, expecting not to be cut out of it until the spring. There were reports of children arriving at their Reception Area greeting place with footwear that consisted only of the uppers, the soles having worn away. More than one school used as a greeting point had to be fumigated after the nit- and parasite-infected evacuee children had been moved on. Middle-class Britain was utterly appalled.

Despite being involved in a terrible war, the British government moved into action on a new front: social welfare. In 1941 the government asked the economist Sir William Beveridge to head a committee looking into the way in which a system of social welfare might be set up in Britain. The Beveridge Report, titled *Social Insurance and Allied Services,* that was published in December, 1942 and accepted by the government in most of its main points in February 1943, became the foundation on which was built the post-war welfare state.

Home Front evacuation in Britain officially ended on 2 July 1945. The official homecoming for evacuated children, which the government had actually begun preparing since 1943, began two months before this and although many children had already returned there were still several thousand, including those evacuated during the V1 and V2 attacks, to be returned to their homes and families.

AN ARMY OF WOMEN VOLUNTEERS

When war did finally come in 1939, thousands of women up and down the land already had well-stocked larders, had bought the blackout materials and sticky tape necessary to prepare their windows for war, knew how to wear the gas masks that had already been issued to adults and children at the time of the Munich crisis (babies got theirs, in the form of a bag into which the baby had to be put, in September 1939), and had made practical plans for a bomb shelter, even if it could only be a very sturdy table in the kitchen. No one, having seen the effects of aerial bombing on the cities of Spain during the Civil War of 1936, was in any doubt that if war came to Britain, then everyone, civilian or serviceman, was in danger of attack from bombs and gas.

However, there was also a strong feeling that simply guarding the home would not be enough. Again and again, the same theme turns up in the diaries and journals, letters to friends and articles in newspapers and magazines written before and during the war: most British women believed it was their patriotic duty to make a contribution to the war effort, while still doing their best to guard their children and families from harm.

Giving a home to children evacuated from the danger zones of the big cities and ports was the first opportunity to help the war effort given to many women. The WVS set up an Evacuation Committee within weeks of its founding in 1938 and by 1939 had its local groups well organised to deal with the business of receiving evacuees. WVS local evacuation committees usually in-cluded members of other organisations, such as the Girl Guides and the Women's Institutes. For the first evacuation wave, local committees

EVACUATION POSTERS
Because the British government were concerned that our towns and cities would be the subject of German bombing campaigns, they encouraged evacuation.

had little trouble in finding enough houses to take in evacuees. Most women were ready to help. Even the writer Virginia Woolf and her husband Leonard found room in their home at Rodmell, Sussex for evacuees. She noted in her diary for 6 September that 'we have carried coals etc into the cottage for the eight Battersea women and children. The expectant mothers are all quarrelling.'

The sudden arrival into their homes of groups of children, especially if those children came from the slums and tenements of deprived inner city

GOVERNMENT GUIDELINES

In addition to their gas mask and identity card, the government recommended that the following items were packed in children's evacuation bags:

BOYS
2 vests
2 pairs of pants
1 pair of trousers
2 pairs of socks
6 handkerchiefs
1 pullover or jersey

GIRLS
1 vest
1 pair of knickers
1 petticoat
2 pairs of stockings
6 handkerchiefs
1 slip (or long vest with shoulder straps)
1 blouse
1 cardigan

Other items that they suggested were included in their suitcases:

1 overcoat or mackintosh
1 comb
1 pair of Wellington boots
1 towel
1 bar of soap
1 facecloth
1 toothbrush
1 pair of boots or shoes
1 pair of plimsolls
sandwiches
1 packet of nuts and raisins
1 packet dry biscuits
packet of sweets (for example barley sugar)
1 apple

areas, was an extraordinarily disturbing business for many householders – and for the children who came into their homes. Many children from really deprived areas did not know how to hold a knife and fork and were unfamiliar with the simple but healthy foods put in front of them. There were numerous reports of children, never having seen a toilet, urinating on carpets.

Mrs Nella Last's comments in the diary she kept for Mass Observation were typical of many heard again and again throughout Britain. 'The country and village people have had the shock of their lives with the sample of children and mothers who have been billeted on them from Manchester and Salford,' she wrote. 'One little boy of eight, after assuring the women that the dirt "would not come off" his legs and neck, was forcibly bathed with hot water and carbolic…. There is a run on Keating's [flea powder] and disinfectant and soap, while children who arrived with a crop of curls look like shorn lambs – but have stopped scratching!'

WHILE THE CHILDREN ARE AWAY

Knowing their children were safe, women found they had spare time on their hands. They needed to find ways of occupying themselves and many turned to doing their part for the war.

As the blue, white and black card many WVS members displayed in the front windows of their homes said, the WVS was a 'housewives service' of Britain's wartime Civil Defence. Where the volunteers of such Civil Defence organisations as ARP and the AFS did much of their work while the air raids and bombings were still going on, the WVS was in the forefront of dealing with the aftermath of air raids and the other results of war. Almost all the hundreds of thousands of women – their numbers were never officially counted – who wore the grey-green uniform suits, coats, berets and felt hats of the WVS during World War Two were paid nothing more than out-of-pocket expenses for their heroic services.

Even before war was declared, the WVS was organising greeters and helpers for the thousands of children evacuated from the perceived danger zones from the first day of September. Soon, they were also helping to provide clothing for the evacuees. Then in 1940, when thousands of troops were suddenly arriving from the horrors of Dunkirk at ports in Kent and along the south coast, the women of the WVS found themselves washing the feet and darning the socks of thousands of exhausted soldiers, while also serving thousands of meals and cups of tea.

A welcome sight in many bomb-damaged cities during the Blitz was a Queen's Messengers Convoy. There were eighteen of these Queen's

1942

OCTOBER
- Second Battle of El Alamein.
- Battle of the Santa Cruz Islands.

NOVEMBER
- Operation Torch – US and UK forces land in French North Africa.
- Germany invades Vichy, France, violating the 1940 armistice.
- Battle of Guadalcanal between Japanese and US forces. Aviators from USS *Enterprise* sink the Japanese battleship *Hiei*. US eventually retain control.
- British forces capture Tobruk and Benghazi.
- A British SOE team blow up the Gorgopotamos railway viaduct in Greece, in the first major sabotage act in occupied Europe.
- The film *Casablanca* premieres in New York.
- A fire in the Coconut Grove night club in Boston kills 491 people.

DECEMBER
- Petrol rationing begins in the US.
- An avalanche in Aliquippa, Pennsylvania, kills 26 people.
- British commandoes raid ships in Bordeaux harbour.
- French Admiral Darlan, a former Vichy leader who had switched over to the Allies, was assassinated in Algiers.

Messengers Convoys, the first one paid for by Queen Elizabeth – hence the convoys' name – and most of the rest of them paid for by overseas generosity, especially American. Each convoy consisted of up to twelve vehicles, equipped to rush hot meals, drinks and fresh water to bombed areas. They were manned by members of the WVS and did particularly valuable work in Coventry, Liverpool and Plymouth in the later months of the Blitz.

The WVS's main task during the Blitz was to provide strong back-up support for the Civil Defence services. Their locally-maintained censuses were invaluable for ARP people assessing the population of bombed streets and houses and they became very practised at organising convoys out of bombed areas. The WVS canteen van, many of which were donated by other countries, including the Dominions, the West Indies and Kenya, became a familiar sight in the middle of clearing-up operations after a bombing raid. The WVS canteens provided refreshments for both the casualties of bombing raids and the Civil Defence workers helping with the clearing-up operations. Members of the WVS also became adept at showing people how to build makeshift brick ovens in the street using the rubble from bombed-out buildings.

Perhaps not quite as familiar a sight as the canteen van, but just as welcome when it did turn up, was the mobile laundry service units that the WVS manned in bomb-damaged housing areas. In Portsmouth, where sixty-five thousand out of the city's total housing stock of seventy thousand were either destroyed or damaged by enemy action, mobile laundries were essential. Rescued clothes and bedlinen would be washed in the units and hung out to dry on lines, hopefully under cover but quite often strung across streets and between bombed-out houses. Many of these units were provided by the manufacturer of the popular washing powder, Rinso, doing its bit to keep the nation's washing clean even if many of the nation's domestic washing machines were being destroyed by the enemy.

At the height of the Blitz in London, local authority rest centres – housed in church halls, schools, office buildings and many other places and manned largely by WVS women – were sheltering around twenty-five thousand people who had been bombed out of their houses. The WVS's national structure geared itself to organising the training of its volunteers in many essentials, from first aid and ambulance work, to cooking for large numbers and sorting and distributing clothes by the ton. By 1941, the WVS's work had moved in directions unimagined in 1938. After Lord Beaverbrook's appeal for household aluminium to help the aircraft industry, it was the WVS which set up pots-and-pans collecting depots in towns and cities. The response of WVS groups in Sussex to the 'Beating the Invader' leaflet was to organise a messenger service of women cyclists who would be able to maintain communications if the invader blocked roads and cut telegraph lines.

For the many thousands of men, women and children who survived a bombing raid with nothing but the clothes they stood up in, the WVS's nationwide network of shops and depots was a godsend. During the war, the WVS centre was the main source of replacement clothing and blankets for people whose homes had been severely damaged or destroyed. WVS clothing centres also provided warm sweaters, scarves, gloves and balaclavas, many of them knitted by WVS members, for the seamen of the Royal Navy and the merchant navy fighting the war at sea in the North Atlantic. Although a lot of the clothing donated to the WVS came from British people, much of it came from America and the Dominions of the Empire, especially Australia, Canada, New Zealand and South Africa. In the second half of 1940, when the Blitz was at its

STICKING TOGETHER
Labelled evacuees join forces as they wait for their train out of London. About eight million
people, including children and their mothers, were evacuated from cities and industrial areas
during World War Two.

FEMALE HANDS TO DECK

While their children are safe in the country, members of the WVS at Winchmore Hill work at St Paul's Institute making camouflage nets which were urgently required for war purposes.

height, the WVS distributed clothing worth around £1.5 million.

By the time the Blitz came to an end in London in May 1941, 241 WVS members had been killed in the bombing, and many more injured. Twenty-five WVS offices and centres had been destroyed, and, of course, there were WVS casualties in many other cities. By this time, over one million women had enrolled in the WVS. The Housewives Service grew considerably during the Blitz, and by the time it was renamed the Housewives Section in 1942, it accounted for 20 per cent of the membership of the whole WVS.

The WVS continued throughout the war and after to be a major force in local voluntary services. In April 1945, the Home Secretary and his Scottish counterpart announced in the House of Commons, the WVS would be fitted into the general pattern of Social Services throughout the country, with its work supported from central funds. Men were not totally excluded from the WVS as they occasionally helped out with such jobs as driving which not many women could do at the time. Their work was very diversified as they staffed hostels, clubs, sick bays and communical feeding centres, opened clubs for mothers and provided transport for hospital patients and undertook welfare work for troops.

It is difficult to stress how important the work of the WVS was during the war-stricken years – the rest centres which provided food and shelter – and their bravery when they had to work so close to where the bombs were falling. During the days of the Blitz, two hundred and forty-one members of the WVS lost their lives trying to help others. Even today the WVS continue their services in various parts of Great Britain, turning out whenever there is a tragedy or accident. The women are all still volunteers and help others in need just as they did during the war years. They have to rely entirely on donations from companies or members of the public.

POPULAR CULTURE
1943

POPULAR SONGS
- *Paper Doll*, The Mills Brothers
- *Sunday, Monday or Always*, Bing Crosby
- *Pistol Packin' Mama*, Al Dexter and His Troopers
- *That Old Black Magic*, Glenn Miller
- *All Or Nothing At All*, Frank Sinatra and Harry James
- *As Time Goes By*, Rudy Vallee
- *Moonlight Becomes You*, Bing Crosby
- *Taking A Chance On Love*, Benny Goodman

The musical *Oklahoma* by Rodgers and Hammerstein opens on Broadway.

POPULAR FILMS
- *For Whom The Bell Tolls*, starring Ingrid Bergman, Akim Tamiroff and Katina Paxinou
- *The Song Of Bernadette*, starring Jennifer Jones and Charles Bickford
- *Stage Door Canteen*, starring Cheryl Walker, William Terry, Marjorie Riordan, Lon McCallister and Margaret Early
- *Star Spangled Rhythm*, starring Bing Crosby and Bob Hope
- *Outlaw*, starring Jane Russell, Thomas Mitchell and Walter Huston

HELPING TO FEED COVENTRY

The first Queen's Messengers Convoy to go into action went to Coventry from Lewisham, in south London, in November 1940. The convoy consisted of four motorcyclists, eight lorries and twenty-seven WVS women, many of whom had had to leave a scribbled note on the kitchen table for their families, as they had packed up for the journey in such haste. By 7 a.m. on the morning after they had left London, they were already in action, distributing hot drinks and sandwiches to the rescue workers and ignoring the delayed action bombs going off all over the ravaged city. In the two days they were in Coventry this first Queen's Messengers Convoy prepared and served fourteen thousand meals to the people of Coventry, while their cups of tea helped wash the blood and dust out of the mouths of the men who were digging the trapped people – and the bodies – out of the rubble.

CHILDREN AND THE WORLDWIDE WAR

The war beyond Britain's shores had far-reaching effects on children, at home and abroad. Even before the war started a steady trickle of children began coming into Britain with their families to escape the increasingly punitive actions of the Nazis in Germany and Austria against non-Aryans, especially Jews, who were stripped of civil, cultural and economic rights. Jewish children were thrown out of state schools in Germany and Austria, which was annexed by Germany in March 1938, later in that year. Because there was no private school system in either country, this meant that Jewish children were deprived of all schooling.

The trickle of Jewish refugees, especially children, from Germany and Austria became, if not a torrent, then certainly a steady stream after the violent 'Kristallnacht' attacks on Jewish property throughout Germany on 9 November 1938. The British government reduced its strict immigration rules to allow Jewish children between the ages of five and seventeen to come into Britain from Europe, but placed quite severe restrictions on them in an effort to ensure that they would not become a tax burden on the country and that their stay would be limited, with 'ultimate resettlement' (ideally in Palestine) the goal to be aimed at by refugee agencies.

Thus began the 'Kindertransport' scheme that

MOBILE CANTEEN

These boys are drinking tea in front of a Food Flying Squad mobile canteen in Coventry. It was part of the Queen's Messenger Food Convoy which was supported by US aid and staffed by women of the WVS, to provide food for people made homeless by German air raids.

brought some 10,000 children to safety in Britain between December 1938 and the outbreak of war in September 1939. They came by train, crossing the Dutch border out of Germany and arriving from Holland at the English ports of Harwich and Southampton. The last train to leave Austria crossed the border with Holland on the day war was declared.

For many of the Kindertransport children, the first experience of life in Britain was within a hastily set-up camp, perhaps in run-down First World War One transit camps or in tents on isolated farms, even, in one case, in un-used greenhouses on a nurseries site. Eventually the children were billeted with foster families, which, as with Britain's own evacuee children, were sometimes good, comfortable and caring, and sometimes the reverse, and found places in schools. When the hastily, ill-conceived internment scheme for 'enemy aliens' was begun, more than a thousand Kindertransport sixteen-year-olds and above were even put into internment camps for a time.

British schoolchildren, seeing yet another kind of stranger in their classes, tended to accept Jewish refugee children in much the same way as they accepted the evacuees from cities and industrial areas; with indifference, tolerance, or irritation, depending on how many of these children there were, and how much difference it made to their own lives. It was not until after the war, when the full, horrifying extent of the Holocaust was revealed that children and their parents began to see the Jewish children from Europe in a new light.

ARRIVAL FROM ANTWERP

Betty Malek, aged three, arrived in London from Antwerp, Belgium with her bags and toys. Antwerp had been bombed by German aircraft and hundreds of people were made homeless.

1943

JANUARY
- Frank Sinatra appears at the Paramount, causing 'bobby soxers' to flood Times Square.
- Soviets begin an offensive against the Germans in Stalingrad.
- The first uprising of Jews in the Warsaw Ghetto.
- Duke Ellington plays at New York's Carnegie Hall for the first time.
- Fifty US bombers mount the first entirely American air attack against Germany.
- Roosevelt becomes the first president of the US to travel via an aeroplane while in office. He meets with Winston Churchill in Morocco to discuss the war.

FEBRUARY
- Germans surrender at Stalingrad in the first big defeat of Hitler's armies.
- Russia reconquers Kharkov.
- Shoe rationing starts in the US.
- Goebbels delivers his Sportpalast speech.
- Members of the White Rose are executed by the Nazis in Germany.
- The Smith Mine in Montana, USA, explodes killing 74 men.
- RAF begin round-the-clock bombing of Tunisia.
- Commando raid destroys German atomic weapons plant at Telemark in Norway.

As for the Kindertransport children themselves, some stayed in Britain and some moved on to the United States, Australasia and, eventually, Palestine and, after 1947, Israel. Almost all of them, when they boarded the trains to safety, left behind parents, siblings and other family members and most of them never saw their parents again. They were orphans, not just of the war, but of the Holocaust, too.

Another group of evacuees to Britain came from the U.K. overseas territory of Gibraltar. Several thousand Gibraltarians were evacuated first to North Africa in mid-1940, then in a merchant shipping convoy that brought them, in appallingly overcrowded conditions, to England from July 1940. Few of the children among them could speak English and during the near four years in which they lived with their families in hostels in London, they were taught there rather than attending English schools.

Although things were very quiet on the Home Front during the early months of 1940, invasion from Europe still seemed so likely that better-off parents, who could afford the £15 that a one-way ticket by sea to America could cost, began stepping up the arrangements that many of them had been making since before the War started to send their children overseas. At the same

---

JEWISH REFUGEES
Jewish refugee children from Germany and Austria arrive at Liverpool Street Station in London with a look of bewilderment on their faces.

PAYING FOR SEAVACUATION

With so many calls on their money supplies to contend with, the government could not make the CORB scheme free. For most of the parents who queued outside the CORB London office – set up, with probably quite unintended irony, in the pre-War 'Temple of Travel', Thomas Cook's stylish Mayfair headquarters – there would be costs to meet. True, their children would be given free passage on the ship, but parents would have to make the same size of contribution towards their maintenance that would have applied if they had been evacuated in Britain. A means test would be used to assess, on a sliding scale, the size of parents' contributions. If the child had been to a fee-paying school at home, parents would be asked to pay £1 a week towards the child's upkeep, plus an extra £15 towards the cost of travel.

time, with the situation in France looking very threatening indeed, the governments of Australia, New Zealand, Canada and South Africa, as well as America, repeated earlier offers of hospitality in even stronger terms than before. In May 1940, the British government decided to accept these offers and put in hand a government-sanctioned scheme to evacuate children overseas.

A Children's Overseas Reception Board (CORB) was set up to arrange such evacuations and to receive the names of children whose parents wished them to be registered for the scheme. Over 211,000 applications, many of them from families who could not have afforded the cost themselves (£15 was the average monthly salary of the great majority of British men in 1940), were received within a fortnight of the CORB scheme opening.

CORB eventually sent just over 2,664 children overseas, most of them to the United States and Canada, but more than 400 of them, with their escorts, to Australia. One reason for this low number was the lack of suitable ships; another

was the lack of enthusiasm for the scheme expressed by Winston Churchill, among others, partly because of the bad effect the scheme could have on national morale, but mainly because of the dangers involved: German U-boats were prowling the Atlantic seaways in great numbers. The government could not guarantee the safety of the children and nor would it agree to making any commitment to bring them back at a particular time. In the end, nearly 20,000 of the 'seavacuees', as children sent abroad came to be called, were sent overseas under private arrangements made by their families.

The 'seavacuation' scheme was dealt a dreadful blow in September 1940 when the SS *City of Benares,* lead ship in a convoy of merchant and passenger ships in the Atlantic, was hit by a torpedo and sunk. There were one hundred children on board, including 90 CORB children being sent to Canada. Eighty-one children perished. The CORB scheme was stopped shortly after, although the government continued to grant exit visas to parents wanting

LEFT: A REFUGEE FROM ENGLAND
Nine-year-old Michael Corrie, a refugee from
England, takes the ferry to Ellis Island in
New York. Evacuated from Bedford, Michael
arrived in New York without an entry visa since
his father had forgotten to give it to him.
The Ellis Island Immigration Station is in the
background.

ABOVE: NBC RADIO CITY
Young refugees, Dennis Collins, John Fenn
and Doreen Davenport speak to their parents
back in England from the NBC Radio City
studios in New York.

1943

MARCH

- In London, 173 people are crushed to death while trying to enter an air raid shelter at Bethnal Green tube station.
- Germans recapture Kharkov from the Soviet armies in bitter street fighting.
- Battle of the Atlantic reaches a climax when 27 merchants ships are sunk by German U-boats.
- First flight of Gloster Meteor jet aircraft in Britain.
- Japanese troops counter-attack US forces on Hill 700 in Bougainville. The battle lasts for five days.
- Meat, butter and cheese rationed in the USA.

APRIL

- Albert Hoffmann writes his first report about the hallucinogenic properties of LSD (lysergic acid diethylamide) after deliberately taking it for the first time.
- Hitler and Mussolini meet for an Axis conference in Salzburg.
- RAF shoots down 14 German transport planes over the Mediterranean Sea.
- Allies bomb Naples, Syracuse and Sardinia.
- 60,000 Jews killed in the Warsaw Ghetto uprising.
- Nazis discover mass grave of Polish officers near Katyn.

to make their own arrangements for their children.

When fourteen-year-old Kenneth Jones left his English school to return home to Chile at the end of 1940 he was accompanied by his mother. Kenneth recalls an eventful start to his voyage to Chile. 'We missed our convoy and had to spend the night on board ship – the night of the first massive bombing of Liverpool docks. We were locked in our cabins with the ship shuddering and rocking with the all-night bombing. Mother was quite calm and therefore so was I. It was just as well we missed our convoy because that was the one that received a great U-boat attack and the *Empress of Canada*, full of children, was sunk.'

When the War was over and the seavacuees returned to Britain, they came back, well fed and well clothed, with strong North American accents, and with an even greater liking for all things American, from music and movies to comics, candy and bubble gum, than their G.I.-influenced contemporaries who had spent the war years in Britain.

The same could not be said for many of the British children caught up with their parents in overseas countries when the War began. While the rules of war meant that accredited diplomats and their families were granted safe passage out of countries with which their own governments were now at war, British workers overseas and their families were not so fortunate. Everyone who has read J. G. Ballard's *Empire of the Sun* will know what happened to the British in Shanghai

BELGIAN REFUGEES
An old man and a young boy, both refugees from Belgium, arrive in London with their worldly belongings.

during the War; even worse was experienced by those British caught up in the capture of Singapore in 1942.

On the whole, however, the children of Britain were saved from the worst that war could do. Britain was not invaded and did not have to be fought for street by street, mile by mile, often by children (twelve-year-old members of the Hitler Youth movement fought the soldiers of the Red Army in the streets of Berlin in 1945), as happened to many of the countries of Europe. There was no mass starvation – indeed, many people agree with the food writer Marguerite Patten, who worked as an adviser with the Ministry of Food during the War, that, on the whole, Britain's children were fed a more basically healthy and nutritious diet between 1939 and 1945 than they were before and since.

BUY WAR BONDS
A World War Two poster featuring three children playing as a menacing shadow of a swastika surrounds them.

HITLER YOUTH MOVEMENT (HITLER-JUGEND)

When Hitler came into power as the German chancellor in 1933, numbers in the Hitler youth movement were relatively small. The years from 1933–1938 determined just how influential the movement was to become. In 1936, membership of the youth movement was made compulsory for all boys aged between fifteen and eighteen and by 1938 there were 8,000 full-time members. Added to this were the 720,000 part-time leaders, often schoolteachers who had been specially trained in National Socialist prin-ciples. They trained the boys in semaphore, arms drill and fitness and, once they passed the necessary tests, were given the 'Blood and Honour' dagger.

During World War Two the youth movement was often used in defence work, but the main object of the movement was to provide the paranoid Hitler with loyal supporters.

CHAPTER SIX
EXTRAORDINARY TIMES

EXTRAORDINARY TIMES

Everyone accepted that the family home was going to be in the front line in the war that started in September 1939. This meant that it would also have to be a bomb shelter, a refuge from gas warfare and a safe and strong store for food and water.

GAS PROTECTION
Three air raid wardens wear a new type of gas mask, designed for the elderly and those with chest complaints.

THE WARTIME HOME

The householder got plenty of safety and protection advice from the government, in the form of an avalanche of pamphlets, leaflets and public notices delivered to every house in the land. However, the onus of putting that advice into practice fell firmly on the householder himself.

An early piece of home-protection advice offered householders by the government was a booklet, *The Protection of Your Home Against Air Raids*, published by the Home Office (price one penny) in 1938. This gave detailed advice on how householders could protect their property from the worst effects of bombs, incendiary devices and gas.

Gas was considered likely to be the most serious thing people would have to protect themselves from – hence the issuing of millions of gas masks, also in 1938. In the house, the Home Office booklet advised, people should create a 'refuge room', in which the fireplace, its flue stuffed with newspaper, should be boarded up with plywood and every crevice and crack in the room filled with putty or soggy newspapers. By the time the war actually started, few people remembered the booklet and fewer – if any – actually created a 'refuge room' in their homes, being much more concerned with ensuring that their blackout arrangements were perfect. By this time, too, the government was thinking along rather more practical lines when it came to protecting families.

The first shelter for family use, provided by the government before the outbreak of war, was the Anderson Shelter, named after the Minister of Home Security Sir John Anderson. Poorer inhabitants in recognised danger areas got their Anderson shelters free of charge; everyone else paid from £6 14s (£6.70) to £10 18s (£10.90) for them, depending on size. The standard-size Anderson shelter, intended for four people,

1943

MAY
- Food rationing begins in the US.
- German plane sinks boat loaded with Palestinian Jews bound for Malta.
- German and Italian troops surrender in North Africa.
- *Batman* appears on the screen for the first time in the US.
- Joseph Stalin dissolves the Comintern.
- Jewish resistance in Warsaw Ghetto ends after 30 days of fighting.
- The Dambuster raids by RAF 617 squadron on German dams.
- The Allies win the Battle of the Atlantic.
- Winston Churchill arrives in US and pledges England's full support to US against Japan.
- The first jet fighter is tested.
- *Archie* comic strip is broadcast for the first time on radio.

JUNE
- Germany shoots down a civilian flight from Lisbon to London, everyone on board dies including actor Leslie Howard.
- A military coup in Argentina ousts Ramón Castillo.
- Eden announces casualties for the first three years of the war – 92,089 killed, 266,719 wounded.

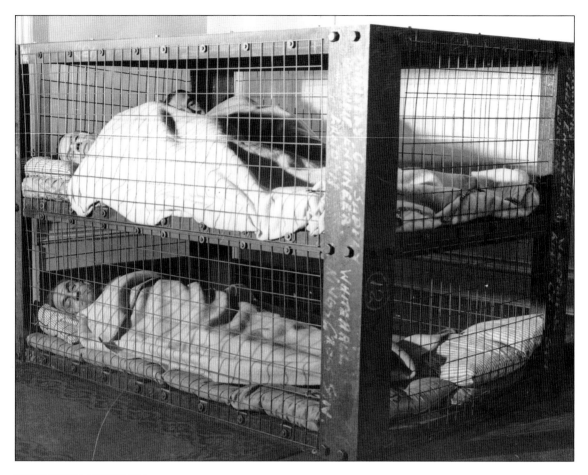

TWO-TIER MORRISON

A group of men in the new two-tier Morrison shelter. It is similar in construction to the original indoor shelter, but housing two beds, one above the other. Where available, the new shelter will be supplied free to householders whose income is not more than £350 a year.

or six at a pinch, was considered ideal for the average suburban family.

The Anderson shelter was a 'sectional steel shelter' intended for erection in the back garden (which meant it was most used in the suburbs, many inner-town houses having no garden), 6 to 15 feet (1.8 to 4.5 metres) from the house. The shelter was delivered in sections made of corrugated iron and had to be erected inside a hole at least 3 feet (1 metre) deep. The earth from the hole was put on top of the finished

shelter to give added protection (and often, later in the war, to make a useful vegetable plot). Digging the hole and erecting the shelter was the householder's responsibility. Because they were partially underground, Anderson shelters were, at best, damp, draughty and cramped. Since they could quickly fill with water when it rained, the fire services spent much of their time in the early months of the war pumping out Anderson shelters.

Eventually people got the hang of making

AFTER THE RAID
The Dallison family leave their Anderson shelter to view the wreckage caused by a nearby bomb explosion the night before.

KEEPING WARM IN THE ANDERSON SHELTER

As the usual methods of household heating could not be used in the Anderson shelter, many ingenious forms of providing warmth were thought up. Drinks could be kept hot in Thermos flasks or in 'hay bottles', which were woollen bags packed with newspaper or straw. Two blankets sewn together made good sleeping bags, and a hot brick, heated in front of the fire for two hours, could be wrapped in something woollen and taken into the shelter to warm a bed. A warming heater could be made from two terracotta flowerpots: you simply fixed a candle at the bottom of one flowerpot (being careful not to block the drain hole) and put the second pot upside down on top of the first one. After a while, the 'heater' would give off noticeable warmth.

their Anderson shelter more damp-proof with the help of leaflets from the government, including a Ministry of Home Security booklet called *Air Raids – What You Must KNOW, What You Must DO*, first published in 1940, then largely rewritten based on Blitz experience in 1941. The shelters, although not strong enough to withstand a direct hit, did give families good protection from near misses and flying fragments.

Also surprisingly effective as a shelter, this time for indoors, was the Morrison shelter, named after the Minister of Home Security, Herbert Morrison, which was issued at the end of 1940. The Morrison shelter was a low, steel cage 6 feet 6 inches (2 metres) 4 feet 3 inches (1 metre 22 centimetres) in area and 2 feet 9 inches (82 centimetres) high, and with a sheet metal top. With enough room in it for a double bed-size mattress, the Morrison shelter could give a couple and their children shelter strong enough to withstand the weight of roof beams and other house debris falling on them.

As with the Anderson shelter, the Morrison shelter was available free to people with an annual income of less than £350, and at a cost of £7 to everyone else. Setting a good example, the prime minister was one of the first to have a Morrison shelter installed in his house, No. 10 Downing Street.

While something could be done to protect people in their homes, there was nothing that could be done to protect the houses. Although building was a reserved occupation, priority was given to the building of factories, accommodation for servicemen and women and other government contracts. House building virtually stopped when the war started and many men who had worked in the building industry of the 1930s, as civil engineers or builders, were, once the initial great increase in government building had ended, sent into the armed forces. At the same time, the government had placed strict controls on the use of building materials. Then came the Blitz. Long before it had ended, it was obvious that replacing destroyed homes and repairing those that were damaged was going to put an enormous demand on men and materials.

With the Blitz at its height, the government began releasing men from the army to work in the Directorate of Emergency Work's special mobile squads, which were sent into local authority areas where they were most needed. In April 1941 a 16,000-strong squad of builders and repairers was sent into London, where some 39,000 houses were either destroyed or had to be demolished. By August, the squad had helped repair 1,100,000 houses, making them at least wind-and-weather-proof and therefore habitable. Another 50,000 houses awaited their attention.

This sort of first aid for housing was all very well in the short term, but it did not provide the country with social housing of either the quality or the quantity that was needed. The housing situation was aggravated by the constant population movements – evacuees to safe areas, workers to new factories thrown up on the outskirts of once quiet towns and villages, and billeted soldiers and civil servants. Then, when much housing repair and rebuilding had taken place, came the V-1 and V-2 attacks of 1944–45 to destroy much more property in the south-

CLEARING UP
Maintenance workers clear rubble in the City of London following an air raid.

THE ENEMY'S HOUSING HIT LIST

A large part of the country's urban housing stock was destroyed by enemy action during the Blitz. The count for properties destroyed reached 3,250,000, with 92 per cent of the total reckoned to be private dwellings.

Some figures for outside London:

• Sheffield, December 1940 – 6,000 people left homeless

• Merseyside, 'May Week' 1941 – 70,000 people left homeless

• Glasgow, Clydeside after raids in March, April and May 1941– only eight out of 12,000 houses left undamaged

• Plymouth, March/April 1941 – 'scarcely a house seemed habitable' to a Mass Observation team sent to the dockyard city

• Portsmouth, May 1941– 60,000 of the city's 70,000 housing stock damaged to a greater or lesser degree.

east than the Blitz bombings had achieved. The housing situation remained dire in many parts of the country throughout the war.

The great wartime increase in the numbers of marriages in Britain also added to the demand for housing – and on furniture to go in them. Young married couples naturally would like to start their new homes with new furniture, but the government was certainly not going to provide the materials, especially the wood, needed to make it. The price of second-hand furniture rocketed, and there was much profiteering in the furniture-making industry, so much so that the government was forced to step in and establish pricing rules and regulations.

By late 1941, officials were talking of Utility furniture, as they had recently talked about Utility clothing. In November 1941, the government decreed that those manufacturers still permitted to make domestic furniture would only be able to make articles from a specified list of twenty pieces, using only a specified maximum amount of wood in their construction. Definitely not among the twenty pieces of furniture were comfortable deep-sprung sofas and armchairs, which would have required heavy upholstery fabrics and metal springs. A couple of months after it was announced, the already very small timber quota for domestic furniture was cut by one-third; the use of plywood, needed in the building of Mosquito fighter-bombers, was forbidden altogether.

CARRY ON COOKING

Despite the fact that there is no glass in her windows after a bombing raid the night before, Mrs Williams carries on cooking regardless.

1943

JULY

- The Women's Army Auxiliary Corps in the US converts to full status and becomes the WAC.
- The Battle of Kursk begins and makes history as the largest tank battle of all time.
- Allied troops invade Sicily in Operation Husky. British soldiers land in the eastern side, American in the southern.
- Rome is bombed by Allied forces.
- Operation Gomorrah begins. Hamburg is bombed by British and Canadian forces. 280,000 buildings are destroyed and 30,000 civilians are killed. The excessive bombing causes a firestorm and a further 42,000 people perish.

AUGUST

- In the US, the Women's Flying Training Detachment and the Women's Auxiliary Ferrying Squadron join together to form the Women's Airforce Service Pilot's – WASP. Each member of freed a male pilot for combat.
- Canadian prime minister, MacKenzie King, meets with Winston Churchill and Franklin D. Roosevelt in Quebec for the Quandrant Conference.
- Germany dissolves the Danish government.
- The USS *Intrepid* is launched.

It was Board of Trade officials, not the manufacturers, who decided on the kind of new furniture that people could buy, high-mindedly believing that they should be 'influencing popular taste towards good construction in simple, agreeable designs . . .' The Board directed that furniture must be strong and serviceable and made using only hardwoods (in practice, this meant mahogany or oak). Panels had to be made from veneered hardboard, all joints had to be morticed or pegged, and screws not pins, should be used. Plastic, a favourite 1930s material for things like handles and wardrobe fittings but now in very short supply in all its forms, was banned.

When the government mounted a Utility furniture preview exhibition in London in October 1942, the near-30,000 visitors were surprised to find that this government-inspired furniture that was being foisted on the nation was of good quality and quite simple in design, with reassuringly clean, solid lines. Today, the best Utility furniture would be called 'minimalist'; at the time, to many it looked austere and even drab, with none of the curly configuration of Arts and Crafts furniture or the colour and geometrical exuberance of Art Deco. But, like it or dislike it, at least it was available – although not to everyone.

In order to ensure a fair distribution of the new Utility furniture, the government made it available only to specified 'priority classes' to whom permits were issued. The classes included people who had been bombed-out and newly-weds setting up their first homes; newly-weds moving into in-laws' homes were permitted one or two extra pieces, but not the full range.

FURNITURE FACTORY
These women are making Utility furniture which will only be available by permit.

LEFT: KEEPING THE ARMY CLEAN
WVS women also washed over 1,500 army shirts every week. Here a member is hanging out shirts to dry from the Aldershot Barracks in Surrey.

ABOVE: WASHING SERVICE
Members of the WVS hang up washing that has been collected and washed by the mobile clothes-washing service, which operates self-contained Rinso units (background) for bomb-damaged households in east and south London.

As well as paying the (government-controlled) price for the furniture, the buyer also had to provide a certain number of units, more for large pieces like a wardrobe, fewer for smaller pieces. A kitchen chair, for instance, could be bought with the purchase price plus just one unit.

Once the Blitz was over and life on the home front settled into a drab austerity, simply obtaining basic consumer goods became very much a matter of being in the right shop at the right time. Certain household basic essentials had to be rationed, to ensure that everyone got at least some of them. Foremost among these was soap, including washing powder, which was rationed in February 1942.

The type of soap powder available to housewives became markedly inferior and manufacturers, such as the makers of Rinso, officially a 'Number One soap powder', published adverts advising people on how best to use it. 'You don't need to boil', said a 1944 Rinso ad,

RINSO
The makers of Rinso advertised their product as the 'Number One soap powder'.

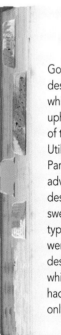

UTILITY FURNISHING FABRICS

Government control of furniture design extended to the fabrics which could be used to cover or upholster it. A small sub-group of the Advisory Committee on Utility Furniture, called the Design Panel, was set up in mid-1943 to advise on the creation of new fabric designs. The splendid geometric sweeps of colour and pattern typical of 1930s Art Deco design were out. Instead, the first two designs, called 'Skelda' and 'Flora', which were introduced in 1944, had small patterns with a repeat of only 3–4 inches (7–10 centimetres)

to keep fabric wastage to a minimum. Fabric weight was low and colour choice small – only rust, green, blue and cream (natural) were available.

POTS FOR THE WAR EFFORT
A Chelsea pensioner adds a frying pan to a heap of pots and pans at the WVS depot at Chelsea, following Lord Beaverbrook's appeal for aluminium to help the war effort.

1943

SEPTEMBER

- Allied troops invade Italy's mainland.
- The Gulf Hotel in Houston, Texas destroyed by a fire, 55 people die.
- Czechoslovakian Julius Fucík, a man in the forefront of the anti-Nazi Resistance, is captured and executed by Nazi soldiers.
- Grace University, a Bible college in Omaha, Nebraska, is established.
- General Dwight D. Eisenhower of the United States announced Italy's surrender to the Allies.
- Following the Great Council of Fascism's decision to depose Benito Mussolini, Hitler commands German paratroopers to rescue Mussolini from his captors. Operation Eiche (oak) was a success.
- An uprising in Naples, Italy, lasts for four days, as people rebel against the presence of the occupying German forces.

OCTOBER

- American forces enter the newly liberated Naples.
- The new government of Italy join the Allies and declare war on Germany.
- Chaing Kai-shek becomes president of China.
- The French Resistance liberate Raymond Aubrac from the Gestapo.

'you simply soak . . . [using the] wartime method, half the water and two-thirds the Rinso', then you sit back at the end of washday and await the admiration of your husband, sitting in his comfy chair and taking his pipe out of his mouth to tell you that you are 'a marvel, darling, running the house and a job too.' Even in wartime, men seldom took any part in housework.

A series of Limitations of Supplies Orders, the first one in 1940, greatly restricted the production of most consumer goods from pottery and cutlery to toys and games. Some household goods were classed as 'fripperies' and their manufacture was prohibited altogether. Housewives might agree that a birdcage or a coffee percolator was a frippery in wartime, but a vacuum cleaner or a refrigerator? By 1943, when new saucepans were almost unobtainable, housewives, most of whom by now were doing part-time jobs as well as running households, were greatly regretting the generous impulse that had made them give their saucepans to the Spitfire Fund back in 1940.

ORDINARY LIFE IN EXTRAORDINARY TIMES

The country might be at war again, but the concerns of ordinary life were still uppermost in the minds of most women in Britain in September 1939. For married women, keeping a comfortable home and food on the table for their families was a major concern, as, of course, it had been since the dawn of history. As for young, unmarried women in Britain, their main object was also an age-old one: securing a partner in life with whom they could establish a home and family of their own.

Marriage in wartime became, for many, something done hastily because call-up papers had arrived in the post, or an all-too-short leave was about to expire. As for that lifetime partnership – that was something to hope

A WARTIME WEDDING
Wartime weddings were usually done in haste just in case the groom was called away on duty.

for rather than to expect as a matter of right. Despite this, the marriage statistics for the six years of the war showed that the rising number of marriages in the late 1930s, perhaps reflecting increasing prosperity in the nation as a whole, was not a glitch: the boom in marriages in the first year of the war produced a record statistic of 22.5 marriages per thousand of the population. Although rates fell during the war, it has been calculated that overall, people continued to marry at the same increasing rate as they had done in the 1930s. In Britain about half a million couples married every year of the war. Women also tended to marry younger than they had in the 1930s; nearly three out of every ten brides in wartime Britain were less than twenty-one years old. The birth-rate also soared, contrary to all expectation, given the gloom and worries about the future resulting from the war. In 1942, a year of terrible austerity, the birth-rate reached 15.6 per thousand, a rate which had not been experienced since 1931. The birth-rate continued to rise throughout the war, to reach a new peak of 20.6 per thousand in 1947. This was not surprising, given that thousands of servicemen were now back home after years away.

GI BRIDES

Three British GI brides with their babies in lifejackets cross the Atlantic to be with their husbands in America.

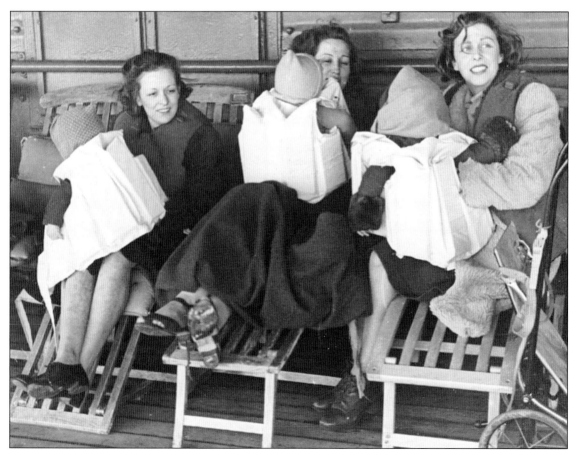

WAITING FOR MUM
Babies sit in line in their prams at the Muriel Green Nursery Centre, St Albans, where they are looked after while their mothers are working for the war effort.

THE UTILITY FURNITURE RANGE

The Board of Trade decided that the young bride wishing to buy Utility furniture for her first home should be able to choose from the Utility furniture range – a double bed, wardrobe, tallboy, dressing chest, dining table, sideboard, easy chair, three dining chairs, a kitchen table and one kitchen chair. These were the items of furniture, the Board of Trade decided, that were needed to fully furnish the average working class home.

The maximum price of the complete set of furniture made in oak was set at £54 9s 9d – about twenty pounds less than the same range in mahogany. The chair on the left is pre-war and is made of fine quality polished wood with decorative carving on the legs. The Utility chair on the right, is plain in design, has a lower back to economise on the wood and is roughly finished with a matte wax. All Utility furniture was stamped with the CC41 'cheeses' below.

MORRISON TABLE SHELTER

The Morrison table sheler was developed because many families had no cellar that could be used as an air raid shelter and insufficient room for an outdoor shelter. The table saved many lives as it was capable of withstanding the weight of debris falling on top of it, although they did not afford much protection in the case of a direct hit.

A side-effect of the failure to predict the wartime rise in the birth-rate was that many items essential to the safe care of babies, including prams, teats for bottles, baby baths and fireguards, were soon either in very short supply or not available at all. As the babies became toddlers then children, their mothers found that there were very few toys for them, the government having banned the production of toys that included a long list of materials, such as rubber, cork, kapok, celluloid and plastics, that were ideal for use in children's toys. As for children's birthday parties, they would have to have streamers, paper chains and paper hats

A MOVE TO THE FACTORIES
Women started to take the place of men in the factories. This woman is making klaxon sirens.

made out of newspaper because there were none of the traditional party papers made during the war, nor could there be bunches of balloons tied to the front gate or crackers to pull at the party table, on which there would probably not be an iced cake. Materials and ingredients for all these were banned or simply not available.

Creating one's first home in wartime was not easy and many newly-married couples had to live with their parents or in-laws at first. Even if they did find a home of their own, they probably had little time to enjoy life in it together, with the young husband soon disappearing into the armed forces and the young wife left to look after the house while carrying on with a job and probably undertaking civil defence activities as well. Thousands of wives and mothers were left to look after the home on their own, to rescue what they could if it was bombed and could not be patched up and to find somewhere else to store their belongings while they searched for a new home. It would not have been easy for them. By the end of 1942 a million or more people were living in houses that would have been condemned in peacetime and another two and a half million families lived in bomb-damaged houses that had been given just very basic first aid.

The coming of war in 1939 put an end to the 1930s house-building boom, and in 1940 the building of new homes came to a complete halt, partly because there were not enough trained builders to construct them, but also because there were no building materials, especially timber. It was not until it became necessary to build camps and accommodation for the hundreds of thousands of American servicemen who began to pour into Britain from mid-1942, that building again became a reserved occupation. In 1943 the War Cabinet at last gave the go-ahead to begin repairs on the estimated one hundred thousand houses that had been made uninhabitable by enemy action in Britain's cities and to build three thousand new cottages for agricultural workers, including Land Girls, many of whom had moved from cities and towns to work for the Women's Land Army in the country.

Then there were the hundreds of thousands of men and women workers who moved from the danger zones to new offices, factories and armament manufacturers in the 'reception areas'. They all had to be accommodated somewhere. Hostels were built or requisitioned, but this still did not meet the demand, and so the burden fell on the householder, especially the housewife, many of whom had already had to take in evacuated children and their mothers. Many ordinary housewives, living peacefully in their homes in what had been before the war quiet market towns far from the noise and bustle of the great cities, suddenly found themselves being required to provide billets in their own homes for these workers.

Furnishing houses – even providing extra beds for billeted workers – soon became as difficult as everything else in wartime. The demand for furniture to furnish newly-weds' homes, to replace that destroyed by enemy action and to replace what was simply worn out, could not be met by furniture makers: neither the workers nor the materials were available to meet the demand. The 'Standard Emergency Furniture' of February 1941, which was plain and simple and made of plywood, was intended as an emergency stop-gap only. Later that year, the government decided that only women and men over the age of forty could be spared to work in the furniture industry. Many women, who rather liked the relatively light and not very dangerous work in furniture factories, stayed on in the industry after the war.

The furniture situation was made worse in November 1942 when the government cut the

FURNITURE PERMITS

As can be seen from the permit above, which is dated 1947, furniture rationing continued after the war.

---

already very small timber quota for domestic furniture by a third. The government responded in the same way as it had with the provision of food: rationing, with coupons and a points system for furniture, and the introduction of Utility furniture.

Utility furniture grew out of the need to make the best use of available materials, providing furniture to a minimum guaranteed standard of quality that would ensure good value for money. At first, the government had tried to counter huge price increases for both new and second-hand furniture (that made after 1900; furniture older than 1900 was 'antique' rather than 'second-hand') by bringing out a Furniture (Maximum Prices) Order in May 1942.

This was soon followed by the announcement of a Utility scheme for furniture. Utility furniture, which was first made available in January 1943, could only be bought with coupons and was available only to three 'priority classes': newly married couples setting up home for the first time, couples needing homes because babies were

on the way, or those who had been bombed out. These priority cases were issued with 'dockets', or ' buying permits', to buy furniture up to the value of a specific number of 'units', depending on the nature of their need for furniture.

Most visitors liked utility furniture because, although basic in design, it was plain and solid, reminding many of the furniture of the Arts and Crafts movement. Reaction was similar in Glasgow and other cities where the furniture was exhibited. The Utility furniture scheme was later extended to include curtain materials, bedlinen and mattresses and the floor covering, linoleum.

EMANCIPATION

As in so many other aspects of life in Britain, World War II dramatically changed attitudes to sex out of wedlock, to marriage itself and to divorce and the birth of children. It wasn't just that women, while remaining the nation's home-makers, discovered that they could also make a major contribution to the world that went on outside the home. They also discovered that it was possible to hold down a worthwhile job while still maintaining a happy home life.

Before the war, women, despite their hard-won experience and training as secretaries, teachers and nurses, had automatically lost their jobs when they married. It was recognised well before the war that this situation would have to change, if only 'for the duration'. Thousands of women were recalled from marriage or retirement to take up their old jobs in teaching, nursing and other professions. By the end of September 1939, the Ministry of Health's Emergency Medical Service had already enrolled fifteen thousand trained nurses and twenty thousand trained auxiliaries.

Although most married women were forced unwillingly to return to their place in the home at the end of the war, post-war society put very different demands on men and women alike than the society of the 1930s had; within a couple of decades of the end of the war, women were going back out to work in numbers that soon exceeded wartime figures.

For many women, having become used to being solely in charge of the home while their husbands served in the armed forces, the end of the war and the return of their menfolk took some getting used to. The majority of women were pleased and relieved to have their husbands and the fathers of their children home; a quite sizeable minority were not. Divorce rates in Britain soared after the war. There were just under ten thousand divorce petitions in 1938, and twenty-five thousand in 1945.

True, many of the post-war divorces were between young couples who had married in haste, when one of them was due to be called up, and were now repenting at leisure. But many more were between couples who found that their wartime experiences had irrevocably changed them and their attitudes towards each other. Loneliness and a lack of sexual fulfilment led many women into adulterous relationships during the war – a fact of life implicitly acknowledged in the many articles in women's magazines that talked about the importance of a woman's loyalty in thought and deed towards her husband serving in the armed forces – so it is not surprising that more than two-thirds of

1943

NOVEMBER
- United States Marines arrive in Bougainville, Solomon Islands.
- Royal Air Forces bomb Berlin causing 131 German deaths and losing 9 aircraft and 53 aviators of its own.
- SS leader Heinrich Himmler orders that 'gypsies' are to be imprisoned alongside Jews in concentration camps.
- Winston Churchill, Franklin D. Roosevelt and Joseph Stalin discuss war strategy at a meeting in Tehran. Within two days they devise Operation Overlord, due to commence with the Normandy Landings in June 1944.
- British troops reach Garigliano River in Italy.

DECEMBER
- The Great Depression in the United States officially ends.
- The Luftwaffe bomb Bari harbour, Italy. An American ship is sunk.
- American Broadcast journalist Edward R. Murrow tells CBS Radio of an RAF overnight bombing raid in Berlin, describing it as 'orchestrated Hell'.
- General Dwight D. Eisenhower becomes Supreme Allied Commander in Europe.
- In Bolivia, a military coup is staged.

divorce petitions in 1945 were on the grounds of adultery.

The other rate that, not surprisingly, soared during the war was that of illegitimate births. One-third of all births in Britain during World War II were illegitimate – at a time when the overall birth rate declined at a rate faster than it had already been doing in the 1930s. It would be natural to assume that many of these illegitimate births occurred because young women could not bear to send their young lovers off to the wars with just a chaste kiss and a wave of the hand. But statistics show that illegitimate births were much higher among older women than younger ones: 'spinsters kicking over the traces as they neared middle-age', as the historian Angus Calder put it. And it should not be forgotten that many fathers were servicemen, and were simply not there to make an honest woman of their pregnant girlfriends.

A much more basic reason for the rise in illegitimacy rates was the suddenly altered lifestyles of young women. Thousands of them were released from the eagle eyes of their parents and the confines of home when they were as young as fifteen or seventeen, often into digs, billets and the shared accommodation of service barracks far from their home towns and villages. Their newly relaxed lifestyles took them after work or off duty into pubs and dance halls where they could forget the drab and austere conditions of their lives. Many girls lost their virginity during one-night stands enjoyed without a thought of the consequences the morrow was all too likely to bring.

At the start of the war, there was nowhere unmarried women could go to get contra-ceptive advice and nowhere 'safe' they could go for an abortion or for adoption advice. Society condemned them for their immorality; even in hospital maternity wards they were segregated from married pregnant women. However, unmarried mothers were accepted back into society – together with their children – more readily than in the past, partly because there were so many of them it helped to desensitise the issue. As in so many other social matters, the conditions of wartime life taught the post-war world to be less condemning of women who gave birth outside the bounds of marriage – and much more accepting of the children, too.

THE EFFECTS OF WAR ON FAMILY LIFE

World War Two affected every aspect of life in Britain, from the cradle to the grave. By the war's end, the nation's idea of what the average British family should be like, and what its place in society should be, had changed markedly.

The first step in creating a family – giving birth to a child – while it was, of course, surrounded by practical problems in wartime, also led to much heart-searching about the standards of maternity care in the country in general. Immediately after the War the provision of well-ordered, nation-wide maternity services was a major element in the development of the National Health Service. Many expectant mothers, evacuated to the country where maternity services were a good deal more patchy, if they existed at all, than in the country's large urban areas, found themselves giving birth in improvised maternity units without anaesthetics (which had to be saved for operations). As the Blitz began, expectant mothers who had been evacuated to country

SAVING WHAT YOU CAN
After their home was destroyed during a German air raid on the East End of London, a father and son load a horse-drawn cart with the family furniture.

houses hastily converted into maternity homes, could count themselves fortunate, whatever the quality of care available. At least they were not having to give birth, probably while wearing a tin hat, to the sound of air raid sirens followed by the crump of bombs landing nearby – or, as in the case of Southampton's general hospital on the first night of the many air raids on the city, by the light of a hurricane lamp, with another mother and her new-born baby pushed for safety under the delivery table. Even more appallingly memorable for some mothers was giving birth in the London Underground during an air raid.

For infants and older children, the arrival of the family's gas masks was probably their first practical indication of the fact that family life

GAS MASKS

Forty-four million gas masks were distributed in Britain before the outbreak of war. Wearing the gas masks was never made compulsory, although at the beginning of the war it was an offence to leave home without it, and the government contenting itself with issuing posters with warnings like 'Hitler will send no warning, so carry your gas mask with you at all times.'

One of the most familiar objects in photographs of children during the September 1939 evacuation is the gas mask in its canvas box strung round every child's neck. The gas masks are conspicuous by their absence in photos of later evacuations. In fact, when it very soon became clear that there were going to be no gas attacks from the enemy, people began leaving their mask at home. Schoolchildren, who did not have this option – they might be sent home to get them if they arrived at school without them – soon began to find other uses for the canvas boxes, such as carrying their sandwiches to school in them.

Child's 'Mickey Mouse' gas mask

UNDERGROUND SHELTER
A trap door in the living room floor provides an additional entrance to the cellar which offered shelter during air raids.

PUTTING ON GAS MASKS
Children at the Cosway Street School in Marylebone, London, try on their gas masks during a gas instruction lesson.

would not be the same in wartime as it had been up till now. The government was concerned that everyone should have a gas mask, originally called 'respirators', because it seemed very probable that the enemy's first attack would be accompanied by the use of the mustard and chlorine gases that had caused such appalling damage on the frontline in World War One.

Children aged between two and five were provided with strangely shaped multi-coloured masks that someone in authority presumably thought would be more acceptable if they were called 'Mickey Mouse' gas masks. Older children were given the same unwieldy and unattractive

gas masks as adults. It was not until October 1939 that babies were issued with their own gas masks, which looked like haversack-shaped bags with a Perspex visor and with a set of bellows which mothers had to keep pumping to get air in the bag.

Everyone was advised to practise wearing their gas masks for at least fifteen minutes every day. Mothers had to oversee their children's practice because they might not have time to help their children as well as themselves and their babies in the event of a gas attack. All schoolchildren were required to take their gas masks to school, where regular gas mask practices were held in

SAFETY IN PLAY
Nursery school children at play wearing gas masks just to be on the safe side.

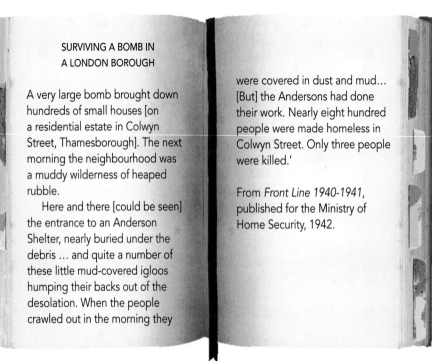

SURVIVING A BOMB IN A LONDON BOROUGH

A very large bomb brought down hundreds of small houses [on a residential estate in Colwyn Street, Thamesborough]. The next morning the neighbourhood was a muddy wilderness of heaped rubble.

Here and there [could be seen] the entrance to an Anderson Shelter, nearly buried under the debris ... and quite a number of these little mud-covered igloos humping their backs out of the desolation. When the people crawled out in the morning they were covered in dust and mud... [But] the Andersons had done their work. Nearly eight hundred people were made homeless in Colwyn Street. Only three people were killed.'

From *Front Line 1940-1941*, published for the Ministry of Home Security, 1942.

the first weeks of the war. While schoolboys might have found wearing gas masks great fun, even 'smashing', for many children, wearing the rubber-smelling, claustrophobia-inducing gas masks remained their most unpleasant memory of the War.

THE ANDERSON SHELTER

There were other, more practical things that children noticed took up a lot of their parent's time. While mother might be busy round the house clearing the understairs cupboard so that it could become an emergency air raid shelter, getting in emergency stocks of torch batteries (soon very hard to find in the shops), candles and blankets, and filling kitchen cupboards with emergency rations, father might be outside in the garden building a very strange object indeed. This was the Anderson Shelter.

The Anderson Shelter, named not after Sir John Anderson, the Home Secretary of the day, as is generally believed, but after Dr David Anderson, the engineer who invented it, was an ingenious solution to a serious problem: how to give ordinary people adequate protection from bombs. Households with an annual income below £250 were given their shelters free of charge. The Anderson Shelter was a corrugated steel construction intended to act as a strong roof erected over a deep hole dug in the garden. The earth from the hole was often put over the shelter, to act as extra protection. Many householders soon began planting vegetables on their Anderson Shelter's roof. In 1942, the Ministry of Home Security calculated that something like a million back-garden 'Andersons' had been built throughout the country.

Although it was usually smelly and damp, and might even fill with water after heavy rain, the Anderson Shelter very successfully fulfilled its purpose, saving the lives of thousands of people throughout Britain. It also provided children

THE ANDERSON SHELTER
Neighbours put up their Anderson air raid shelters in their gardens.

with some of their best memories of the war. If you had a torch with batteries, you could wrap yourself in blankets and pass the time reading books and comics, or even do your school homework. If the only faint light at night came from the candle under an up-turned flower pot that served as a heater then you could tell each other stories or listen to your mother or father telling you one. The stories of recently seen cinema films – which could be stretched out over several sessions, serial-form – passed the time in many air raid shelters.

Not every family had an Anderson Shelter, even if they had space for one. The family of Mary Murphy, who was born in Chingford in Essex in 1939, did not have an Anderson Shelter. Her father, who had fought at Gallipoli in World War One, and then served as a special policeman in the City of London after 1939, had such terrible memories of helping dig out victims after air raids that he refused to even consider building one. He had no intention of letting himself and his family be buried alive.

Thus, when the V1 flying bombs began their devastatingly indiscriminate attacks on southern England in 1944, five-year-old Mary found herself standing in the garden, her father holding her hand tightly as they watched the searchlights criss-crossing the night sky and listened to the sound of a doodlebug engine getting nearer

and nearer, knowing that when the sound of the engine cut out she was to start counting to fifty during the eerie silence that followed. If she got to fifty before there was a loud explosion, that meant that the doodlebug had passed over them. 'I remember the fires after the doodlebugs exploded. Sometimes the whole horizon was ablaze,' Mary recalls.

Another very familiar air raid shelter, also distributed free to low-income families, was the Morrison Shelter, which was designed for families without gardens or for those people living in flats and other accommodation. This was a box-shaped shelter with a large and strong steel plate on top, which could be used as a table during the day and used as a double bed, or, if it had an inner shelf, as bunks for a family, at night. By November 1941 more than half a million Morrison Shelters had been made for use by families throughout Britain.

Mary Murphy's family did have a Morrison Shelter in their front room. During air raids, Mary got into the habit of retreating into the Morrison Shelter with her beaten-up teddy bear, her faithful doll and her tabby cat, John.

The most famous of all Britain's air raid shelters was the London Underground. At the height of the Blitz in September 1940, an estimated 177, 000 men, women and children were sheltering in tube stations from the devastation being wrought above them. Although photographs show that many of the children who were taken down into tube stations for the night took games, toys, books and even knitting with them, suggesting that the Underground played a big part in sheltering children during the War,

SLEEPING UNDERGROUND
Children climb into their bunks in an underground air raid shelter.

POPULAR CULTURE
1944

SONGS
- *Don't Fence Me In*, Bing Crosby and The Andrew Sisters
- *Swinging on a Star*, Bing Crosby
- *I'm Making Believe*, Ella Fitzgerald and The Ink Spots
- *I Love You*, Bing Crosby
- *D-Day*, Nat King Cole
- *Shoo-Shoo Baby*, The Andrew Sisters
- *Saturday Night (Is The Loneliest Night Of The Week)*, Frank Sinatra
- *It Could Happen To You*, Jo Stafford
- *First Class Private Mary Brown*, Perry Como

HIGH-GROSSING FILMS
- *Meet Me In St Louis*, starring Judy Garland and Margaret O'Brien
- *Going My Way*, starring Bing Crosby and Barry Fitzgerald
- *Since You Went Away*, starring Shirley Temple and Jennifer Jones
- *Hollywood Canteen*, starring Bette Davis and Joan Crawford
- *Double Indemnity*, starring Fred MacMurray and Barbara Stanwyck
- *Gaslight*, starring Ingrid Bergman and Charles Boyer
- *Cover Girl*, starring Rita Hayworth and Gene Kelly
- *To Have And Have Not*, starring Humphrey Bogart and Lauren Bacall
- *Laura,* starring Gene Tierney and Dana Andrews
- *Henry V*, starring Laurence Olivier and Robert Newton
- *The Fighting Seabees*, starring John Wayne and Susan Hayward

THE MAN OF THE HOUSE
The eldest boy in the family takes the place of his fighter pilot father by pouring the afternoon tea for the rest of his family.

in fact only about 9 per cent of the population used communal shelters. For most families, shelter from air raids was sought in Anderson and Morrison Shelters, in the cupboard under the stairs or even under the kitchen table: strong tables were much in demand during the War.

For families bombed out and left homeless after an air raid – which, in London after the end of the main Blitz in May 1941, meant one Londoner in every six – there was often a very long wait until something better than temporary accommodation in a shelter or a relative's home could be found. It was not until 1943 that the permanent repair of damaged houses, using good quality materials, could begin or the building of new homes could get under way.

In the meantime, in the big cities, local authorities' social services, helped by volunteers, did what they could. In London's East End, the WVS evacuated children under five and the London County Council found billets for school-age children. Some local councils set up services so complicated that mothers, dealing with one official to get their children: new ration books, identity cards, and to get the children billets together, would give up in despair.

As the War dragged on, children found that far more disturbing than long hours spent in shelters, days and nights hearing bombers flying overhead and bombs dropping, even the loss of their homes, was the absence of their parents. As conscription bit deeper, so more and more men were called up as age limits were extended. Even if one's father was not called up into the services, he could still be absent from his family because of his job or because he spent many nights on ARP or fire-watching duties or in the Home Guard. It really was an army of fathers and grandfathers, brothers and uncles.

Many women were also absent from home much more than had ever been known in Britain. The needs of wartime industry took more and more women into essential wartime industries or into a wide range of voluntary work, including the WVS, first aid posts and British Restaurants. Even when she stayed at home, one's mother might be occupied in some form of war work, including out-work for munitions factories, which she and friends and neighbours could do at home on the kitchen table.

PROVIDING FOR WAR ORPHANS

While thousands of children could be looked after by grandparents, often even being sent to live with them out of the danger areas, many more charities and voluntary organisations had to fill child-care gaps. Children were also helped by the increased provision of state-backed childcare facilities and the development of such things as British Restaurants, which allowed

more and more women to work outside the home as the War went on. By 1944 seven million of the sixteen million British women aged between fourteen and fifty-nine had jobs in civil defence, industry or the armed forces. Far worse for children than the absence from home of their parents was the death of one or both parents. Families with men fighting for their country lived in dread of the delivery of the telegram that told them their husband or son had been killed in action. Then there were the many children who survived an air raid that destroyed their home or shelter and left one or both parents and other members of their families dead.

Good Housekeeping ran a story in the December 1944 issue called 'Nobody's Children' which addressed the problem of what to do in the long term with thousands of homeless children. One of the organisations that helped with the problem was Dr Barnardo's homes for children.

Thomas John Barnado, a Dubliner born in 1845, arrived in London just when a cholera epidemic was sweeping through the East End of London. It left many children homeless and without parents as the epidemic claimed more and more lives. Barnado, seeing thousands of children living on the streets, opened his first school in 1867 giving poor children the chance of a basic education. Barnado was so deeply affected by the orphans he found literally sleeping on rooftops and in gutters, that he devoted the rest of his life to helping destitute children. His first boys home opened in Stepney in 1870 and he never turned a single boy away, saying that every child deserved the best possible start in life. By the time of his death in 1905, the charity he had so fondly formed, ran 96 homes caring for more than 8,500 children.

During the war Dr Barnado's provided 25,000 meals for the 7,500 homeless children under their jurisdiction. Today, Thomas Barnado's legend lives on as it has become the leading children's charity in the UK, responsible for the care of over 11,000 children and their families.

Providing proper care for war orphans became an important part of the post-war Welfare State's programme, which built on the foundations laid by such war-time organisations as the WVS, working in tandem with charities like Barnardo's and service organisations like SSAFA (Soldiers, Sailors and Airmen's Families Association).

LIVE FOR TODAY

Other serious consequences for family life in Britain that resulted from the war were great rises in illegitimacy rates and in divorce, both a direct result of the widespread wartime attitude of 'live for today for tomorrow we may be dead'.

Despite such very sad and distressing problems, for the majority of the children of the war years life was surprisingly good. While it is true that the passing of time mellows memories, many adults who grew up during the War seem to have been not much disturbed by the actions of the enemy or by wartime deprivations. There was a certain excitement about living through extraordinary times coupled, for some, with a feeling that, since 'what will happen will happen', one may as well just get on with things.

As Patricia Houlahan, who spent the war in her family's house in the naval city of Portsmouth remembers, she and most of her friends were not much bothered by the day-to-day problems or aware of the horrors of war:

'We just got on with things. Even after whole nights spent in the Anderson shelter or next door in our neighbour's brick shelter, we always went off to school the next morning. Bombs and rockets did not bother me. The flares that the German dropped to guide their bombers to Portsmouth scared me much more. To this day, I cannot bear to listen to or look at fireworks.'

DR BARNADOS

Young boys from the Dr Barnados home in Hawkhurst, Kent try on experimental gas masks. Dr Barnados opened hundreds of children's homes across the UK during World War Two. The government required owners of large buildings to allow them to be used for the war effort, lots of Dr Barnado children were evacuated to these houses in the country.

CHAPTER SEVEN

CHILDREN AND THE WAR

CHILDREN AND THE WAR

Two of the most important areas of children's daily life in wartime Britain — how they were fed and how they were clothed — were both very quickly brought within government rationing schemes. The government had had some experience of rationing food during World War One, but what was planned now — and indeed, had been planned for some time — was something on a much bigger scale altogether.

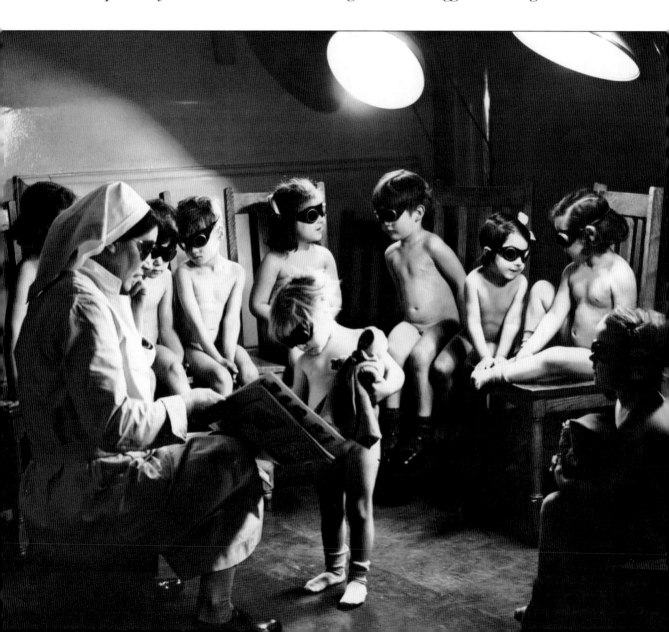

Statisticians and planners had long recognised that the availability and price of food was of national importance at all times as a symbol of the nation's well-being and prosperity. But in times of war it took on even greater significance: a country at war needed a well-fed and healthy population to keep wartime industries working at full capacity and to ensure that, once the war was over, there would be a generation of healthy, well-fed children to take over.

When ration books were first issued in January 1940, children under six (later reduced to under five) were given their own ration books, coloured green to distinguish them from the buff-coloured ration books of older children and adults. Children aged between five and sixteen (later eighteen) also got their own ration books, coloured blue, from 1943. Expectant mothers were directed to obtain a child's green ration book from their local Food Office before their baby was born. As children were not exempt from having a National Registration Identity Card, no child was exempt from having a Ration Book: the Imperial War Museum in London holds in its archives the ration book issued to Her Royal Highness Princess Elizabeth, of The Royal Lodge, Windsor Great Park on 16 January 1940.

Ration books, which were brought in partly to prevent hoarding, were filled with coupons allocated to specific foods. This allowed the Ministries of Food and Health to ensure that everyone got a fair share of foods, such as meat, dairy products, cooking fats, milk, sugar, preserves and eggs, that were regularly available.

1944

JANUARY
- The *Daily Mail* makes history as the first transoceanic newspaper.
- The Battle of Monte Cassino begins, consisting of four battles spanning five months.
- Meat rationing ends in Australia.
- Soviet troops start the offensive at Novgorod and Leningrad.
- British troops cross the Garigliano River.
- An earthquake in San Juan, Argentina, kills 10,000 people.
- Berlin is hit by 2,300 tons of bombs, courtesy of the Royal Air Force.

FEBRUARY
- American soldiers land and capture the Mashall Islands within two days.
- Jewish actor and director Kurt Gerron was bribed into shooting a Nazi propoganda film entitled *The Fuhrer Gives A Village To The Jews*. This followed a prank against the Danish Red Cross, who were tricked by Hitler's men into believing a concentration camp was a happy community. Gerron completed the film and was later gassed.

LACK OF SUNLIGHT
A nurse watches over a group of children in Bermondsey, London, as they sit under sun-ray lamps to help make up for the deficiency in sunlight and the lack of certain items of food, such as fruit, during the long winter months.

A VERY IMPORTANT NUMBER

Identity cards, which everyone, young and old, was issued with at the beginning of the War and had to carry at all times, so that it could be produced when someone in authority asked to see it, had a personal number, unique to the card's carrier. The National Registration Number was also used on such things as ration books, so it is not surprising that many people can still reel off their wartime Identity Card number without a second's hesitation. Jane Elliott, given her Identity Card when she was a pupil of Harrogate Ladies College, remembers that its number was KIAB 413, while that of Martin Wagrel, at school in Aberdeen, was SUFD 203.

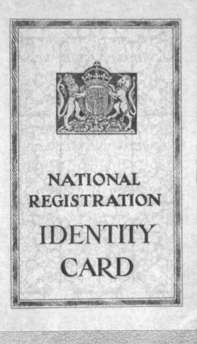

A HEALTHY TREAT
Three young children enjoy a portable, healthy snack – a carrot on a stick. Ice cream was not available during war time rationing.

These foods were not rationed all at once in January 1940, but were added to the ration books over a period of eighteen months or so. Fruit and vegetables were never rationed, but as fruit quickly became very scarce, with fruits from overseas, like oranges and bananas, being seldom seen, most children ate many more fresh vegetables than fresh fruits during the war. A high point of the war for many children came in July 1942 when a 'personal points' scheme covering chocolate and sweets came in. Now everyone over the age of six months could buy, or have bought for them,

8oz (250g) of chocolate and confectionary every month without using up precious food coupons. Chocolate bars, rather smaller than before the war and often wrapped in greaseproof paper to save precious tinfoil, became a regular item in many children's shopping baskets, despite the fact that the chocolate was powdery and not as smooth as it had been and was also, much of it, dark because of the shortage of milk.

Beside chocolate bars there might also be in a child's shopping basket, paper bags, or screws of paper (if just a pennyworth was purchased) containing such delights as acid drops, fruit drops, bulls' eyes, humbugs, liquorice comforts and many other sweets. After a time the chocolate and sweet ration went up to 16oz (500g) before dropping back to 12oz (375g), where it remained until sweet rationing was finally ended in 1953, eight years after the war ended.

Children, except those under five, who got half the meat ration and orange juice instead of tea, were allowed the same ration quantities as adults. Another concession for small children was being allowed three eggs a week; they also got double the allowance of dried eggs as adults when these were introduced. A points system, brought in later, gave everyone sixteen points a month which could be spent as one chose on a range of foods covered by the points rather than by the coupons in ration books, including tins of corned beef, Spam, and pulses like split peas or dried beans.

Mothers, clutching their children's ration books as well as their own would use much of the time spent standing in queues outside shops deciding which of the several books in their shopping bags would have its meat coupons removed and which would be used for butter,

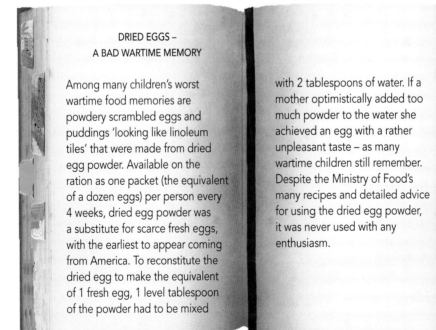

**DRIED EGGS –
A BAD WARTIME MEMORY**

Among many children's worst wartime food memories are powdery scrambled eggs and puddings 'looking like linoleum tiles' that were made from dried egg powder. Available on the ration as one packet (the equivalent of a dozen eggs) per person every 4 weeks, dried egg powder was a substitute for scarce fresh eggs, with the earliest to appear coming from America. To reconstitute the dried egg to make the equivalent of 1 fresh egg, 1 level tablespoon of the powder had to be mixed with 2 tablespoons of water. If a mother optimistically added too much powder to the water she achieved an egg with a rather unpleasant taste – as many wartime children still remember. Despite the Ministry of Food's many recipes and detailed advice for using the dried egg powder, it was never used with any enthusiasm.

eggs or sugar. They might get their children to carry the sheets of newspaper that many of them took to the shops for wrapping up their purchases. Children's health and nutrition were major priorities during the war. As well as providing free immunisation against such childhood diseases as diphtheria, the government also developed several schemes aimed at ensuring children's nutritional needs were met. Among them were the National Milk Scheme

FOOT INSPECTION
A row of toddlers, evacuated from London during the Blitz, have their feet inspected at their new home in a 15th-century mansion house in Kent.

and the Vitamin Welfare Scheme. The creation of the long, grey-looking but undeniably very nutritious National Loaf and Household milk – dried milk powder that was turned into milk by mixing the powder into water – benefitted children as much as adults.

The National Milk Scheme was a development of a scheme begun in the 1930s to get milk to children from the poorest families. The wartime scheme, begun in 1940, was by 1944 getting free milk to nineteen out of every twenty children entitled to it. The pre-War schoolchildren's free or subsidised milk scheme was also continued and extended so that something like three-quarters of state school children were getting a third of a pint of subsidised, very nutritious milk in school every day.

Of course, not every schoolchild liked his or her school milk. To begin with, it was room temperature, if not actually warm, and there was often dust on the cardboard top because the crates of milk had been sitting in a school corridor or outside in the playground. But it was easy enough to blow the dust off, push in the central button on the top with the end of your straw, and then drink the milk. And if you were permitted to drink it in class, it made a break from lessons.

The Ministry of Food considered that providing infants and young children with vitamin foods was so important that coupons for vitamin foods, including orange juice and cod liver oil, were included in a revised children's ration book, called the R.B.2. As well as this, the Vitamin Welfare Scheme was set up in December 1941 as a follow-up to an earlier

1944

MARCH
- The 16th Academy Awards is held in Grauman's Chinese Theater.
- Narva and Tallinn, Estonia, are attacked by Soviet air forces.
- Just outside Salerno, Italy, a train stalls in a tunnel and 521 passengers choke to death.
- In Northern Italy an anti-fascist strike begins.
- Louis Bulchater, the leader of crime syndicate Murder Inc., is executed in Sing Sing prison.
- German troops occupy Hungary in Operation Margarethe.
- The Fosse Ardeatine massacre takes place in Rome as a retaliation against the previous days partisan attack. Over 600 people die in the massacre, among them Italians and Jews.

APRIL
- The United Negro College Fund is founded in the United States.
- In Devon, England, American troops stage a rehearsal for the Normandy landings. During the rehearsal, named Exercise Tiger, an Allied convoy was attacked and 749 American troops were killed.

FOR WHAT WE ARE ABOUT TO EAT…
Children say a prayer before a meal at a crèche which was formed to enable factory working mothers to leave their children safely during the daytime.

PICCADILLY TUBE STATION
People take shelter in Piccadilly tube station overnight bringing their personal belongings and makeshift beds with them.

scheme aimed at countering vitamin deficiency in infants by issuing free blackcurrant juice and cod liver oil. Now the blackcurrant juice was replaced by concentrated orange juice, much of which came from the United States as part of the Lend-lease scheme.

The Ministry of Food did its best to inform mothers of where they could get the orange juice and cod liver oil to which they were entitled. But bureaucracy, as ever, got in the way, making mothers apply first to a Food Office, which might be in another town, for their free coupons and then sending them somewhere else,

such as a welfare centre, clinic or distribution centre, to get them. Many mothers never availed themselves of the scheme and three-quarters of the cod liver oil made available by the Ministry was not used. The unpleasant taste of cod liver oil did not help, of course, and many mothers preferred to give it to their children in the form of a spoonful of the much more pleasant malt extract with added cod liver oil and orange juice.

By the time the war ended in 1945, one child in three was getting a meal, free or subsidised (at a cost to parents of just four or five pence, the

YES, WE HAVE NO BANANAS

Bananas were so seldom seen in Britain during the war that not only was a song about the lack of them very popular in East End community singalongs, but many children, like little Annabel Rudland in Stevenage, who was six when the war ended, remember when the first bananas arrived from the West Indies when the war was over. Probably Annabel, like many others, had not been deceived by a wartime children's pudding which, although called 'Mashed Bananas', had actually consisted of cooked parsnips and pieces of the grey National Loaf mashed up with a little sugar and a few drops of banana essence. Annabel, being too young, would have missed out on the time when, a full consignment of bananas having made it safely to Britain, the Ministry of Food decided that a 'special ration' of one banana should be given to every child over fourteen.

price of a child's ticket at the cinema) at school. For many of these children, the school meal, often including vegetables grown in the school's own allotment, was the most nutritious of their day. For those schools that did not have their own canteen, the nearest British Restaurant – another very successful scheme to get cheap, nutritious and off-ration food to people in wartime – made an excellent substitute.

For children at boarding schools mealtimes left mixed memories. Kenneth Jones, at school in Devon, does not remember ever being bothered by the rationing.

'Every Monday morning we were issued with our personal ration of sugar and butter. There was always a lot of bartering in accordance with our personal tastes – "I will swap half my sugar for half your butter". Then, one day a week we would spend the afternoon helping local farmers and were given a smashing tea with Devonshire clotted cream, strawberries, home-baked buns etc. We boys certainly didn't suffer, at least during the early years of the war.'

Joan Elliott, whose school was evacuated from Harrogate to the imposing Swinton Castle on the Yorkshire moors remembers the grandeur of her surroundings, but also being hungry and, in the cold of winter, getting chilblains. The thought of the tins of water biscuits back at home in the cellar air raid shelter was often tantalising. It was a Red Letter Day when Lady Swinton, encountered in a lift in the castle, offered her a peppermint.

Trying to ensure that their children were adequately fed remained a constant worry for mothers, and keeping them well-clothed soon began to worry them almost as much. They were still wrestling with the problems of food ration books, coupons and points when the government introduced clothes rationing in

June 1941. Now every man, woman and child in the country had another ration book, again with one's identity card number on the front, to deal with.

The basic clothes ration was sixty-six coupons (later in the war reduced to sixty) per person per year, except in the first year of clothes rationing when the coupons had to last fifteen months. When it was realised that the purchase of a new winter coat would mean handing over thirteen coupons along with payment, while a pair of men's trousers took eight coupons and a dress eleven, mothers knew that new clothing was not going to figure regularly in their children's lives. It was all very well for *Good Housekeeping* magazine to tell mother that she could buy a delightful 'Buster Utility suit', including a shirt and lined trousers for her little boy for just ten shillings and twopence, plus four clothing coupons, for reality did not always match up with the optimistic tone women's magazines tried their best to convey during the war. More than one wartime child still remembers the annoyance of having to give up clothing coupons so that an older brother or sister, now old enough to leave school and take on a job, could buy new trousers or a coat to go to work in.

On the other hand, recalling the ingenuity with which they and their mothers 'made do and mended', provides many an amusing memory. Just as well as she remembers the arrival of the first banana in her home, Annabel Rudland remembers the excitement of going to the nearby Henlow RAF base with her mother to buy used parachute silk for making into nightgowns and underwear.

For other girls the memories centre on learning to knit. Although new wool became increasingly hard to buy and was rationed, anyway, with one clothing coupon needed to buy one 2oz (50g) ball, there were always many old jumpers that one's brothers and sisters had grown out of that could be carefully washed, unravelled and knitted up again into something with an entirely new, although rather curly and wrinkled, look. This re-use of odd bits of wool accounted for the wonderfully striped jumpers, cardigans, gloves and hats worn by many children – and their mothers – during the war.

When the Utility Clothing scheme was adopted in 1941, children's clothes were included in it. Because the scheme was devised by the government to control both the amount of precious raw materials used in the manufacture of clothing and the amount of the finished fabrics put into garments, everyone assumed the clothes would be unattractive. In fact, because ten leading designers, including Queen Elizabeth's dressmakers Norman Hartnell and Hardy Amies, were involved in the design of the clothes, they turned out to be both well-designed and of good quality. Where girls, with their natural liking for ribbons, buttons and bows, may have felt they were losing out was in the introduction of something called Austerity regulations. These drastically limited the amount of frills and decorations that could be put on clothes, for both adults and children.

For most people, buying new clothes, whether Utility or Austerity, rationed or not, played a very small part in daily life. A much bigger role was played by the business of making do with

NO FRILLS OR BOWS
There was only a limited range of children's clothing available during the period of rationing in World War Two.

what clothing you had and mending it – again and again and again. 'Make do and mend' was another slogan, like 'Dig for Victory', dreamed up by the propaganda men and women of the Ministry of Information (MoI) for the Board of Trade, the government department responsible for clothing, in an effort to make shabbiness not just acceptable but a patriotic duty.

Again like the 'Dig for Victory' campaign, children were as much a target of the 'Make do and mend' campaign as their parents, with many leaflets and posters from the Board of Trade being aimed specifically at children. 'Useful jobs that girls can do – to help win the war' and 'Simple jobs boys can do themselves – and so help win the war' were the headlines on two.

The poster aimed at boys gave quite detailed instructions on how to mend a table leg or do simple electrical repairs, but also, in a departure from the norm, on how to sew on a button or darn a sock. The girls' poster, while concentrating on the business of making, repairing and looking after clothes, also threw in instructions on how to refix a loose knife handle or sort out a sticking drawer. Looking after clothes was a theme carried on in many girls' schools, with instructresses coming in from outside to advise girls on how they could make their school clothes and uniforms last longer by being let out, patched and added to so that they would continue to fit growing girls.

Children in the German-occupied Channel Islands would have envied their mainland counterparts and their reasonably available, even if rationed, food and clothing, however limited in quantity. Rationing, curfews and censorship

1944

MAY
- Jean-Paul Sartre publishes his existenstial play *No Exit*.
- In Sevastopol, Ulkraine, Soviet troops drive out the German forces, despite Hitler's demands that they, 'fight to the last man.'
- Soviet troops liberate the Crimea.

JUNE
- A coded message is sent by the BBC for the benefit of the underground resistance in France, warning them that the invasion of Europe is imminent. The message used the first line of the poem *Chanson d'automne* by Paul Verlaine. When the second line was broadcast, the resistance knew the invasion would take place within 24 hours.
- Operation Overlord begins. 155,000 British troops land in the beaches of Normandy, France in the most impressive amphibious military attack in history. France is liberated from Germany and the Nazi hold on Europe begins to weaken.
- Germany launches a V1 flying bomb attack on England.

A GROUP PROJECT

During the school holidays children were encouraged to do some gardening at a school in Cobham in Surrey.

THE TRAUMA OF WAR
Young patients sit on their mothers' laps at Miss Dane's clinic in Lewisham, London. The clinic treats children who are traumatised by the war.

of books and newspapers were all imposed on the Islanders from the beginning of the Occupation.

As the war went on and Hitler decided to turn the Channel Islands into an 'Atlantic Wall', things got very much worse. The staple diet was reduced to root vegetables while blackberry and rose leaves and dock weeds were used to make 'tea'. While British mothers – although perhaps not their children – were irritated when soap rationing was imposed without warning in February 1942, at least they had enough to keep their families and their homes and clothes clean. Soap was in such short supply in the Channel Islands that the smallest cut on unwashed skin would fester and leg sores, dubbed 'Occupation ulcers' by one doctor, were common.

GOING TO SCHOOL IN WARTIME

The education system was turned upside down when war broke out. There was chaos and confusion for weeks after the evacuation scheme for schools was put into action on 1 September, the day on which it had been planned to coincide a return to school after the summer holidays with the raising of the school-leaving age from fourteen to fifteen, which now did not happen for another eight years. Thus, many fourteen-year-olds who, in peacetime, would have had another year's schooling, found themselves being treated as young adults in a nation at war, able not only to get themselves paid jobs, but also to help with Civil Defence work, including fire-fighting, auxiliary nursing, ARP work and much else.

Under the schools evacuation scheme, schools in the Reception Areas could, if necessary, operate a shift system, usually two shifts a day, but occasionally three, so that an evacuated school could share the premises with the local school. This system was in operation, more-or-less successfully, by the middle of September, although in both the Reception and the Neutral Areas, the re-opening of many schools was delayed by the need to complete the provision of shelters, which all schools were required to have. If the school grounds allowed it, shelters were dug in the playground, but many schools had to use inner corridors without windows as their main shelters. In some very small, usually primary schools, no shelters could be provided, and children regularly practised running home as quickly as possible in the event of an air raid warning – which, since these were in areas hopefully far from air raids, ought not to be very often, if at all.

There were, not surprisingly, many problems to be overcome in integrating large groups of children from the large cities into schools in quiet towns and villages far from urban life. It was all very well for children used to having their school to themselves, with desks for everyone, to be told, when being shunted about to make room for the newcomers, that 'There's a war on, you know, we must all make adjustments.' Differences

A LOGISTICAL NIGHTMARE

The problems encountered by the education authorities of the London outer suburb of Croydon in keeping track of their school-age children were typical of those experienced by many local education authorities. According to a post-war report undertaken by Croydon Corporation, there were more than twenty thousand school pupils in Croydon in 1939, most of them in elementary schools, where five out of six children in England and Wales spent all their school lives. In the weeks and months after evacuation, schools and their teachers were scattered from one end of England – Penzance in Cornwall – to the other – Newcastle-upon-Tyne. Once in the 110 different places to which they were sent, weeks went by before many teachers found permanent places to set up their classrooms. Teachers were reduced to appointing a regular meeting point every day, from which their pupils would be marched off to whatever place was available to house them that day.

in dress, behaviour, accent and language were swiftly noted and led, if not to a ganging-up in the playground, then certainly to a tendency for the newcomers to gather together in a self-protecting group. There were many playground fights during those difficult weeks of evacuation, and not always between the local children and the newcomers: sometimes the fighting would be between boys from different parts of London's East End.

In the Evacuation Areas, in theory now without school children and school teachers, as many as two thousand state elementary and secondary schools (which were a mixture of technical schools and grammar schools) were taken over by the Civil Defence services and put to use as shelters for those left homeless by bombing, as storage areas, ARP posts, first aid posts and other things. As many families did not send their children out of the Evacuation Areas, there were soon many thousands of children running wild and unsupervised in Britain's cities. To these numbers were gradually added hundreds more as evacuated mothers and children began to drift back to the cities. Many of these children got what education they could by joining home tuition classes organised in private houses, in pubs and in other distinctly non-educational surroundings.

Although the government acknowledged the inevitable at the beginning of November 1939 and permitted the reopening of state schools in the Evacuation Areas, where parents wanted them, it was not until mid-1941, more than a year after the Board of Education had re-introduced compulsory education, that enough schools had re-opened to get all children off the streets, and

back into full-time education. A major reason for delays in opening was the time it took to sort out the details of shelter construction, including how strong they should be and who, whether the local authority or the Board of Education, would pay for them. For many children in Britain's most deprived areas, there was a very long period without the free milk and free meals to which they were entitled in schools. As for the scabies, headlice and other parasites that had so shocked the nation in 1939, these went virtually untreated in many working-class elementary schools until the middle of 1941, when school medical inspections got back to their pre-war frequency.

Many independent or public schools, which educated only one schoolchild in every ten in England and Wales, in 1939, evacuated themselves to the country, many of them to large country houses and stately homes. Perhaps the most important public school evacuation of the war was that of the famous Worcestershire boys' school, Malvern College, to Blenheim Palace, birthplace of Winston Churchill, who replaced Neville Chamberlain as Prime Minister in May 1940. While the boys of Malvern College found themselves in classrooms and dormitories hung with famous paintings and valuable tapestries depicting the military successes of Churchill's famous ancestor, the 1st Duke of Marlborough, their old college was taken over by the government's Telecommunications (or radar) Research Establishment in May 1942. Where there was some truth in the saying that the Battle of Waterloo had been won on the playing fields of Eton, there was even more in the quip that World War Two was won on the playing fields

TIME FOR PLAY

A group of young evacuees in Monmouthshire, Wales, find plenty to alleviate their homesickness. Some have never seen a climbing frame before, such as this one situated in a local playground.

FIELD CLASSES
A group of evacuees having an open-air maths lesson in a hayfield near a village in Monmouthshire, Wales.

of Malvern College – especially the junior boys' playing fields, which soon disappeared under experiments involving the ground radar devices that did more than anything else to give victory, especially in the air, to Britain and her Allies.

Double-shift education was first experienced in Britain, because of a shortage of teachers, during World War One. It had been something of an educational disaster, and the teaching profession was anxious to avoid the same thing happening after 1939. Trying to ensure that full-time schooling continued led to many shifts and stratagems, from holding classes out-of-doors in parks and fields in good weather – fortunately, September 1939 was a very fine summer – to taking over any suitably big enough building or large room in buildings. Church halls, village halls, large rooms in public houses and even

HOW TO BE A TEACHER

At the outbreak of war, there were two main kinds of teacher in English state schools: qualified and unqualified. Qualified teachers were those who had completed courses at teacher training colleges. Unqualified teachers were teachers who had not gone to a training college, perhaps staying on as unqualified teachers at the school where they had finished their schooldays as pupil-teachers. It was possible for unqualified teachers, especially in more remote village schools, to pass all their learning and working lives in the one school. As the war went on, a third category of teacher began to appear in elementary schools. These were 'supplementary teachers', who needed only to be over the age of eighteen and to have been vaccinated to qualify to help teach the nation's children.

theatres and cinemas were all turned over to the business of educating the nation's children.

As with other aspects of life in Britain, there had long been a marked difference between the standards of teaching and the facilities available in middle-class state schools and those available in schools in poorer, working-class and inner-city areas. It was a difference exacerbated by the war. While the obvious problems and deficiencies of state school education in Britain had become of increasing concern to the government throughout the 1930s, the children of the war years also had to grapple with many serious practical problems.

As more and more young men were called up into the armed services, the lack of qualified teachers became a problem. Many people, recalling their wartime schooldays, have vivid memories of the increasing age and female gender of their teachers. Some schools ended the war with all-female teaching staffs, many of whom were married – something not permitted before the war – and many more of whom were well past retirement age and therefore trained in an earlier age. Children began to experience the sort of teaching, involving much chanting of arithmetic tables and the rules of spelling, that their grandparents had known. In secondary or 'selective' schools where subjects like Classics were still on the timetable, vicars, who had never taught in their lives, found themselves trying, often without much success, to keep order in increasingly large classes instead of instilling the rudiments of Latin and Greek into their pupils.

Almost as difficult for Britain's state school children as the lack of well-qualified teachers was the lack of all kinds of teaching equipment, including such basic materials as pens, pencils and paper. Paper was in short supply, and bits of paper of every kind were hoarded carefully. Many children used newspaper for painting on during art lessons, and squared-up bits of

1944

JULY

- Minsk is liberated by Soviet troops.
- During a circus performance in Connecticut, USA, the main tent catches fire and more than 100 children die.
- Soviet troops occupy the Baltic Islands.
- Claus von Stauffenberg attempts to assassinate Adolf Hitler by placing a bomb (inside a suitcase) in a conference room. The attempt was unsuccessful and the assassin was later executed.
- Canadian and British forces take Caen.

AUGUST

- Anne Frank and her family are discovered by the Gestapo following a tip-off from a Dutch informant.
- An undersea oil pipeline is laid between England and France.
- Polish radicals liberate a concentration camp in Warsaw. 348 Jewish prisoners are freed.
- Operation Overlord is completed as the Allies liberate Paris.

paper on which to practise their cross-stitch and other embroidery stitches. Wartime economy paper in exercise books was full of woodchips, and the exercise books themselves were in such short supply that children had to use them very carefully. Some schools resorted to guillotining exercise books in half, so that every child in a class had some sort of book in which to write.

Then, there were the poor quality pencils. Made out of cedar wood – unpainted, because to give them a smooth, colourful coating would be to waste paint – their lead was thin and broke easily. Some schools cut pencils in half as well as exercise books, and many teachers gathered up the pencils at the end of lessons and put them away carefully. Fountain pens were also in short supply, so most children wrote with dip pens, dipping the nibs into inkwells filled with inferior ink, which it was the responsibility of the class's ink monitor to mix up from a powder. Indian ink, always very scarce, often disappeared altogether from the classroom.

But worse than the lack of basic materials was the absence of text books from the classroom. From the infant classes' readers to the texts of Shakespeare's plays needed by pupils anxious to pass their School Certificate and Higher School Certificate exams, text books became increasingly difficult to replace as the war went on. Of course, for many older children, exams in wartime took on a special, not necessarily all bad flavour. There was the thrill of being able to write on your exam paper that your exam had been 'interrupted by an air raid warning for one hour and forty minutes', while the interruption itself, during which you had very carefully not talked to your fellow pupils in the shelter and

A WARTIME LESSON
Peter Neve and other children, learn how to fit a gas mask during a drill at school.

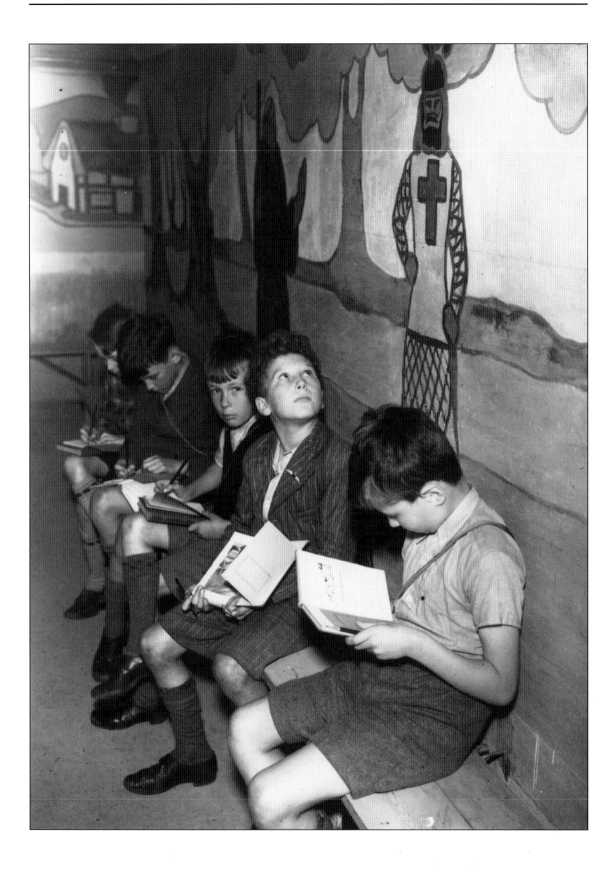

SCHOOLS AND THE NIGHT AIR RAIDS

As with most things, schools in the bombing areas soon devised a rule covering absence from school in the event of a night-time air raid. If the all-clear sounded before midnight, children were expected to be in school before 8.45 the next morning, no matter how many hours they had spent in the Anderson shelter or in the cupboard under the stairs. Only if the all-clear had sounded after midnight could children come into school in late morning, in time for their school dinner. In London, children who spent their nights in an Underground station were assumed to have had a reasonable night's sleep – which, perhaps after many nights of practice, they did. In a good few cases, of course, there was no school to return to after an air raid. One in five of the nation's schools was badly damaged by bombs during the war.

certainly not discussed the paper with anyone, at least allowed you to marshal a few facts in your head.

Many older schoolchildren 'doing their bit for the war effort', found that exams got in the way. Joining an ARP team, being in the Girl Guides or Boy Scouts, perhaps helping with a Cubs group or helping in your local hospital one night a week left little time for revising for exams. Many men and women, recalling their war-time schooldays, think that they only passed their School Certificate because the examiners were extra kind.

Many schools put a lot of time into the 'war effort', both in school and outside. School assemblies gave head teachers a chance to keep their pupils up to date with the course of the war and to read out letters sent from the war zones by former teachers and pupils. Some children would say years later that the only geography they were taught in school during the war involved studying maps of the various parts of the world where British troops were fighting. There was a lot of practical help, too. Many schools sponsored particular parts of the armed services, with naval vessels being popular. Girls, following the lead of Princess Elizabeth and Princess Margaret, who were photographed knitting socks for servicemen, might knit balaclavas, thick socks and mittens for sailors on the Arctic convoys and pupils would write letters to crew members. For schools in country areas, the 'war effort' was more likely to consist in helping the 'Dig for Victory' campaign by taking

SCHOOL AIR RAID SHELTER

Boys from the St John's School in Redhill, Surrey, have a lesson in the school air raid shelter. The historical murals on the walls were all painted by the pupils.

SAFETY UNDERGROUND
Children at their lessons in an underground air raid shelter.

CLASSROOM POST OFFICE
Schoolchildren line up to pay at their classroom post office where they raise money during
Warship Week. Local charity organisations, churches and schools also provided the crews of
adopted ships with gloves, woollen socks and balaclavas. Children would often write letters and
send cards to the crew to keep up their morale.

half days out of school to help local farmers with the harvest.

This positive, patriotic approach to the war no doubt helped many schoolchildren safely and confidently through their schooling, which may not have included such frills as cookery lessons or outdoor sports, but in most cases gave them a good grounding in the three 'Rs'. But there is

no denying that many children were deprived of a decent education during World War Two and ended up, if not totally illiterate, then certainly very educationally below standard. National Conscription, brought in for men at the beginning of the War, did not end until the late 1950s, by which time it was clear that far too many young men called up into the post-war services had a poor grasp of basic skills such as reading, writing and simple maths.

Also by this time, however, the reformation of education in England and Wales signaled by the Education Act of 1944 was beginning to show positive results. R. A. Butler, who was president of the Board of Education for much of the war, steered through Parliament the Education Act of 1944 that led the way to a comprehensive reformation of the education system in England

A 'ROVING' TEACHER

A 'roving' teacher holds a class in the living room of a house in Beckenham, Kent. Many homes have been turned into temporary classrooms while local schools are shut due to bombing, so that the children are never more than two minutes from home.

LESSONS IN GROOMING
A couple of toddlers groom themselves in front of a mirror in the garden of Muriel Green Nursery Centre in St Albans.

THE BUTLER EDUCATION ACT

As well as raising the school leaving age to fifteen, which the post-war Labour Government put into effect in 1947, the Education Act of 1944 reorganised secondary education in England and Wales. The elementary schools that had been the only school experienced by the majority of children were replaced, at secondary level – that is, at age '11 plus' – by a tripartite system that, it was hoped, would allow a more democratic 'parity of esteem' among school children. The Act provided for grammar schools for the more academically able children, technical schools for those with a more technically-minded bent, and secondary moderns for those children not comfortable in either of the first two categories. In practice, things did not work out quite as R. A. Butler and his Board had hoped. During the 1940s and 1950s, local authorities built few technical schools and the majority of children were educated in secondary modern schools, some of which demonstrated very low expectations of their pupils indeed.

and Wales (but not Scotland, which had its own education organisation).

PLAYTIME

'Total war' did not mean there could be no playtime for children. Rather, it meant that playtime was something to be enjoyed at home rather than away from the home environment. Certainly, for many, the greatest playtime of all – the annual holiday, usually to the seaside – became a thing to look forward to when the war was over. It was not just that many beaches were now out of bounds, hidden behind barbed wire, concrete anti-tank blocks and other anti-invasion devices. There was also the problem of how to get there. Petrol rationing kept family cars up on blocks in the garage 'for the duration', and all those posters at railway stations and elsewhere asking 'Is your journey really necessary?' made families think twice about leaving home.

Sports and games stopped being a regular school activity, sometimes because playing fields were taken over by air raid shelters or 'Dig for Victory' vegetable plots, but also because schools were not encouraged to have their children gathered together out-of-doors on playing fields. This was particularly so in those parts of the country most at risk from enemy action.

Front Line 1940-1941, a Ministry of Information booklet, published in 1942 and telling the 'official story of the civil defence of Britain, 1940–41', noted that the children of London became 'very expert shelterers and Blitz citizens. They made a practice of using as their special

---

WASHDAY
Three girls play at doing their washing at a wartime crèche installed at Dallington.

SHRAPNEL HUNTERS
Children in a street in South London sort shrapnel, anti-aircraft shell fragments, which they have collected as their contribution to the war effort.

play-pitch the sites of their demolished homes, where they could on summer evenings in 1941 be seen soldiering with sticks and mounting guard in some symbolic play understood only by themselves.' The photograph accompanying the text shows four boys swinging round a decapitated lamp-post on both ends of a length of rope tied to it, using the piles of bricks scattered around them as jumping-off points. Probably the boys, like many others throughout Britain, made a hobby of collecting shrapnel from the streets

and bombsites. For many children, the best place for outdoor sports was in the street outside their homes. With few, if any, cars about, streets were an ideal playground.

Patricia Houlahan, who was eight when the war started, lived in heavily bombed Portsmouth throughout the war. Of Portsmouth's 70,000 houses, 63,000 were damaged in one way or another during the attacks on the city and its dockyards in 1940-41. Not surprisingly, none of Patricia's wartime schools offered outdoor sports

THE HAZARDS OF STREET PLAY

The Luftwaffe did not confine its activities to the hours of darkness, especially when they were making 'hit and run' raids on coastal towns and dockyards. Children playing in the streets became used to stopping their play long enough to look up try to identify the planes flying low overhead. Sometimes German planes were not what they seemed to be. Patricia Houlahan, playing in her Portsmouth street, vividly recalls one such plane. 'We were used to seeing bright yellow training planes in the air above us during the day,' she remembers. 'One day, we children playing in the street saw a bright yellow plane flying very low over us and did not take much notice. Then, it dropped a bomb on the nearby railway line and flew off.' The enemy had thought up a new way to disguise its planes. The children did not stop playing in the streets.

at school, so she played often on the street.

As going out after dark, even if only to go a few houses away to discuss homework with a friend, was difficult and even dangerous during the blackout, especially in the winter, most evening playtime was spent at home with the family. The centre of attention in most living rooms was the wireless set. Even though she was only an infant, living in Stevenage in Hertfordshire, during the war, Annabel Rudland can remember to this day the way her father carefully positioned on the dial of her family's wireless the numerous paper dots that would allow him to tune in quickly to all the long-wave stations for the latest news of the war, at home and abroad.

'The wireless was huge, with twelve valves that glowed brightly and which needed constant renewing. Sometimes the noise and crackle of the long-wave stations was awful, but my father sat there listening carefully to the news from those far off places.'

The British Broadcasting Corporation (the BBC) was Britain's greatest provider of news, information, morale-boosting propaganda and – most important of all – entertainment during the War. As well as all the still well-remembered 'family' programmes such as Tommy Handley's *ITMA* (It's That Man Again), Richard Murdoch's *Much Binding in The Marsh*, Arthur Askey's *Band Waggon* and *The Brains Trust* and light music programmes, many involving dance bands playing at such famous London hotels at the Savoy, the BBC produced numerous programmes especially for children.

Foremost among these was *Children's Hour*, which was taken off the air in September 1939 because the powers-that-be at the BBC considered it too lightweight for wartime. It was pretty quickly brought back on the air and for the rest of the war, led by 'Uncle Mac' (Derek McCulloch) and others, was required listening for thousands of children. One of *Children's Hour's* best-known young broadcasters was the

1944

SEPTEMBER
- Anne Frank and her family are transported to Auschwitz.
- A V2 rocket hits London.
- Brussels is liberated by the Allies.
- The Soviets declare war on Bulgaria.
- The Allied Operation Market Garden begins in the Netherlands and Germany. Nine days later the Allies withdraw.
- Antwerp, Belgium, is liberated by the British.

OCTOBER
- A German jet fighter is shot down over Holland by the Royal Canadian Air Force.
- Winston Churchill and Joseph Stalin meet in Moscow to discuss Europe's future.
- Serial killer Marcel Petiot is apprehended in a French station. Petiot is believed to have murdered more than 60 people.
- In Auschwitz, 800 gypsy children are killed.
- Anne Frank and her sister Margot are moved to the Bergen-Belsen concentration camp.
- Allied troops land in Athens.
- Hitler orders the establishment of the Volksstrum – a military force comprised of citizens aged between 16 and 60.

King's elder daughter, 16-year-old Princess Elizabeth, who made a short broadcast to the children of Britain and the Empire from Windsor Castle in October 1940. The princess finished her talk by calling her sister Margaret to join her at the microphone to say goodnight.

It was not long before toy and game manufacturers began giving their products a patriotic war-time flavour. Wooden jigsaw puzzles, printed in bright colours, were particular favourites, especially with boys, who enjoyed putting together pictures of British fighter planes in the air over England's green and pleasant land or, as the war progressed and British troops began operating abroad, battle scenes with outcomes favourable to the allies.

Girls – and their mothers – spent a lot of time knitting, using up scraps of wool to make stuffed toys for babies and infants and dolls with up-to-the-minute clothes, such as the uniforms of the men's and women's services, for older girls. French knitting, done on a wooden cotton reel with four small nails hammered into the top, was also popular with girls. Even though she was only little, having been born in 1939, Mary Murphy remembers spending many hours at home in Chingord, Essex, making place mats, pot holders, tea cosies and egg cosies out of her French knitting.

Board games, played round the family table, were another popular play activity. While *Ludo* and *Snakes and Ladders* were always family favourites, other board games based on Home Front themes such as the work of ARP wardens, fore-fighters and others also appeared from Britain's toy and game manufacturers. Games like *Battleships* took on a new dimension in wartime, and extra fun could be got out of a dartboard with a picture of Hitler's face pasted on it.

Boys like collecting things. Bits of shrapnel were very popular – you could compare the size of your pieces with those of friends at school

TUNING IN
In the evening at home, families would often tune in to hear the news on the radio with gas masks at the ready.

THE WIZARD OF OZ
Jack Haley as the Tin Man, Bert Lahr as the Cowardly Lion, Judy Garland as Dorothy, Ray Bolger as the Scarecrow and Frank Morgan as the Doorman to the Emerald City in *The Wizard of Oz*, 1939.

the day after a bombing raid. Then there were cigarette cards, which now put their subjects on a war footing, replacing the portraits of cricketers and other sportsmen popular in the 1930s with things like gas masks, accompanied by instructions on how to put them on, or home protection advice. Also very collectable were cap badges from servicemen, including, after 1942, those worn by American servicemen. There were great dangers in collecting, especially for children exploring in the grounds of munitions factories or on testing ranges, but also on bomb sites where unexploded bombs could lurk.

Children's publishers, despite wartime economies which meant that paper, in short supply anyway, was also of poor quality, soon swung into wartime mode. Leading children's writers, like Richmal Crompton, who had been

delighting children – and their parents – since the early 1920s with stories about a mischievous boy called William Brown, quickly began putting their characters into wartime settings. Captain W. E. Johns, whose Flight Commander Bigglesworth, known to all as Biggles, had been flying in a daredevil kind of way since the early 1930s, put Biggles into stories in Norway and during the Battle of Britain.

While paper restrictions meant that comics, like adults' magazines, were much reduced in size and page extent, those comics that survived – and several pre-war favourites, like *Tiger Tim*, did not – also turned to war times themes for the adventures of their favourite characters, as did the heroes and heroines of such newspaper comic strips as *Rupert* (in an English national paper) and *Oor Wullie* and *The Broons* (both of

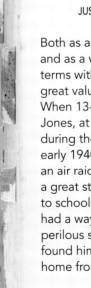

JUST ANOTHER MOVIE

Both as an escape from reality and as a way of coming to terms with it, the cinema was of great value to wartime children. When 13-year-old Kenneth Jones, at home in Croydon during the school holidays in early 1940, got caught up in an air raid, he not only had a great story to take back to school in Devon, he also had a way of dealing with the perilous situation in which he found himself. 'I was travelling home from London when the sirens started. The bus was obliged to stop and discharge its passengers. There was no air raid shelter close, so we just stayed in the street while, above, the Germans were coming in to bomb Croydon airport. They were engaged by Hurricanes and a dog fight developed right over our heads, just like in the movies! I couldn't wait to get home to tell my friends how lucky I had been to have a front seat watching two German planes going down in smoke.'

which appeared in Scottish papers). *Dandy's* regular character, the amiable giant Desperate Dan put his weight behind the war effort, turning drainpipes into pea-shooters to bring down enemy aircraft and skimming across the sea flat stones large enough to take out enemy warships.

Publishers of boys' comics, including *Rover, Wizard, Skipper* and *Hotspur* all brought war themes into their pages, including German spies, secret codes and, in *Hotspur*, a teacher at a boys' public school laying down his life for the British Secret Service. *Dandy* and *Beano* introduced specifically wartime characters into their publications. *Dandy*, for instance, had 'Big-hearted Martha, our ARP nut' and *Beano*, whose favourite enemy comic character was Musso da Wop, a 'big-a-da-flop' whose generals issued spaghetti to tie their soldiers' boots, also made fun of Adolf Hitler and Hermann Goering by

MINISTRY OF INFORMATION
A van belonging to the Ministry of Information, travels the country stopping at villages to show mainly documentary films.

GIs IN TOWN
An American soldier helps some children with their skipping. He is watched by his comrades in a town street in the south of England. The street is lined with military equipment waiting to be shipped to France.

way of characters called 'Addie and Hermy, the Nasty Nazis'.

When US servicemen began arriving in Britain in 1942 they brought with them, as well as apparently endless supplies of candy, their comics. Now British children began speaking American slang and thrilling to the exploits of a new and very different set of comic-book heroes, such as the supercop Dick Tracy (sporting a two-way wrist TV) and the amazing Superman, with his X-ray vision and ability to fly through space.

Outside the home, one of the most popular children's leisuretime activities of the war years was 'going to the pictures'. At the outbreak of the war, the government, assuming an immediate bombing onslaught on Britain, closed all cinemas. It was soon realised that the effect of this on national morale was catastrophic, and cinemas were re-opened within weeks. In fact, cinema provided everyone, young and old, with their greatest escape from the war. It was estimated that three-quarters of the British adult

ABOVE AND OPPOSITE: HELLFIRE CORNER
Although thousands of children had been evacuated from the town, many children are still to be seen playing at 'hellfire corner' in Dover. It gots its name because it was the section of town that took the brunt of the German bombing raids.

population considered themselves to be cinema-goers during the war, buying between twenty-five and thirty million cinema tickets every week. As for Britain's children, they were even more avid cinema-goers than adults, with a great proportion of children going to the cinema more than once a week.

While most small children went to the cinema with their mothers, or with older siblings, as more and more mothers, especially from the working classes, took on jobs during the war so more and more children went by themselves. The Ministry of Information, noticing the great popularity of the cinema among children, focused their short information and propaganda films shown in cinemas on a wide age-range. Many children remember the wartime documentaries and Ministry of Information 'shorts' with particular pleasure. While many of the most popular children's films of the war years – *The Wizard*

1944

NOVEMBER

- Franklin D. Roosevelt is re-elected to a fourth term in office.
- 16 people are killed and 50 injured when in a passenger train accident Aguadilla, Puerto Rico. The train was travelling at excessive speeds as it went down a hill, causing the train to derail.
- Generals Jan Golian and Rudolf Viest, two commanders of the Slovak National Uprising, are captured and executed by German forces.

DECEMBER

- The Battle of the Bulge begins.
- The Malmedy Massacre takes place. German soldiers kill 90 of their prisoners of war.
- A private plane carrying Glenn Miller disappears in heavy fog en route to Paris from Britain. Neither the crew or Miller are seen again.
- The WASPs disband.
- The Red Army take Estonia.
- Hungary declares war on Germany.
- Fighting breaks out between communists and royalists in newly liberated Greece.
- Hundreds of thousands of Japanese soldiers die in the Battle of Leyte.
- American forces drive back German soliders at Bastogne.

of Oz, *Bambi* and *Fantasia*, for instance – were American in origin, with the films of Walt Disney being well to the fore in the popularity stakes, especially with younger children, there was also plenty of home-grown filmmaking talent in Britain, much of it in the hands of the great cinema mogul J. Arthur Rank. Older children, of course, took as much pleasure as grown-ups in the musicals, romances and war films which made up a large output of wartime film studios, both British and American.

Most cinemas changed their programmes at least twice a week, and there was always more than just one feature film on the programme, plus an interlude from the Mighty Wurlitzer, the massive theatre organ that had been introduced in picture palaces in the 1920s and remained a feature of cinemas, except the very smallest, until the 1950s.

Rank's Odeon and Gaumont cinema chains ran Saturday morning cinema clubs specially for children, with tickets on sale at just a few pence. While much of the fare shown at cinema club mornings was American comedies, Westerns, serials and cartoons, there was also a sprinkling of films from a part of Rank's empire called Gaumont-British Instructional.

One popular leisuretime activity among older children that took on a new meaning in wartime was the youth group or youth club. Although many youth clubs were forced to close when war was declared, often because their young leaders were called into the services, the government was quick to mobilise those, such as the Boy Scouts and Girl Guides and the Boys and Girls Brigades, that were left. As early as 1938, Lady Reading, founder of the WVS, was in close (and secret) contact with the headquarters of the Girl Guides, asking for lists of Guides prepared to help the WVS with its local evacuation arrangements.

During the War, Boy Scouts and Girl Guides and other youth groups were to prove their value

TENDING THE WOUNDED
A group of children in Worthing, Sussex, formed their own Air Raid Protection and first aid parties, with uniforms, casualty clearing stations and all the trappings of the grown-up world.

BADGES WITH A DIFFERENCE

Boys and girls who joined the Boy Scouts and Girl Guides in peacetime, planning to earn an armful of badges for a wide range of indoor pursuits and outdoor activities, found themselves working for a very different kind of badge. For the Boy Scout intent on doing his bit in wartime there was a National Service badge to be won, while for Girl Guides, the badge to work towards was the War Service Badge, for which extra annual stripes could be earned. While many of the ways in which the badges could be earned involved the use of peacetime skills – erecting tents, weeding allotments or shopping for the blind, for instance – many more, such as distributing gas masks, directing traffic during blackouts (having already helped paint white stripes on kerbs and lampposts so that pedestrians and motor traffic would notice them in the blackout), helping in first aid and ARP posts and, if they were old enough, being motorcycle messengers or telephone operators.

to the war effort in many ways. Some of those ways, such as Girl Guides leading crocodiles of newly arrived evacuee children to their billeting officers or Boy Scouts staying in camp while helping picking fruit for jam-making, were more fun than dangerous. But those Girl Guides who offered first aid help in ARP posts and Boy Scouts who got on their bikes to deliver messages between ARP posts and the police in front-line towns and cities, were often working in highly dangerous conditions.

Annual holidays away from home became almost impossible for most families during the war. One way round this problem, which also helped with the major wartime problem of having enough workers to bring in the harvest, was to organise harvest camps for town children. Started in a small way at the beginning of the war, there were by the summer of 1943 more than a thousand camps in England that could accommodate 63,000 children during their summer school holidays – and get the vital food harvests safely gathered in.

The government, all too well aware of the need for children to get a break away from the day-to-day restrictions and deprivations of wartime and to get out in the fresh air and sunshine as much as possible, also developed a scheme to encourage people to take 'Holidays at Home'. Local councils throughout the country were urged to provide concerts and other entertainments in public places, especially local parks, which were carefully kept as attractive-looking as possible, given wartime conditions and the fact that many public spaces were ploughed up for allotments.

Truth to tell, there was little more that the government could do than to 'encourage' people to take time off and enjoy leisure activities. It was up to parents to do whatever was possible for the children. And, also truth to tell, most children in Britain got on with their lives during the war much as they would have done in peacetime. As Patricia Houlahan says now, 'Most of my friends and I were not aware of the horrors of the war. We did not notice the absence of 'frills' and got on with things, including playing and entertaining ourselves.'

ACTING AS MUM
Some Girl Guides were responsible for looking after babies while their mothers were at work.

POPULAR CULTURE 1945

SONGS
- *Sentimental Journey*, Les Brown and Doris Day
- *Rum & Coca Cola*, The Andrew Sisters
- *Till The End Of Time*, Perry Como
- *My Dreams Are Getting Better All The Time*, Les Brown
- *On the Atchison, Topeka and the Santa Fe*, Johnny Mercer
- *I Should Care*, Frank Sinatra
- *You Belong To My Heart*, Bing Crosby
- *I'm Beginning To See The Light*, Harry James
- *Laura*, Woody Herman

HIGH-GROSSING FILMS
- *The Bells Of St Mary's*, starring Bing Crosby and Ingrid Bergman
- *Leave Her To Heaven*, starring Gene Tierney and Cornel Wilde
- *Spellbound*, starring Ingrid Bergman and Gregory Peck
- *Anchors Aweigh*, starring Gene Kelly and Frank Sinatra
- *The Dolly Sisters*, starring Betty Grable and June Haver
- *Weekend At The Waldorf*, starring Ginger Rogers and Lana Turner
- *Mildred Pierce*, starring Joan Crawford
- *The Lost Weekend*, starring Ray Milland and Jane Wyman
- *Saratoga Trunk*, starring Gary Cooper and Ingrid Bergman
- *Diamond Horseshoe*, starring Betty Grable
- *The Valley Of Decision*, starring Gregory Peck and Greer Garson
- *Love Letters*, starring Jennifer Jones

COLLECTING PAPER
Cub scouts bundle up old newspapers. Many aspects of the scouting movement were based on Lord Baden-Powell's own experiences during military training. Baden-Powell was fifty years old and a retired army general when he decided to form the scouting movement, and his revolutionary ideas helped to inspire thousands of young people from all walks of life.

RUINED SUBURB
Inhabitants of a bomb-damaged London suburb sit sunbathing among the ruins.

CHAPTER EIGHT

THE FOOD FRONT

THE FOOD FRONT

In the 1930s, much of Britain's food came from abroad, shipped in from most of the countries of the Empire, from North and South America and Europe.

Another war in Europe that inevitably involved shipping in the world's major seaways would obviously have a catastrophic effect on imports of food into Britain. The British government's advanced planning for war therefore included establishing a Ministry of Food in 1937.

Once war was declared, the Ministry of Food and its minister, Lord Woolton, played ever-growing parts in everyone's lives. Lord Woolton was immortalised in the name of perhaps the most famous recipe to come out of World War Two, the Woolton Pie. This was a vegetable-based concoction that at its most basic, and without the help of extras like a cheese sauce or cream, was a less than exciting dish.

A constant flow of recipes, including Woolton Pie, and food advice in booklets, leaflets, pamphlets and information adverts called 'Food Facts', featuring such characters as Potato Pete and Doctor Carrot, came from the Ministry's Food Advice Division. Their intention was to keep housewives well-informed about the nutritional value of foods, especially vegetables and fruit, and to offer guidance for preparing interesting meals from the suddenly limited range of foods available. A team of home economists, including the redoubtable Marguerite Patten, still one of Britain's leading cookery writers, carried on the Food Advice Division's work through Food Advice Centres, which were set up all over the country.

THE KITCHEN FRONT

One of the greatest helps to housewives trying to feed families well with limited resources was the BBC Home Service's five-minute programme, The Kitchen Front, broadcast at 8.15 a.m. from Tuesday to Friday throughout the war. The timing, after the 8 o'clock news bulletin, was intended to catch housewives before they went out to do their shopping – which soon involved long hours of queuing. The programme, with contributions from a wide range of people, including the cookery writer Ambrose Heath, Marguerite Patten, the actresses Elsie and Doris Waters and even Lord Woolton himself, soon attracted a large audience. Within a couple of weeks of the first programme 30,000 people had written in asking for recipes.

THE PRICE OF SUGAR
A London shopkeeper puts up a sign announcing the new price of sugar as revealed in the budget. The price has risen by a penny a pound.

1945

JANUARY

- Auschwitz concentration camp is evacuated.
- Hungary agrees to armistice with the Allies.
- American troops cross the Siegfried Line into Belgium.
- Birkenau concentration camp is liberated.
- American and Filipino forces free 813 prisoners of war from Japanese captors in Cabanatuan City, Philippines.
- Supplies begin to reach China.

FEBRUARY

- The Yalta Conference begins; Winston Churchill, Franklin D.Roosevelt and Joseph Stalin attend.
- The last V-2-rocket is launched at Peenemünde.
- Ecuador, Peru, Chile and Paraguay join the United Nations.
- 30,000 US Marines land in Iwo Jima with the intention of capturing the two airfields. The Battle of Iwo Jima begins.
- The SS *General von Steuben* is sunk by the *Soviet submarine S-13.*
- Budapest, Hungary, is captured by Soviet forces.
- Dresden, Germany, is bombed by the Royal Air Force. 3,900 tons of bombs and incendiary devices were dropped on the city over four raids.

The Ministry of Food's greatest task during the war and for nearly a decade after it was to oversee the fair distribution and rationing of basic essential foods. Food rationing, which was introduced in January 1940, was organised by the Ministry through 1,300 local offices throughout the country.

Rationing of basic foods was brought in gradually, starting with bacon, ham, sugar and butter in January 1940. In March, meat was rationed and in July tea, margarine, cooking fat and cheese. In March 1941, jam, marmalade, treacle and syrup were all rationed and in June the distribution of eggs was controlled, as was, in November, the distribution of milk. The last of the war-time rationing came in July 1942, when sweets were put on the ration list.

The eggs available on the ration were often not whole eggs, but dried egg powder, sold in packs or tins. Quite a lot of this notoriously difficult to use, much-disliked product came from the United States. Dried egg was pure egg with all its moisture removed.

A complicated system of ration books, coupons and points controlled the distribution of rations through food shops. Every person in the country had a ration book, containing on its front cover the same details about the person that was on his or her identity card. Ration books could only be used at retailers whose names and addresses were listed in it (and who kept in their shops counterfoils of the list in the book). Of course, it could be said, that rationing had its good points too, because it meant that everybody got their fair share of what was available. For people in the lower income bracket, it meant that they were getting more food during the war than before. People were better educated about food, as the government campaigned for the public to eat more vegetables. They also provided cod liver oil and orange juice for children. Things

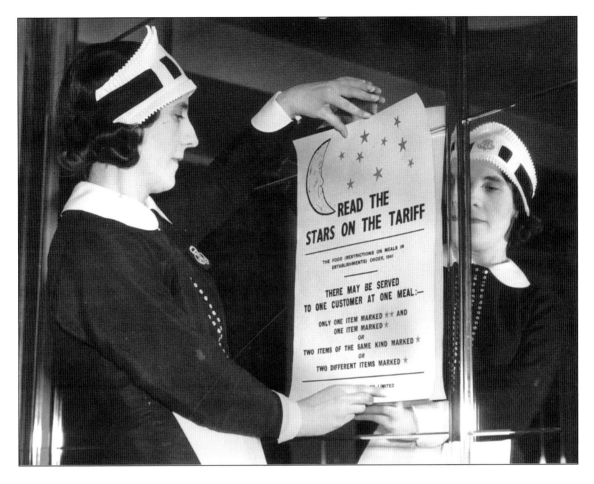

RATION MENU
A 'nippy' waitress at a Lyons' teashop puts up a poster to explain the new rationing system, which ranks scarce food according to stars.

like fish were never rationed, as they were virtually unobtainable and, if they were on sale, the queues were so long that people had to wait for hours with no promise of what they were getting when they reached the front. The ration book was designed to show exactly when and how many coupons had been used to purchase the various rationed foods. Children's ration books, called RB2, included spaces for the extra foods, such as orange juice, that children were allocated. (Children were helped in other ways,

oranges, for instance, when available being kept solely for children until they had been in the greengrocer's display for five days.)

As well as the coupons, there was a monthly points system giving 16 points that could be spent on 'extras'; one can of fish or meat or 2lb (900g) of dried fruit, for example, would use up all 16 points, whereas only one point (plus the 8d/3H pence purchase price) would get the housewife an 8oz (250g) packet of Krisvita Crispbread. The British people were finally able

LATEST PRICES   LATE NIGHT FINAL

Nicholson's Gin

IT'S CLEAR
IT'S GOOD

Evening Standard

La Coquille

LONDON, FRIDAY, SEPTEMBER 1, 1939   ONE PENNY

AN ADULT'S WEEKLY RATIONS

The colour of your ration book was very important as it made sure you received the right amount and types of food needed for your health and family.

Buff-coloured ration books – Most adults had this colour.
Green ration books - Pregnant women, nursing mothers and children under 5. They had first choice of fruit, a daily pint of milk and a double supply of eggs.
Blue ration books – Children between 5 and 16 years of age. It was felt important that children had fruit, the full meat ration and half a pint of milk a day.

Although the amounts varied slightly, depending on availability, the following amounts were what one adult could expect to have of the rationed foods each week:

Bacon and ham – 4oz (100g)

Meat – 1 shilling and 2 pennies (6 pence)-worth of what was available; sausages were not rationed, but were rarely seen, and offal was sometimes part of the ration

Butter and cheese – 2oz (50g), although sometimes 4 oz (100g) and even 8oz (225g) of cheese was available

Margarine and cooking fat – 4oz (100g), sometimes only 2oz (50g) of the latter

Milk – 3 pints (1800ml), sometimes dropping to 2 pints (1200ml) 'Household' milk, which was skimmed or dried milk, was sometimes available as 1 packet every 4 weeks

Sugar – 8oz (225g), which had to cover baking and jam-making as well as one's cup of tea, although, if it was available, extra sugar would be issued at jam-making times

Preserves – 1lb (450g) every 2 months

Tea – 2oz (50g)

Eggs – 1 whole egg, if available, but sometimes dropping to 1 every 2 weeks; the dried egg ration was 1 packet every 4 weeks

Sweets – 12oz (350g) each 4 weeks.

to tear up their ration books in June 1954, when meat was the last food to come off the ration.

While the Ministry of Food was in the forefront of giving advice about optimum use of the foods available, the Ministry of Agriculture was the government department responsible for the production of as much food as possible in wartime Britain. By the late 1930s, after nearly twenty years of cheap imports of food, especially diary products, meat, cereals, fats, sugar and fruit, British agriculture was very much given over to pasture. This would have to change – and rapidly.

The Emergency Powers Act gave the Ministry of Agriculture the power, often used with draconian thoroughness, to make that change. Throughout the war, the Ministry of Agriculture, working through War Agriculture Committees (soon referred to as 'War Ags') set up in every county, directed and controlled the production of the food that fed the nation.

1945

MARCH
- Anne Frank dies of typhus in Bergen-Belsen concentration camp. Otto Frank, her father, is the only member of the Frank family to survive the Holocaust.
- Princess Elizabeth joins the ATS as a driver.
- Finland declares war on the Axis powers.
- The Battle of Iwo Jima ends.
- Soviet forces take Vienna.
- Adolf Hitler orders that all industries, machine shops, military installations, transportation and communications facilities in Germany are destroyed.
- The 17th Academy Awards ceremony is held, broadcast via radio for the first time.
- Mandalay, Burma, is liberated by British troops.

APRIL
- Harry S. Truman succeeds Franklin D. Roosevelt as US President
- Ohrdruf concentration camp is liberated by American troops.
- The Bergen-Belsen camp is liberated.
- Benito Mussolini and his mistress, Clara Petacci are executed by Italian partisans. Their bodies are hung by their heels on public display in Milan.
- Adolf Hitler and his wife, Eva Braun, commit suicide.

MILK MOUNTAIN
Twelve million tins of powdered milk from North America and New Zealand being stacked in cardboard boxes ready for distribution in Britain during World War Two.

TINNED FOOD
A shop assistant arranges newly arrived tinned meats from the United States as part of the Lend-lease agreement.

THE U-BOAT THREAT TO BRITAIN'S FOOD

Germany sent its U-boats and its surface navy into the Atlantic with the fixed intention of starving Britain into surrender. In the early months of the war, it looked as if they might well do so. While at home Britain sat through the Phoney War, at sea her merchant navy bore the brunt of an all-out German attack. In September, October and December 1939, and again in January and February 1940, nearly 200,000 tons of merchant shipping were sunk, with their cargoes, each month. These figures, so bad that the government suppressed them, got even worse later in the year, with over 500,000 tons of merchant navy convoys going to the bottom of the ocean in June 1940. This loss of vital food and other supplies, running at about 400,000 tons a month well into 1941, was compounded by the loss of several large European food sources, sucked into the Axis powers' war machine.

A 'Ploughing-Up' campaign, begun in the spring of 1939, persuaded farmers (with an incentive payment of £2 an acre) to switch from growing animal feed on grassland to growing grains such as oats, wheat and barley, and vegetables like potatoes and sugar beet for human consumption instead. The Ministry of Agriculture hoped that by harvest time in 1940 there would be an additional 1.7 million acres of farmland devoted to growing food. Farmers, many of them using horse-drawn tractors and ploughs because of petrol rationing, had achieved this change several months before that date.

While this was going on, the Ministry of Agriculture also tried to bring into production as much hitherto unproductive land in their counties as they could, including marshland, barren hillsides, scrubland ignored for centuries and much else. The mechanisation of farming gathered pace during the war, as did the use of fertilisers. By the time of the last full war-time harvest, that of 1944, Britain was able to feed itself for 160 days a year – forty days more than in 1939.

It was not just the farmers who fed Britain during the war, they were helped by some 36,000 Land Girls who were pitched into agriculture from the civilian life of offices, beauty salons, department stores and domestic service. Every local authority with a park or public garden or land that could be turned into allotments, every householder with land at the back or front of the house was urged to 'Grow More' and 'Dig for Victory'.

The Ministry of Agriculture's allotment scheme allowed local councils to make use of

LAND ARMY FASHION

Two land army girls sporting straw hats and dungarees, catching pitchforks while leading their carthorse to work on the fields.

DIG FOR VICTORY
A woman does her part for the war effort by growing vegetables on her allotment in London.

every piece of land not in full use that they could borrow or rent at an agreed agricultural rent from its owner or occupier. The land was turned into allotments that the government hoped would be taken up by people without gardens of their own and used to grow vegetables and fruit.

In November 1939, the ministry had asked for half a million people to come forward and take up an allotment. In September 1940, by which time the 'Dig for Victory' and 'Grow More' campaigns, backed up by dozens of posters and leaflets, were in full cry, the government asked for another 500,000 people to take them on. By this time, Defence Regulations had been amended to allow allotment holders to keep hens, rabbits and pigs on their allotments. Within a couple of years, it was estimated that more than half the country's manual workers were growing food in allotments or gardens.

Many suburban garden lawns were ploughed up and flower beds dug over, to be replaced by vegetable plots, herbs and fruit bushes. Even the Anderson shelter was brought into use in the wartime garden, marrows and other vegetables being grown on its curved, earth-covered roof and mushrooms and rhubarb in its damp interior. Room was also found in many back gardens for a hen run, for ducks and rabbits and even for pigs.

With bacon being rationed, the pig, which could be kept quite easily in a back-garden sty, came to occupy a large part in many a garden-owner's 'grow more' thinking. A Pig Keepers Club, with nearly 7,000 local offshoots, was set up to give people advice on keeping pigs, not just in the back garden but at the back of office blocks and in factory and other workplace yards as well. Pig-swill bins, into which people put every scrap of food waste that could not be used in the home, appeared on many street corners. Local councils had the job of emptying the pig-swill bins and cooking the swill for at least an hour to kill germs and toxins before allowing

DIGGING FOR VICTORY

One of the most famous slogans of World War II, 'Dig for Victory' was first used in London's *Evening Standard* newspaper, in a leader pushing the government's Grow More campaign. Its succinct mixture of practicality and patriotism made 'Dig for Victory' the perfect propaganda slogan, and the Ministry of Agriculture was quick to pick it up. Its first official use was on a leaflet issued in November 1939, calling for people to take up an allotment.

Within a year, Dig for Victory had become a full-blown campaign in its own right, often promoted side by side with the Grow More campaign, and much used in the advertising of food-related products.

FIREMEN'S PIGS
The Wyse Pig Club – Firemen at an AFS (Auxiliary Fire Service) station in south-west London raise
pigs as part of the war effort.

KEEPING A FIRM HOLD
Three land army girls keep a firm hold on their chickens as they move them into their coops for the night.

1945

MAY

- As Nazi Germany surrenders, V-E Day (Victory in Europe) commemorates the end of World War Two in Europe.
- Following Hitler's death, Karl Dönitz succeeds Hitler as President of Germany. Joseph Goebbels succeeds Hitler as Chancellor of Germany.
- Joseph Goebbels and his wife kill their six children and then commit suicide. Karl Dönitz appoints Count Lutz Graf Schwerin von Krosigk as the new Chancellor of Germany.
- The Fall of Berlin is announced by the Soviet Union.
- Neuengamme concentration camp is liberated.
- The poet and author Ezra Pound is arrested for treason in Italy.
- Canadian troops enter Amsterdam.
- The Sétif massacre takes place in Algeria. Thousands die as French troops and released Italian POWs kill an estimated 6,000 to 40,000 Algerian citizens.
- Former head of the Nazi SS Heinrich Himmler, commits suicide in British custody.
- William Joyce ("Lord Haw-Haw") is captured. He is hanged in January 1946.
- Hermann Göring is captured by the United States Army.

it to be used as pig feed. While it was fine for workplace pig clubs or the policemen at Hyde Park station in London to keep pigs (fattened on scraps from the local big hotels in the case of the Hyde Park station pigs) and kill and replace them with a new litter every six months or so, despatching the animals in the back yard could be a major problem for families, especially if the animals in question had become family pets. At least with hens, this dreadful end could be put off for a long time, during which the hens provided the family – and local people – with a supply of fresh eggs.

The availability of fresh eggs dominated the thinking of housewives at all levels of society. Vita Sackville-West, creator of one of England's loveliest gardens at Sissinghurst in Kent, mentioned eggs in *Vogue* magazine in July 1943: 'Perhaps country-dwellers are better off than town-dwellers. The egg problem, for instance, isn't so acute, because most of them keep a few hens. The price and staleness of vegetables doesn't worry them, because they grow their own . . .' Vita Sackville-West was right in that throughout the war it was much easier for people with the space of the countryside or large country gardens around them to grow more and to dig for victory than it was for people in urban areas.

Not all food was eaten at home, of course, and the Ministry of Food was soon having a big say in the business of eating out, beginning with eating at work. Well aware that properly fed workers were healthier workers, the government early in the war made it compulsory for

---

WEEKLY RATIONS

Women helped to keep the steel mills running during World War Two. These two women take a well-deserved break by smoking a couple of their 40-a-week cigarette ration.

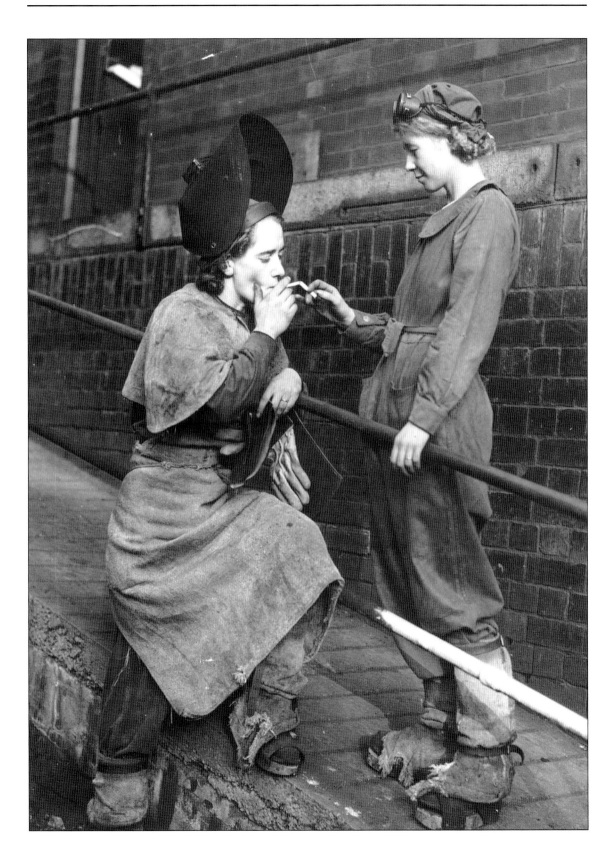

ORDERED EATING

Among the government directives covering eating out in wartime, the Meals in Establishments Order 1942 dictated what diners could choose to eat in restaurants. The menu card for VE Day, 8 May 1945, at Simpson's-in-the-Strand in London explained it: 'By the terms of this Order it is not permissible to serve or consume more than three courses at any meal; nor may any person have at a meal more than one dish marked * [meat and fish dishes] and one dish marked § [egg and vegetable main courses], or alternatively, two dishes marked §. Dishes unmarked may be ordered instead of those marked, or in addition to them, provided that the limit of three courses is not exceeded, nor the maximum permitted price [5 shillings, or 25 pence].'

factories to install workers' canteens. By the end of 1944, there were 30,500 canteens in workplaces all over the country.

The canteens were kept supplied with the raw ingredients for nutritious meals, with plenty of tea and, in factories with more than 200 employees, cigarettes as well. The cigarettes were another piece of positive lateral thinking by Lord Beaverbrook. He noticed that many workers in Sheffield's hard-pressed factories, when they heard that cigarettes were available in the city, took time off to queue for them. He persuaded the government to release supplies of precious American Lend-lease Virginia leaf cigarettes to larger factories, where they were sold at a rate of forty cigarettes per worker per week.

During the Blitz, when so many people were bombed out of their homes or their cooking facilities were damaged or destroyed, Communal Feeding Centres were set up. Soon re-named, at Winston Churchill's suggestion, the more attractive British Restaurants, these unpretentious eating places were open to everyone. Supplied with otherwise hard-to-obtain cookers, pots and pans, crockery and cutlery by the Ministry of Food, British Restaurants provided more than adequate meals at very low prices – 1d for a bowl of lentil soup, 6d or 8d for a main course of rabbit pie and vegetables, 2d for sultana roll or rice pudding, and whole meals for children for 4d – for thousands of people up and down the country throughout the war. Although their number never reached the 10,000 the government had hoped for, by 1944 there were enough British Restaurants to serve an average of 600,000 meals a day in the towns and cities of Britain.

The government ensured that schoolchildren were properly fed by providing school meals. By February 1945, Britain's schools were dishing up 1,850,000 meals every day. There was even some help for workers in the fields, though this was limited because of the rationing of petrol, and the WVS managed to operate a few of their

MOBILE CANTEENS

Several voluntary organisations operated mobile canteens to provide hot meals to those people who lived in bombed-out areas of London. Their work was co-ordinated to ensure that the canteens were directed to where the need was greatest.

BUSINESS AS USUAL
Signs outside small restaurants proclaiming WE ARE CARRYING ON! HITLER WILL NOT BEAT US! show the efforts of most Londoners to maintain a semblance of normality throughout the ongoing German air raid attacks on the city.

mobile canteens in country areas. At the top end of the scale, grand hotels and restaurants flourished in the early years of the war. Since most of the expensive foods and drinks that made up their menus were not rationed, they were available to anyone prepared to pay for them. And many people were. As the diarist and politician Sir Henry 'Chips' Channon noted in his diary in November 1940, there must have been a thousand people on the dance floor of the Dorchester Hotel the night he dined there with friends. 'London lives well: I have never seen more lavishness, more money spent, or more food consumed than tonight.... The contrast between the light and gaiety within, and the blackout and roaring guns outside was terrific....'

Such lavishness and high-living caused

considerable resentment among the ordinary population, many of whom felt that people should pay with their ration coupons for food in restaurants, just as they paid for it in shops. A Gallup Poll in early 1941, drawing attention to this growing resentment at the obvious inequality between the rich and the less well-off as far as food and diet went, prodded the government into taking action. There was not a lot they could do, although the Ministry of Food did try to get a grip on things by putting an upper limit on the price of meals and on the number of courses that could be served during a meal. But there was no way of stopping people eating two or three meals in two or three different restaurants in one day, should they so wish.

A HEALTHY DIET FOR ALL

The surprising thing about life in wartime Britain, which before the war relied on its merchant fleet – like its navy, the largest in the world – to bring to Britain much of its food from all parts of the world, was that nobody starved. Many people often felt hungry, but seldom desperately so. In fact, nutritionists and food experts – the well-known food writer Marguerite Patten, for instance – believe that, on the whole, Britain was very well fed during World War Two, being provided with one of the most nutritionally sound diets the nation had ever known.

Government planners recognised that should war come, there would very quickly be reductions in food imports once German U-boats were at large in the North Atlantic, as this was where all merchant shipping bound for Britain, whether from North America or much further away, ended up. They thought they could plan for this, perhaps even without having to bring in rationing, which had become necessary towards the end of World War One.

1945

JUNE
- The Four Powers – the US, Britain, the Soviet Union and France – all sign the declaration of German defeat.
- King Haakon VII of Norway returns with his family to Oslo after five years in exile.
- British troops capture German foreign minister Joachim von Ribbentrop.
- Japanese situation becomes hopeless and there are mass suicides among the Japanese forces on Okinawa.
- William Joyce (Lord Haw-Haw) is charged with treason.
- General Eisenhower addresses a joint session of the US Congress.
- The Battle of Okinawa ends as US Army and Marines finally take over. 112,000 Japanese and 12,500 Americans are killed and another 36,000 are wounded.
- The USSR capture the Free Republic of Schwarzenberg.
- The United Nations Charter is signed.
- Fifty nations meet in San Francisco and sign the World Security Charter establishing the United Nations.
- President Truman approves plans for the invasion of Japan starting on 1 November 1945.
- Chinese forces invade Indo-China.

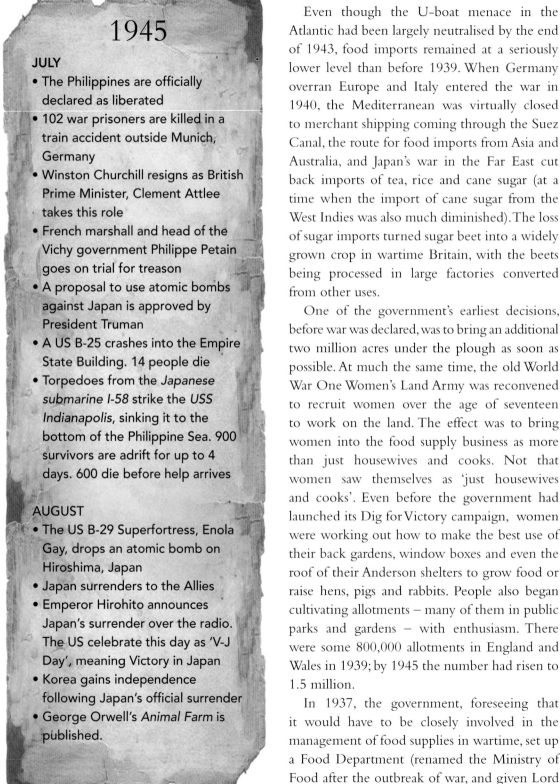

1945

JULY
- The Philippines are officially declared as liberated
- 102 war prisoners are killed in a train accident outside Munich, Germany
- Winston Churchill resigns as British Prime Minister, Clement Attlee takes this role
- French marshall and head of the Vichy government Philippe Petain goes on trial for treason
- A proposal to use atomic bombs against Japan is approved by President Truman
- A US B-25 crashes into the Empire State Building. 14 people die
- Torpedoes from the *Japanese submarine I-58* strike the *USS Indianapolis*, sinking it to the bottom of the Philippine Sea. 900 survivors are adrift for up to 4 days. 600 die before help arrives

AUGUST
- The US B-29 Superfortress, Enola Gay, drops an atomic bomb on Hiroshima, Japan
- Japan surrenders to the Allies
- Emperor Hirohito announces Japan's surrender over the radio. The US celebrate this day as 'V-J Day', meaning Victory in Japan
- Korea gains independence following Japan's official surrender
- George Orwell's *Animal Farm* is published.

Even though the U–boat menace in the Atlantic had been largely neutralised by the end of 1943, food imports remained at a seriously lower level than before 1939. When Germany overran Europe and Italy entered the war in 1940, the Mediterranean was virtually closed to merchant shipping coming through the Suez Canal, the route for food imports from Asia and Australia, and Japan's war in the Far East cut back imports of tea, rice and cane sugar (at a time when the import of cane sugar from the West Indies was also much diminished). The loss of sugar imports turned sugar beet into a widely grown crop in wartime Britain, with the beets being processed in large factories converted from other uses.

One of the government's earliest decisions, before war was declared, was to bring an additional two million acres under the plough as soon as possible. At much the same time, the old World War One Women's Land Army was reconvened to recruit women over the age of seventeen to work on the land. The effect was to bring women into the food supply business as more than just housewives and cooks. Not that women saw themselves as 'just housewives and cooks'. Even before the government had launched its Dig for Victory campaign, women were working out how to make the best use of their back gardens, window boxes and even the roof of their Anderson shelters to grow food or raise hens, pigs and rabbits. People also began cultivating allotments – many of them in public parks and gardens – with enthusiasm. There were some 800,000 allotments in England and Wales in 1939; by 1945 the number had risen to 1.5 million.

In 1937, the government, foreseeing that it would have to be closely involved in the management of food supplies in wartime, set up a Food Department (renamed the Ministry of Food after the outbreak of war, and given Lord

DIG FOR VICTORY POSTERS
A selection of posters used to launch the government's Dig for Victory campaign.

A WARTIME GARDEN IN LANCASHIRE

At the height of the Munich Crisis in 1938, Nella Last devised a plan to make the best use of her garden in Barrow-in-Furness. Within a day of war being declared in September 1939, as she wrote in the diary she kept for Mass Observation, she had revived and polished up her plan. She would 'keep hens on half the lawn. The other half of the lawn will grow potatoes, and cabbage will grow under the apple trees and among the currant bushes. I'll try and buy this year's pullets and only get six, but when spring comes I'll get two sittings and have about twenty extra hens in the summer to kill,' wrote the indomitable 'housewife, 49', as she described herself at the start of her diary. 'I know a little about keeping hens and I'll read up.' Her husband laughed, but said 'Go ahead'.

Woolton as its head). One of the Ministry of Food's first big jobs was to organise the drawing up of a National Register of adults, children and infants as a prelude to issuing everyone with their ration books.

The government, misreading, not for the first time, the mood of the people, put off actually beginning the rationing of food because it thought the move would be unpopular. In fact, the general feeling was that rationing would give everyone a fair share of what was available, so that when the government did start rationing food, beginning in January 1940 with bacon, sugar and butter, no one complained.

Ration books were to become the bane of everyone's life, especially for the wife and mother who did the family shopping. One could not just walk into the nearest shop, buy what one wanted and hand over the ration book for the correct coupons to be deducted. Every ration book had to have written inside it the names of the retailers the customer was registered with; counterfoils of the registration forms were kept by the shopkeeper. This was because shops were allowed only enough rationed foods to cover registered customers, plus some extras to allow for servicemen and women at home on leave.

Ration books and coupons, plus the monthly points system, allowing the purchase of 'extras', such as a can of fish or meat, or specific weights of dried fruits or pulses, gave shopkeepers headaches, too, because they had to file carefully the registration counterfoils, fill in dozens of forms for the Ministry, count all the coupons they took, and then take the forms and coupons to their local Food Office. Shopkeepers had to

MAKING THE MOST OF AN ANDERSON SHELTER

Women needed to find ways of making the best use of their back gardens. Window boxes and even the roof of their Anderson shelters were used to grow fresh vegetables.

THE NATIONAL LOAF

Bread was not rationed during the war – although it had to be after it, largely because of poor world wheat harvests just after the war. Although something like a seventh of the nation's flour milling capacity was destroyed during the Blitz, women could still buy white bread, and the white flour for making their own, until about mid-1942. By this time, the amounts of wheat getting into the country from abroad were so low that the extraction rate for wheat had to be greatly increased so that much more of each precious grain of wheat could be used. The wartime National Wheatmeal Loaf was not popular, despite everything the Ministry of Food said about its nutritional value. It was coarse and grey and many people, including Ernest Bevin, the Minister of Labour, complained – loudly, during a meeting of the War Cabinet – that it was indigestible. Even though the greyish colour was offputting, it was still highly nutritious and the high extraction rate meant that there was more bread to go round.

WARTIME HARVEST
After the wartime announcement that rye could now be used in Britain's bread, women volunteers were asked to gather the wartime harvest.

be fully aware of all the alterations to the rations, such as changes in quantities and prices, that the Ministry was constantly making.

Queuing, often for hours, outside shops in all weathers became a way of life for women during the war. With just one or two shop assistants behind the counter to find, weigh and wrap every woman's purchases, and to take the correct number of coupons from the family's ration books, shopping became a very long process.

The Ministry of Food did its best to help relieve the boredom and austerity of wartime food, at the same time waging constant war against waste: 'Food is a munition of war. Don't Waste It' said the Ministry's posters. The

Ministry produced a long series of 'Food Facts' booklets, leaflets and pamphlets intended to keep housewives well informed about what foods were available, what their nutritional values were, and how they could be best prepared and used in cooking. The last-mentioned was very needed, especially when unfamiliar items like dried egg powder and skimmed milk powder (called household milk) first appeared, to be followed later in the war by even more unlikely things like snook and whalemeat.

Feeding people after air raids, both in the immediate aftermath, and for weeks and months afterwards while power lines and gas supplies were restored and houses rebuilt, was a major headache for the government. It was one that women played a big part in relieving, especially the women of the WVS, bringing their mobile canteens and Queen's Messengers convoys to the sites of air raids. The WVS were also good at demonstrating how to build efficient temporary ovens in the street, using bricks and rubble from damaged buildings. Then there were the housewives themselves, increasingly adept at building their own temporary cooking facilities in the garden or the street, and, of course, sharing their own undamaged kitchens with less fortunate neighbours.

When the Food Leaders scheme, a development of the Food Convoys and the Food Flying Squads that replaced them, was launched nationally in 1944, most of the fifteen thousand Leaders appointed before the end of the war in 1945 were WVS housewives. Their job was basically a public education task: to advise people how to make the best of what foods were available so that everyone would have a diet that was nutritious enough, even if not always very delicious or interesting, to keep them in good health.

THE ART OF BEING THRIFTY

The art of being thrifty during wartime was a necessity and people quickly learned to make do with what they had in the cupboard. Most of the kitchen staples such as meat, eggs, butter, margarine and cheese were rationed, so it was down to the housewife to do something innovative with what she had. Every scrap of food was reused; what wasn't eaten on one day would be dished up as something different tomorrow. The average family just couldn't afford to throw anything away, even bones from the butcher would make a tasty broth that could last several days.

They were strange times – a lot of queuing. Sometimes you wouldn't even know what you were queuing for, but you would stand in line anyway just in case it was something you wanted. Queuing became a social occasion and very often a necessity. What you couldn't buy you went without, or alternatively grew your own in any available space you had.

You had to make smarter food choices and develop new ways to give your family adequate nutrition on the products that were available. So if you think growing your own and recycling are ideas developed in the 21st century, think again, we inherited these from our wartime cousins.

AN ALLOTMENT EXHIBITION
On 1 April 1941, Councillor A. J. Blake who was chairman of the Wartime Allotments Committee, held a megaphone and a sack of onions before launching an allotment exhibition in Hornsey, London.

THE RURAL PIE SCHEME

A splendid WVS initiative, begun at harvest time in Cambridgeshire in 1941, when they supplied a daily hot pie service to the workers in the fields, led to the Rural Pie Scheme. The Ministry of Food, seeing how the WVS women had managed to cook and distribute some seventy thousand pies, was soon advising local authorities on how they could launch similar schemes, using commercial catering firms, to ensure that agricultural workers got a nutritious lunch every day. At its peak, the Rural Pie Scheme was carrying pies and other snacks to agricultural workers in the fields around some five thousand villages at an average rate of one and a quarter million snacks a week.

WARTIME RECIPES

Here are a couple of recipes that were favourites with many housewives because they used ingredients that were readily available and were quick and easy to make. Women were told to think of food as the munition of war, and were encouraged to read food leaflets issued by the Ministry of Food. Women's magazines also gave some useful tips on making the most of what was in your larder. Items like mashed potato were often substituted for flour and sour milk instead of cheese, especially when you had used up all the coupons from your ration book. Another tip which was popular with the kids at pudding time was how to whip up some fake cream. Beat two egg whites until they are stiff, add 2 oz of icing sugar and 1 teaspoon of lemon juice and serve with some fresh fruit.

SAUSAGE AND SULTANA CASSEROLE

Ingredients:
1 lb sausages
1 large onion, chopped
2 oz sultanas
1 cooking apple
Pinch of mixed herbs
Stock
Salt to taste

Method:
1. Chop the onions and fry until they become translucent.
2. Place the onions in a casserole dish and then fry the sausages until they are starting to brown.
3. Place the sausages in the casserole, with the remainder of the ingredients and cover with stock.
4. Cook in a slow oven for 35–40 minutes.

VEGETABLE ROLL WITH POTATO PASTRY

Ingredients for pastry:
4 oz mashed and sieved potato
½ teaspoon of salt
8 oz plain flour
3 oz fat
2 tablespoons of baking powder

Method:
1. Sieve all the dry ingredients together.
2. Rub the fat into the flour and gently mix in the potato. Add just enough water to make a fairly dry dough.
3. Knead well.

Ingredients for filling:
1½ cups of any mixed boiled vegetables, diced
1 pint thick gravy
Salt and pepper
A little chopped parsley

Method:
1. Take ½ lb of potato pastry and roll out on a floured board.
2. Moisten the vegetable mixture with a little of the gravy.
3. Spread the vegetables on to the pastry leaving 1 inch all the way round.
4. Season to taste with salt and pepper.
5. Roll up and seal the edges well so that the gravy cannot seep out.
6. Place on a well greased baking try with the sealed seam underneath.
7. Brush the top of the roll with milk.
8. Bake in a moderately hot oven for 35–45 minutes.

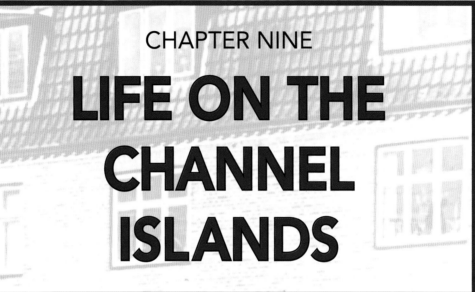

CHAPTER NINE

LIFE ON THE CHANNEL ISLANDS

LIFE ON THE CHANNEL ISLANDS

Hitler certainly made his mark on the Channel Islands during the war, a mark that can never be obliterated. Under his direct orders, his soldiers were told to make the islands into an impenetrable fortress by building walls of steel and concrete right round the islands, having a claustrophic effect on the inhabitants.

BUILDING DEFENCES
The Germans place an anti-aircraft gun on Guernsey close to the sea during their occupation of the Channel Islands.

The Germans occupied the five Channel Islands – Jersey, Guernsey, Alderney, Sark and Herm – from 28 June 1940 until 9 May 1945. For the occupants of the islands, these years were long, bitter and agonising. Everyone lived on a knife edge, afraid of what was going to happen next.

The Channel Islands were in a precarious location right on the edge of the Normandy Coast and Churchill seemed resigned to the fact that he would be unable to protect them from invasion despite valiant attempts to save Allied forces who were stranded off the French coast. This meant that the people of the five islands were left completely defenceless and they began to fear the worst.

The islanders' fears were founded in May 1940, when they became aware that they were directly in the path of the advancing German army. Panic set in and the inhabitants had to make the heart-wrenching decision whether to leave their homes and possessions and flee to the safety of England, or whether to stick it out. Frightened that they would be attacked at any moment, over twenty-three thousand people lined up in St Helier on the island of Jersey to register for evacuation. The problem was there were only a handful of boats available to take the frightened islanders to the relative safety of the mainland. The government of Guernsey offered to evacuate all children of school age, giving parents the choice of whether their children stayed with them or evacuated with their school. On the island of Jersey, the majority of people felt they wanted to stay. Only about seven thousand people actually managed to get off the islands, the remainder had to return home and wait for the inevitable invasion. Why the Germans wanted the Channel Islands is unclear, it held no purpose other than the fact they could say they occupied some British territory.

ATLANTIC WALL

If you take a look at the remnants of the fortifications built by the Germans today, you could not fail to be amazed at the sheer scale of Hitler's undertaking. His paranoia and fanatical urge to defend the islands against attack took barely two and a half years to complete. He formed the Organisation Todt to oversee the construction programme which he called 'Atlantic Wall' defences. These gigantic installations, like the observation tower below at Les Landes, Jersey, were, ironically, hardly ever used.

HUNGER IN THE CHANNEL ISLANDS

The people of Britain came through the war reasonably well fed and in reasonable health. The same could not be said for the majority of Channel Islanders. Within months of the German invasion in July 1940, the people of the Channel Islands were facing severe food shortages and by the time they were liberated in May 1945, many were close to starvation. Between the two dates were years of families hiding what food there was from the German occupying forces and of housewives cooking their food and baking their bread (made from a mixture of corn, water and salt, and called 'hard bake') in communal ovens because there was no fuel for home ovens. Eventually, many were eating either potatoes, including the peelings, or cabbage soup day after day – and eating any slugs found among the cabbage leaves because of their precious protein content. Tea was made from brambles and jelly from seaweed.

THE ARRIVAL OF THE GERMANS

The Germans arrived on 1 July 1940, astonished that they could land on islands that were seemingly totally defenceless. They approached the islands with caution, expecting a fight, but instead they could land and take over control without the hint of any trouble. Just prior to their arrival, not realising that the islands had been demilitarised, the Germans sent a squadron of bombers and attacked the harbours of Guernsey and Jersey fully believing they were being guarded by Allied troops. In St Peter Port, Guernsey, the Germans mistook a convoy of trucks carrying tomatoes ready for export as Allied trucks and forty-four innocent islanders lost their lives.

The Germans quickly consolidated their positions on the islands and demanded that white crosses should be painted in prominent places to signify surrender. Senior government officials arranged to meet the invading forces, but were met with stern opposition and they were forced to hang massive swastikas from their town halls and other government buildings.

Realising they were up against a much greater force, the islanders handed over control of the government and the courts to the Germans, who quickly passsed new laws enforcing the occupation and its ideology. To bring the islands in line with the rest of Europe, the Germans even changed the time zone from GMT to CET and made everyone drive on the right-hand side of the road instead of the left. Life on the islands took a completely different turn and everyone became cautious of what they said or did for fear of retribution. This was particularly true of the Jews. They were already aware of the Nazis hatred of their race, and a register was created that listed the names and addresses of all the Jews. Any businesses run by Jews had to display a yellow notice to that effect.

To enforce their occupation, the Germans restricted movement and forced anyone over the age of fourteen to carry ID cards and everyone had to comply with an imposed curfew. All radios were confiscated and if anyone was caught listening to the BBC they were punished with imprisonment. They allowed the printing of one newspaper, but this was carefully censored before being allowed on the press.

Cars were requisitioned by the Nazis and shipped to the mainland with very little compensation to the owner. Any farms were taken over by the Germans and an inventory was made of all clothing and other goods owned by the islanders. Strict rationing was brought in and within months of the occupancy, islanders were facing severe food shortages, many close to starvation. Fishermen were seen as a threat to security, so any boats in and out of the harbours had to be licensed and were only allowed to fish during daylight hours under heavy supervision.

Many islanders reverted to their original tongues – Guernésiais in Guernsey and Jèrriais in Jersey – so they could speak freely without fear of being overheard. Many of the German soldiers were familiar with both French and English, so the indigenous languages enjoyed a brief revival.

THE CONCENTRATION CAMPS OF ALDERNEY

Alderney was given the name of 'island of silence' due to the fact that so little is known about what happened there during the occupancy. What we do know is that the Germans built four concentration camps there – Lager Norderney located at Saye, Lager Borkum at Platte Saline, Lager Sylt at La Foulère and Lager Helgoland which was in the northwest corner of the island. The camps came under the control of

Organisation Todt who used prisoners to build bunkers, gun emplacements, air raid shelters and other concrete fortifications. By January 1942, the four camps had a total of over six thousand inmates, many of whom never survived. There is no official figure of how many inmates died, as the German officer left in charge of the facilities, Commandant Oberst Schwalm, burned the camps to the ground and destroyed all records before the island was liberated by British forces.

The only one that remains today is the one at Lager Sylt and then only the entrance gateway is intact along with a few concrete bases of the remainder of the buildings. It is a quiet and dismal place, a grim reminder of what the inhabitants of Alderney had to endure.

FORTIFICATIONS

The fortification of the Channel Islands became a complete obsession with Hitler, who made immense preparations against the attack of the islands – an attack which never came. His plans came to fruition on 20 October 1941, when he issued a directive which laid down that the islands were to be converted into what he called 'impregnable fortresses'. Engineers were flown to the islands so they could begin conducting a geographical survey to determine exactly what was required to defend the island. Because of the islands' close proximity to France, it was soon realised that by placing artillery batteries on the islands and also on the French coast, it would be possible to make the islands Hitler's desired 'impregnable fortresses'. The Todt constructed in Jersey alone no fewer than seven coastal artillery batteries. The infantry were supplied with eighty field guns and anti-tank guns in deep concrete bunkers, as well as fifty-one tank turrets mounted on the so-called Tobruk emplacements. All this weaponry had to be housed somewhere, and more than two hundred and fifty concrete bunkers creating thousands of square metres of storage space and underground tunnels were ordered to be constructed for this purpose.

UNDERGROUND BUNKERS
One of the massive underground bunkers built at St Ouen's Bay in Jersey.

PETROL RATIONING
Due to petrol rationing by the Germans during their period of occupancy, the islanders had to use every resource to get by. Here a motor bus is being pulled by a team of horses.

There were huge underground bunkers which were never completed and an entire coast defence system against every possible form of invasion. All the defences were built by prisoners of war and it brought an immense amount of despair and death during their construction. It is estimated that as many as four out of every ten of these workers lost their lives.

Today there is little to see of all these futile defence works, those that remain are memorials to the international band of workers who slaved for Hitler's war machine. The bunkers are left as phantom-like holes in the ground, there are towers overgrown with weeds and several gun emplacements that never saw the firing of any ammunition. Most of the islanders do not welcome these reminders, it is only visitors to the islands that want to know their history.

LIBERATION

It was the Normandy landings in 1944 which heralded the end of the German's occupation. By August of that year, St Malo had been forced to surrender which meant the supply route to the islands had been severed. For eight months the islanders and their captors had to endure near starvation as no supplies got through. Liberation was in sight when, on 8 May 1945, HMS *Bulldog* sailed into St Peter Port. The next day the islanders were informed by the German authorities that the war was over. A resounding cheer of relief could be heard on every street.

CHAPTER TEN
FASHION AND BEAUTY

FASHION AND BEAUTY

Where the Ministry of Food was, appropriately enough, in charge of ensuring that the nation was adequately fed during the war, it was the Board of Trade that dictated in an increasingly draconian manner, the style, shape and fabric content of the clothes bought. Every man, woman and child in the country was affected by clothes rationing which lasted the duration of the war and for four further years when the conflict was over.

Although people accepted that clothing fabrics would be in short supply, it still came as a shock to many when clothing was actually rationed, like food. When the President of the Board of Trade announced immediate clothes rationing on 1 June 1941, the reason given was to 'provide fair distribution of available supplies'. But the government was also intent, not only on reducing consumer spending, but also on cutting the numbers of workers tied up in clothing textile manufacture when they could have been more usefully employed in war production. Clothes rationing in Britain did not end until 1949.

To prevent hoarding, price rises and the development of a 'black market', clothes rationing was kept a closely guarded secret until it was announced. It was a year before the first clothes ration books were issued. They contained sixty coupons and were intended to last until the end of July 1943. In September 1943, the allocation dropped to forty coupons, rising again to forty-eight coupons in 1944. In September 1945, with the war over, the allocation dropped down to a mere thirty-six coupons a year, largely because of a serious shortage of workers in the nation's textile mills.

Clothing ration coupons came in three different colours – green, brown and red – and were intended to cover use by numerous different categories of people, including workers, such as miners, with special clothing needs, expectant mothers, new babies and 'certain older children' who might be growing too big for children's clothes, was a sign that clothes rationing was not going to be simple. And, indeed, it turned out to be nightmarishly complicated, so much so that the government had to issue a booklet, called *The Clothing Quiz*, to help people understand the system.

The Board of Trade's clothes rationing lists attempted to include most items of clothing

READ ALL ABOUT IT
A couple of holidaymakers read about clothes rationing in the *Sunday Pictorial*.

LOST RATION BOOKS

Losing a clothes ration book was a serious thing. A book lost in a bombing could be replaced by the local Assistance Board, but any other loss, unless 'exceptional need' could be proved, probably meant the replacement was unlikely. In the early months of clothes rationing, people were recompensed for the 'loss' of food or clothing ration books with loose coupons – something like 27,000,000 during the first year. But the system was so abused that the Board of Trade cracked down on the use of loose coupons, brought in a complex coupon banking system, and ruled that only coupons in books were acceptable in shops. It even employed its own snoopers, who visited clothing shops trying to buy clothes with loose coupons.

that the British man, woman and child might wish to buy for both their working and private lives, and were therefore both lengthy and, occasionally, esoteric (for example, leggings, gaiters or spats, requiring three coupons for adults, two for children). Coupon requirements included: twenty-six for a man's suit, eighteen for a woman's (also the amount for a lined winter coat); a man's shirt took five coupons, a woman's cotton or rayon dress seven coupons (but her winter woollen dress needed eleven); men's socks ('half-hose, not woollen, or pair of ankle socks not exceeding eight inches [20 centimetres] from point of heel to top of sock when not turned down') took one coupon, a pair of women's stockings (soon very hard to get anyway), two coupons. Babies' knitted booties required half a coupon. One slight relief was that hats did not require coupons.

With these lists beside them, people could work out in advance their clothing purchases for the coming year or so. The foolish blew their allocation early in the summer then found that, come autumn, there were no coupons left for essential winter clothing. Even if people had the right number of coupons, they often found that they simply could not afford the purchase price of the garments they wanted, for the price of clothing rocketed in the early years of the war: a made-to-measure suit, 14 guineas (£14.70) at the start of the war, was soon costing up to £42, and pretty nighties, a delightful present at 25 shillings (£1.25) became something to consider very seriously when their price reached £12 or more.

The Board of Trade, when planning the regulations for the Utility clothing scheme, decided that only four basic outfits should be available – a top coat and a suit, in both men's and women's styles, and, for women, an afternoon dress and a cotton overall dress. The rules governing their manufacture were strict, and were based on using as little fabric as possible. Suits and coats, which could not be double-breasted, had narrow lapels, men's trousers were made without turnups, and women's skirts were all made to the same (shortish) length, regardless of the fact that British women were not all the same height. Numbers of buttons and pockets were restricted and embroidery or lace trimmings were forbidden. The cut of the garments was practical, pared-down and almost military in outline – and thus very much in tune with the wartime mood.

MAKE DO AND MEND

The limited availability of new clothing made looking after the contents of one's existing wardrobe of huge importance. 'Make Do and Mend' and 'Sew and Save' became two more additions to Britain's growing list of wartime slogans. In fact, making do and mending became everyone's patriotic duty, although many women must have thought that the president of the Board of Trade, Hugh Dalton, was going a bit far when he told the readers of *Good Housekeeping* magazine in August 1943 that 'to wear clothes that have been patched and darned – perhaps many times – is to show oneself a true patriot. The "right" clothes are those we have worn for years, and the wrong ones those we buy, when we don't absolutely need them'.

Making do with the clothes one already had involved the use of considerable ingenuity,

CLOTHING RATIONS
A woman uses her clothes ration book to buy some new underwear at Woolworths.

NUMBER OF COUPONS REQUIRED

WOMEN AND GIRLS

	Adult	Child
Lined mackintosh or coat	14	11
Jacket, or short coat	11	8
Dress or frock – woollen	11	8
Dress or frock – other material	7	5
Gym tunic	8	6
Blouse, sports shirt, cardigan or jumper	5	3
Skirt	7	5
Overalls or dungarees	6	4
Apron or pinafore	3	2
Pyjamas	8	6
Nightdress	6	5
Petticoat or slip, combination or cami-knickers	4	3
Other undergarments, including corsets	3	2
Pair of stockings	2	1
Pair of socks (ankle length)	1	1
Collar, tie or pair of cuffs	1	1
Two handkerchiefs	1	1
Scarf, pair of gloves, mittens or muff	2	2
Pair of slippers, boots or shoes	5	3

CHEAP CLOTHING
Women often saved their coupons by buying cheap clothes like this blouse and dungarees.

displayed by homemakers and manufacturers alike. Darning, patching and repairing everything from precious silk stockings to one's husband's trousers became, if not a patriotic duty, then certainly a way of life.

Manufacturers did help, producing special trouser-bottom protectors, for instance, or offering a service whereby last year's winter coat could be turned into this year's stylish suit, for a price that did not need to include precious clothing coupons.

Many women also became adept at re-using fabric to sew new clothes on their carefully maintained pre-war sewing machines. Because knitting wool, like dress fabrics, was soon in short supply (and both were rationed, anyway), it became a regular job to unpick old hand-knitted garments and re-use the wool to knit something that looked new and smart: the wartime fashion for striped knitwear grew out of the practice of using old knitting wools together with a few balls of new wool.

Women's magazines, too, although much reduced in size and page extent because of paper rationing, continued throughout the war to help boost morale by offering women much useful and often wonderfully imaginative advice on eking out and making do with the contents of their family's wardrobes.

A theme common to most women's magazines was that it was their readers' patriotic duty to look smart, not just for themselves but for their menfolk returning from the war. *Good Housekeeping* emphasised the theme through many articles covering everything from turning elderly fur coats into warm waistcoats or slip-coats (and using the bits left over for fur collars and mitts) and titivating hats or making 'becoming turbans' with a yard of jersey fabric to making 'cheerful sleeveless pullovers' to 'spice

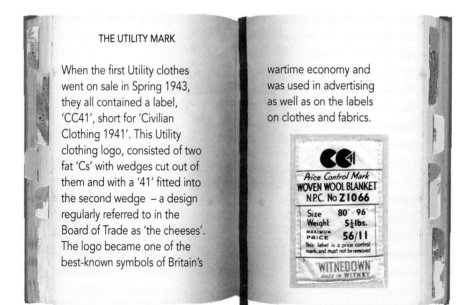

THE UTILITY MARK

When the first Utility clothes went on sale in Spring 1943, they all contained a label, 'CC41', short for 'Civilian Clothing 1941'. This Utility clothing logo, consisted of two fat 'Cs' with wedges cut out of them and with a '41' fitted into the second wedge – a design regularly referred to in the Board of Trade as 'the cheeses'. The logo became one of the best-known symbols of Britain's wartime economy and was used in advertising as well as on the labels on clothes and fabrics.

UTILITY CLOTHING
Models at Bush House, London, display clothes made from government utility materials at the
first mixed mannequin show ever held.

up tired frocks'. At the same time, the magazine did not allow their readers to mis-use their
clothing coupons, regularly reminding them
how long the current allocation of coupons
had to last (usually for a dispiriting number of
months ahead).

KEEPING UP APPEARANCES

Another theme put forward by women's magazines was the importance of keeping up
appearances in wartime. Having your hair
permanently waved, for instance, was not considered frivolous; rather, it was a necessity for

women doing war work to keep 'the hair always neat and pretty', as one perm solution manufacturer put it in a women's magazine advert. And, as *Vogue* put it at the height of the war, 'during World War II it becomes female citizens' patriotic duty to "put their face on", encouraged by the film industry. This gives lipstick respectability.'

To give Hugh Dalton and the Board of Trade their due, they recognised that it was essential to keep up the morale of Britain's women in wartime and tried to make essential cosmetics, perm solutions and the like available – sometimes. But anything of a 'cosmetic' nature, whether women's lipsticks, rouges and vanishing creams, or men's razors and razor blades, were always in short supply, and people got used to keeping an eagle eye on the contents of shop shelves or of keeping an ear open for rumours in pubs and streets about things being 'available', often in street markets or, almost as often, 'round the back of the pub' or on the 'black market'.

Women found many ingenious substitutes for scarce cosmetics. Boot polish replaced mascara on many dressing tables, although dark-lashed women used petroleum jelly to give their lashes a thickening gloss. Beetroot juice reddened lips and rose petals steeped in red wine for several weeks were used as a substitute for rouge.

As for those precious pre-war silk stockings, well, clever lateral thinking and illusion had to replace them – even after the GIs arrived from North America with their miraculous nylons. Tan-coloured creams were painted over legs, and a brown line was drawn up the back of each leg to give the impression that the legs' owner was wearing stockings. Enterprising beauticians

1945

SEPTEMBER
- Japanese prime minister Hideki Tojo (in office for most of World War Two) attempts suicide to escape facing charges at a war crime tribunal.
- As American troops occupy southern Korea and the Soviet Union occupy the north, Korea becomes indirectly divided.
- A typhoon in Japan kills 3,746 people.
- Australian forces liberate Batu Lintang camp in Sarawak, Borneo.
- British troops are ordered to leave India by Mohandas Ghandi and Jawaharlal Nehru.

OCTOBER
- The United Nations is established.
- The Detroit Tigers win the World Series.
- The first ballpoint pens go on sale in America, selling at $12.50.
- In France, women are allowed to vote for the first time.
- The former premier of Vichy France, Pierre Laval, is executed by firing squad for treason against France.
- Norwegian Nazi leader Vidkun Quisling is executed for treason.

NO MORE LADDERS
During stocking rationing, a beautician at the newly opened Leg Beauty Bar at Kennard's store in Croydon, paints stockings onto a customer's skin.

HOME-MADE JACKETS

To beat wartime rationing, women took to making their own clothes, for example simple skin jackets with knitted sleeves as seen here.

set up leg-painting booths where women could have 'stockings painted on their legs' in the shade of their choice for 3d [just over 1p] a leg. The stocking crisis was such that the Church of England eventually issued a statement saying that it was perfectly acceptable for women to come to church without wearing stockings or hats. Thus another step along the road of social revolution was taken in wartime Britain.

LOOKING GOOD ON LESS

When the women's pages of Britain's national newspapers and women's magazines published articles emphasising the importance of women making the best of themselves in wartime, and not just because it was important to look their best when their husbands came home, they were simply following government guidelines. Keeping up the nation's morale was seen by the government as essential to winning the war.

Women's magazines accepted the morale-boosting part they were expected to play from the outset. As *Vogue* put it in their September 1939 issue: 'We can't speak for the future in

DARNING SOCKS
Evacuees are taught how to darn their socks at Baron's Estate in Hampshire.

CLOTHES EXCHANGE
To extend the clothes rationing system, the Women's Voluntary Service set up a depot where children's clothes could be exchanged.

these times, but on the date this goes to press, *Vogue* is still at the old addresses... We started our ARP arrangements in August 1938, and had them all ready last March. So with the consent – indeed, at the desire – of our staff, we remain on the job, in the places where our various departments can best serve their customers.' In other words, whatever their jobs, whatever their class in society, Britain's women were all going to 'see it through' together.

Fabrics and textiles for home dress-making, which had enjoyed a boom among women in the 1920s and 1930s with the availability of inexpensive, easy-to-use sewing machines, quickly became hard to find from early in the war, as did wool for knitting. First came restrictions, imposed by the Board of Trade, on the use of many textiles, including silk and artificial silk, rayon, leather, wool, cotton and flax (for linen). Silk was needed for parachutes, and wool for uniforms.

It is possible that the prime minister himself had something to do with the late date for clothes rationing. As Oliver Lyttelton, president of the Board of Trade in 1940–41, recalled in the ITV television series, *The World at War*, Churchill was opposed to anything that might dampen civilian morale and thus affect output and lengthen the time needed to win the war. But, to Oliver Lyttelton, the reason for bringing in clothes rationing was a simple matter of manpower, with the difference between rationed clothes and free clothes being four hundred and fifty thousand workers. As for the morale argument, Oliver Lyttelton told Churchill that he thought 'the population wanted to do something, particularly the women, after Dunkirk, to feel they were part of the war.'

Oliver Lyttelton turned out to have a more sensitive finger on the national pulse than the prime minister did. There was little complaining about and a general acceptance of clothes rationing, with people 'glad to be a little bit shabby and [feeling] that they were doing

A USE FOR SILK
A WAAF woman uses a Singer sewing machine to stitch a bundle of parachute silk.

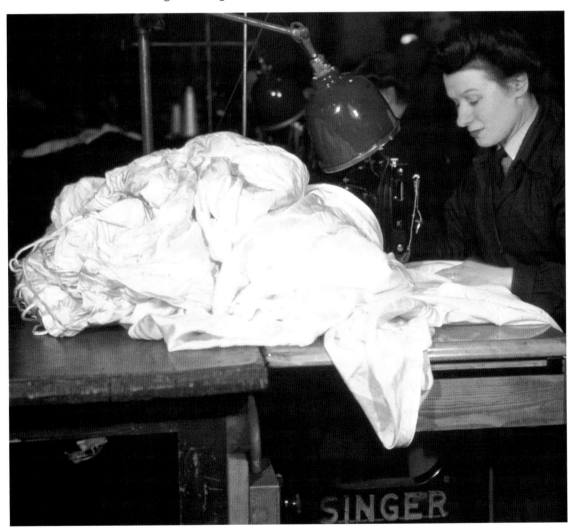

AND THE WAR RAGES ON
The cover of *Picture Post* in August 1944, shows a young woman relaxing on a British beach with a book; but a tangle of barbed wire reminds her that the war is still raging in Europe.

their stint', as Lyttelton put it.

People might have been less accepting of the need to be a bit shabby if they had known that clothing rationing would not end in Britain until 1949. Anyway, as many people discovered very quickly, there was always the black market, which thrived in the early days of clothes rationing because people could claim that their coupon books had been lost or stolen and have them replaced by handfuls of loose coupons.

At the same time as clothes rationing was introduced, the government's propaganda machine swung into action under the banner of another of its famous wartime slogans: 'Make Do and Mend'. Much of the make do and mend campaign now seems both patronising towards women and very 'nanny state'. Women did not need Her Majesty's Stationery Office to issue posters, emanating from the Board of Trade, advising them to 'Go through your wardrobe' and sort out clothes for mending or refurbishing, or to 'Make Do and Mend' by sewing 'decorative' patches over worn parts, keeping clothes packed away from moths, and unpicking and re-knitting sweaters. Women could work out such things for themselves.

It is possible that without the advice included in a Board of Trade booklet, few women would have thought to make themselves skirts out of their husband's old plus-fours or turn his waistcoat into a top for themselves by adding sleeves knitted from odd balls of wool. But perhaps they would have, for women showed great ingenuity in making themselves clothes out of the unlikeliest material during the war.

With so many women looking smart in the uniforms of the auxiliary services and the various Civil Defence units, many others doing men's work in dungarees and trousers, and even volunteers wearing uniforms – the WVS's winter great coat was designed by the London fashion house of Digby Morton – it is not surprising that women's fashions took on a distinctly military style during the war. The two-piece suit, with its short, square, shoulder-padded jacket and knee-length straight skirt is ubiquitous in photographs of this period. Women wore their suits to work, when they went out in the evenings and even for their wedding: after all, the young man whose arm every bride held was almost invariably wearing a service uniform.

Children, like their parents, were issued with clothes ration books, so it is not surprising that knitting and sewing clothes for their children became just another important task that women had to find time for during the war.

Perhaps the most difficult aspect of wartime women's beauty was the maintenance of a head of shining, well-cut and well-maintained hair. A shortage of metal hair pins, hair cosmetics, shampoos and perming solutions accounted for the greatly increased use of hairnets and the popularity of the head-covering turban. Despite such problems, fashionable women's hairstyles, based on longer hair, became increasingly complicated, with hair being rolled into many different styles. The styles were even given patriotic names, such as the 'Victory V' or 'Victory Roll', the 'Montgomery's Sweet' or

THE VICTORY ROLL
The actress Rita Hayworth favoured the Victory Roll hairstyle and many women emulated her chic style.

CHAPTER ELEVEN

ARTS AND ENTERTAINMENT

ARTS AND ENTERTAINMENT

Of the many regulations issued in the days after war was declared, few were as dismaying to everyone as the one which announced that 'All cinemas, dance halls and places of public entertainment will be closed until further notice' and that 'football matches and outdoor meetings of all kinds which bring large numbers together are prohibited until further notice.'

Just about the only public 'entertainment' left to an already distressed and deeply worried nation were – apart from those museums and art galleries that chose to keep most of their holdings on display – pubs and the BBC's one remaining on-air radio station, the Home Service.

Once it was seen that Britain was not going to be subjected to pre-invasion mass bombing, these dreadfully morale-deflating restrictions on public entertainment were relaxed. By mid-September 1939, places of public entertainment, museums and art galleries were open again and a football programme was under way.

A QUESTION OF SPORT

In the long run, outdoor events suffered more restrictions than those entertainments that took place indoors. Men could only 'go to the dogs' at weekends because, in order to prevent people taking time off work, mid-week greyhound racing was forbidden.

Horse racing suffered from petrol rationing, which curtailed people's ability to get to the race courses, and many sports had their playing fields and facilities requisitioned anyway.

Tennis fans had to accept that the courts at Wimbledon were now being used by the Home Guard; even worse, the hallowed Oval cricket ground in London had briefly become a POW camp. Football, like greyhound racing, became a daytime-only activity, the floodlighting of sports grounds clearly being out of bounds for the duration. By October, football matches – initially a programme of friendly matches with crowds limited to fifteen thousand in 'safe' areas and to eight thousand elsewhere – were being played not in the league that was suspended, but within a new regional competition format that cut the amount of travelling teams had to do. Ground managers had to employ raid spotters, who kept a look out for enemy aircraft and sounded a siren or some sort of recognised warning, if they spotted any while matches were in progress. Of course many of the players had been persuaded to join the Territorial Army anyway, starting with fourteen members of Bolton Wanderers. Harry Goslin, the team captain for Bolton Wanderers spoke to his players before a home match against Sunderland – 'We are facing a national emergency. But this danger can be met if everybody keeps a cool head and knows what to do. This is something you can't leave to the other fellow, everybody has a share to do'. Other clubs quickly followed suit, persuading their players to do the same thing.

And then of course there were the 'missing' Olympic Games of 1940 to be held in Sapporo, Japan and 1944 scheduled to be held in London, both of which were cancelled because of the war. The Olympic Games resumed in 1948 and were held in London. Of course, even though the war was over, Europe was still ravaged from such a major conflict. When it was announced that the Olympic Games were to be resumed, many questioned whether it was wise to hold such a prestigious event when many European countries were still in ruins.

WARTIME DERBY

Airmen watch the field as it passed the winning post in a wartime Derby in June 1940. The winner of this particular race was Pont l'Eveque ridden by Sam Wragg. It was being run at Newmarket where it was held from 1940–45, returning to Epsom after the end of World War Two.

1945

NOVEMBER
- The Nuremberg Trials begin.
- A tsunami in Balochistan (Pakistan) is caused by an earthquake, killing 4,000 people.
- Charles De Gaulle is elected as head of a provisional government in France.
- 88 German scientists are brought to America to assist in the development of rocket technology, causing much controversy.

DECEMBER
- General Eurico Gaspar Dutra is elected president of Brazil.
- The United States join the United Nations.

GOING TO THE CINEMA

At first, the blackout kept many people at home in the evenings, but it was not long before the lure of the cinema outweighed the difficulties of getting there and home again through dark streets. Few cinemas closed, even during the worst days of the Blitz (unless completely destroyed, as some sixty London cinemas were during the war), although there were temporary closures for war damage repairs. Many cinema managers found that their dress circles were distinctly under-patronised, except by courting couples, during the Blitz. Going to the pictures became Britain's most popular away-from-home activity during the war. The country's approximately 5,000 cinemas, many of which had room for 2,500 seats, attracted millions of customers. By 1945, ticket sales had reached thirty million a week, despite regular increases in ticket prices.

Cinemas (and theatres) dealt with bombing raids by announcing during the performance that an air raid warning had been received, leaving their patrons to decide for themselves if they would take shelter, perhaps in the building's

DOING THE WARTIME POOLS

During the war, even in the darkest days of the Blitz and the V-1 and V-2 bombings, people could dream of winning the jackpot on the pools. The football pools continued throughout the war, offering betting on regional competition matches or on the 'War Cup' competition that replaced the FA Cup in March 1940. All football pools were pooled to form the 'Unity Pool', with the names of eight pre-war pools promoters, including Littlewoods and Vernons, at the top of the coupon. No less than one shilling (5p) could be invested on one coupon.

MOBILE FILM SCREENS
A crowd watches a film about the RAF on an outdoor screen from the back of a truck. The mobile screenings were used to raise money for weapons and general war effort during the days of the Battle of Britain.

basement, or continue watching the show, which was not stopped. As the war went on and a general shrug-of-the-shoulders fatalism set in, more and more people stayed in their seats.

British film makers did not have the country's cinemas to themselves, for a large part of the output of Hollywood reached Britain during the war. One of the longest-running and most popular films in the country was *Gone With the Wind*, which played to packed houses from its opening in London's Leicester Square in April 1940 until the end of its run in the summer of 1944 (see page 349 for more detail).

Theatre life, especially in London, was rather different from that of the cinemas. When the Blitz was at its height, many theatres, attracting very small audiences and therefore disastrously low ticket sales, closed altogether, leaving only the Windmill Theatre, purveyor of nudity and comedy in London, to carry on.

The worst of the Blitz over, theatre-going got into its stride again, with musicals, both British and American, being particularly popular, while comedies proved more popular than political or war-themed dramas, because they offered the greater escape from what was going on outside the theatre. The problems of the blackout made matinees particularly attractive choices for many, while evening performances in many theatres began as early as six o'clock – and with the pre-war evening dress convention for everyone in the stalls conspicuous by its absence.

Outside London, once theatres were permitted to open again, repertory theatres suffered for a time from an influx of London West End stars moving to the safety of the provinces and into touring productions, where their star quality drew audiences away from local theatre productions. On the whole, however, theatre outside London took on a new vigour during the war, taking advantage of the general recognition that cinema and the theatre could do much to boost morale in wartime. Actors were able to claim exemption from military service, provided they were in more-or-less full-time work in the theatre or films (two consecutive weeks out of work, and military service loomed). Many stage and film actors managed to combine quite lengthy periods of military service with making films or acting in the theatre. Both Laurence Olivier and Ralph Richardson, for instance, spent some time in the Fleet Air Arm.

The Entertainments National Service Association (ENSA) was formed, at the instigation of the distinguished theatre director Basil Dean, to take entertainment to the services and those connected with them in Britain and overseas. Sometimes unfairly mocked for the quality of its shows – there were people who said that 'ENSA' stood for 'Every Night Something Awful'. ENSA took its morale-boosting light entertainments all over Britain and overseas to the many places where British troops were fighting; ENSA's jokes were said to get bluer the nearer the troops were to the front line.

Despite the popularity of the cinema and, to a lesser extent, theatres, concert halls, dance halls and pubs, the home remained the place where the vast majority of people got most of their entertainment. While low-wattage light bulbs and wartime economy standard (i.e. poor quality) paper made reading at night difficult for some, curling up with a good book remained a particularly popular way of passing an evening at home – or in the ARP post or anti-aircraft gun emplacement. Particularly popular wartime reading included the crime stories of Agatha Christie or Raymond Chandler and the classics of an earlier, quieter age of fiction-writing, such as the works of Charles Dickens and Anthony Trollope. The publishing of new books was drastically reduced during the war, with the 1945 total number of books published being less than half that of 1939.

GETTING READY FOR TOUR
An ENSA (Entertainment National Services Association) touring group, prepare for a tour at their headquarters in Drury Lane, London.

THE IMPORTANCE OF RADIO

For families at home together, radio provided the greatest entertainment. Well aware that it was responsible as much for keeping people's spirits up as for keeping them fully informed about the war's progress, the BBC provided hours and hours of dance music, variety shows and comedy shows on its Home Service. During the day, programmes aimed at specific audiences – householders with *The Kitchen Front* and *In Your Garden*, children with *Children's Hour* (deemed

too flippant for wartime in September 1939 and cancelled, but hastily re-instated), factory workers with *Workers' Playtime* and *Music While You Work* – filled the airwaves. In February 1940, the BBC launched the *General Forces Programme*, aimed specifically at the men and women of the armed forces, and including programmes like *Forces Favourites*, *Calling the Forces Everywhere* and *Navy Mixture*. Vera Lynn, the 'Forces' Sweetheart' and the most popular singer of the war, became famous through her appearances

LISTENING TO THE WIRELESS

Nine million wireless receiving licences were issued in Britain in 1939 – enough to ensure that some ninety per cent of households had a wireless. Manufacturers responded to wartime demand by producing both wirelesses and radiograms with increased short-wave facilities and better tuning systems. There were more battery-operated models, too. Thus, even if you were sitting in your blackout-dim house or holed up in your Anderson shelter, you could listen to the wireless.

There is no doubt that the wireless was important during the dark days of war, it was a lifeline to inform people of exactly what was happening. No one ever missed the news, listening avidly to what Churchill had to say. Everyone believed that he was the right man to run the country, he gave people inspiration, he gave people encouragement and above all they believed he was a man who could forecast the future of the country. It didn't matter where you were, at nine o'clock in the evening there would be a mass exodus as people said to each other, 'Come on, you'll miss Churchill, you know he's on at nine o'clock'.

It was also the time of the big dance bands such as Glenn Miller and Joe Loss and people would huddle round the fire in their living room to give them a brief respite from the terrors of war.

on the *Forces Programme*. When the BBC began rebuilding its radio network in the summer of 1945, the *Forces Programme* was renamed the *Light Programme*. It and the Home Service were joined by the *Third Programme* in 1946, the year when television began broadcasting again. (Shut down completely in 1939, British television did not really begin to establish itself as a mass medium until the Coronation of Elizabeth II in 1953.)

At night, the family would gather round the wireless in the living room to enjoy together such comedy programmes as ITMA (*It's That Man Again*), starring Tommy Handley, Kenneth Horne's *Much Binding In the Marsh*, and the rather more intellectually challenging *Brain's Trust*. And there were hours of ballroom dance music, led by such famous band leaders as Henry Hall, Geraldo, Victor Sylvester and, later in the war, the American Glenn Miller, and often broadcast direct from such glamorous places as the Savoy Ballroom. It was while sitting round the wireless in the living room that most people first heard of the great events that were happening in their country and in the rest of the world. Neville Chamberlain announced that the country was at war with Germany on the radio and Winston Churchill, his famously rumbling deep voice already familiar to his listeners, announced the end of the war in 1945 on the BBC Home Service, before he officially informed the House of Commons.

The war made radio performers and news-readers – no less than comedy stars and band leaders – the celebrities of the age. The BBC placed great emphasis on the names as well as the voices of their newsreaders being familiar – 'This is the news and this is Alvar Lidell reading it' – because it lessened the likelihood of German broadcasting of morale-damaging propaganda being believed.

The notorious Irish-born William Joyce (called

'Lord Haw Haw' because of his upper-class accent), who broadcast pro-German propaganda from Hamburg and regularly picked up an audience of millions during the Phoney War, lost most of his audience when the war got serious. The BBC lessened the chances of German imposters being able to copy English accents successfully by using many more people like the northerner Wilfrid Pickles who spoke with regional accents rather than with the 'Received Pronunciation' that had been de rigeur for newsreaders (along with wearing dinner jackets to read the evening news) in the 1930s.

Thus the BBC, a bastion of pre-war middle-class values, made a major contribution to the social revolution that World War Two brought about in Britain.

THE DANCE HALL

Dance halls were a place to let off steam, to forget what was happening in the world and most of all meet a pretty girl or a handsome soldier. In fact the dance halls were full of servicemen, some of them not looking old enough to have even left home, let alone be fighting for their country. The dance hall was the place they could forget what might be ahead of them, and they often did this by partaking of too much liquor.

NINE O'CLOCK BROADCAST
Even down the local pub, the landlord would turn on the wireless at the strike of nine o'clock so that people could hear Churchill's latest broadcast.

WHATEVER HAPPENED TO GLENN MILLER?

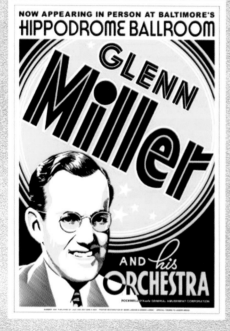

Glenn Miller, the famous bandleader, was at the peak of his career during World War Two. Despite entertaining the people at home and keeping up the morale of the troops with his music, Miller didn't feel he was pulling his weight and decided he wanted to follow his fellow bandleader, Artie Shaw, into the services. Unfortunately, at the age of thirty-eight, Miller was too old to be drafted so, after first being turned down for the Navy, chanced his luck with the Army. He was delighted to be accepted and his band played their last concert in New Jersey on 27 September 1942. Miller was assigned to the Army Specialists Corps with the rank of captain, where he created his own band with fifty players, carrying on his formidable morale boosting with his own special brand of music.

On 15 December 1944, Miller boarded a single-engined plane bound for Paris where he was to make arrangements for his band to play. Tragically, this plane never reached France and it was a mystery for several years as to what had happened as no wreckage was ever found. Later it was revealed that the RAF had been on a bombing mission to Germany that day and, as it was not possible to return with a full load of bombs on board, the planes would have released them over the English Channel. Sadly, Miller's little plane was flying below the RAF and a witness (an RAF navigator) claimed he saw a small plane crash into the sea at the time when their bombs were released.

Drinking made them feel invincible and, with a woman in their arms they could pretend everything was normal. Of course the women felt the same way, because no one really knew whether they would survive another day.

From 1942 to 1945 it is estimated that as many as half a million GIs arrived in Britain. The Yanks, as they were called, created quite a stir with the people of Britain; they simply weren't used to their culture especially as most people had never even met an American let alone heard their accent. With them, the Americans brought a whole new approach to life. Their relaxed, easy going manner and catchy phrases caught the eyes of the ladies; especially as most GIs could afford to be generous, bringing with them nylon stockings, sweets and fruit, all of which had been hard to get since the start of the war. However, most of all they introduced a whole new style of dancing. The one dance that really caught on was the Jitterbug. This was a rather lively and acrobatic form of dancing which made the previous more mundane ballroom dances seem rather boring. Everyone wanted to learn the Jitterbug and needless to say the GIs with their good looks, charm and rather bizarre ways were only too happy to teach the British women their style of dance.

WARTIME DANCE HALL
A dance event for both British and American service personnel was held at the Covent Garden Opera House in London.

It caught on quickly, and many of the more traditional British dance halls and their proprietors were horrified at this new style of dancing with its 'sexy' undertones. It wasn't long before 'No Jitterbugging' signs started to appear outside the dance halls. Signs, however, were not going to stop this new craze; it seemed everyone wanted to Jitterbug and nothing was going get in their way. The young women, in particular, loved the Jitterbug, it was a welcome break to the long hours spent in the munitions factories or working on the land. It gave them a chance to let their hair down, even if it was only for a few hours.

British dance halls were never the same again and most probably contributed to the fifty thousand women who became GI brides. The Jitterbug never really went away even when most of the Americans had returned home, it just got a new name and a less energetic style and became known as rock 'n' roll.

WARTIME CELEBRITIES

In the beginning of the war, many cinemas and attractions were closed, for fear of being destroyed by bombs that people were certain would be coming. But as time went on, and destruction didn't, many cinemas began to reopen, and going

DOING THE JITTERBUG
This move was called the Jiggerbug 'swing'.

DOWN ARGENTINE WAY
A poster for the 1940s 20th Century Fox musical romance *Down Argentine Way*, starring American actor Don Ameche, actress Betty Grable and dancer Carmen Miranda.

to the movies became a very popular pastime. In 1939 more than half of the British population were going to the cinema each week. Spending ninety minutes engrossed in Hollywood and not worrying if your house was blacked out enough, or if bombs were falling from the sky outside was sure to provide an excellent distraction. As the war progressed, the attendance figures rose. By 1945, thirty million were visiting their local cinema a week. While the cinema showed many propaganda films which boosted public morale, they also showed films from a variety of genres, giving way to a whole host of celebrities that emerged as the famous faces of the wartime.

Gone With the Wind will always be remembered as a classic of the golden age of Hollywood. Clark Gable and Vivien Leigh starred in this story of rural America during the Civil War. It was released in the United States but didn't reach London till 1940. It was first shown during the Blitz and proved so popular it was on the bill constantly for four years.

Judy Garland certainly launched her career in this era. *Wizard of Oz* debuted in cinemas in 1939 as the first film to be shot in technicolor. The adventurous and original storyline, outlandish characters and wonderfully vibrant set appealed to adults and children alike. Judy Garland went on to star in many successful films of this era, perhaps most memorably, *Meet Me in St Louis,* in 1944.

The 1940's pin-up Rita Hayworth started her career in the 1939 film *Only Angels Have Wings,* in a small, but important, role opposite Cary Grant and Jean Arthur. It was here that her fan base was established, and soon she was landing jobs alongside Fred Astaire, Joan Crawford and James Cagney.

In 1940, Hollywood heavyweights such as Henry Fonda, Betty Grable, Joan Crawford, Katherine Hepburn, Clark Gable, Ginger Rogers and Vivien Leigh ruled the silver screen. Henry Fonda was the star of many films during this period, but when the time came to enlist in the Navy he did his duty, and was quoted as saying, 'I don't want to be in a fake war in a studio'.

Betty Grable was not just admired for her acting skills, but also for her looks. Her most famous assets were her legs, insured by her studio for $1,000,000 and giving way to her nickname, 'million dollar legs'. At the peak of her box office reign, she was photographed in her swimsuit, with her hand on her hip and peering cheekily over her shoulder, cementing her status as one of the original pin-ups. This picture became popular with many GI's and is one of the enduring images of wartime celebrity.

Ginger Rogers was well known before the war for her partnership with Fred Astaire, but in 1940 the pair were fired as their studio faced bankruptcy. Rogers carried on with her career regardless and won an Academy Award for Best Actress for *Kitty Foyle* in 1941. She went on to star opposite mega stars such as Doris Day, Marilyn Monroe, Cary Grant and Ronald Reagan.

British actor David Niven worked in the United States during the 1930s as a film actor. When Britain declared war in 1939 he returned home and enlisted in the Army. In February 1940, he met British prime minister Winston Churchill at a dinner function. Niven recorded in his autobiography *The Moon's a Balloon*, that Churchill had remarked to him, 'Young man, you did a fine thing to give up your film career to fight for your country. Mark you, had you not done so – it would have been despicable.'

The very talented recording artist and actor Frank Sinatra is one of the most famous celebrities of all time. His music in particular appealed to people of all ages, especially 'bobby soxers'. This was a term coined in 1940 relating to over-zealous teenage girls who responded to Sinatra with hysteria and fainting. By the 1950s 'bobby soxers' took on a new meaning as schoolchildren practiced dancing wearing socks and no shoes, to protect the wooden floor they danced on. In 1943 Sinatra was called up to the war effort but was declared exempt from joining based on his perforated eardrum; allegedly this caused some derision amongst the general public. As they waved husbands, fathers and brothers off to war, Sinatra appeared to be constantly surrounded by beautiful women and making piles of cash. In the end, however, his reputation survived unscathed and he remains to be one of the biggest names in showbiz.

A musical contemporary of Sinatra was Glenn Miller. Miller was a musician and big band leader from 1939-1943 and toured dance halls and playhouses, keeping people dancing with his signature tunes. Sadly he met an early death when his plane crashed into the sea (see page 346).

Bing Crosby is another figure of wartime entertainment and credited with keeping GI morale up during World War Two. During the 1940s Crosby continually made box office smashes and is perhaps most loved for his classic 1942 single *White Christmas* – a staple song at any Christmas party.

CASABLANCA
Dooley Wilson, Humphrey Bogart and Ingrid Bergman star in the 1942 Warner Brothers' classic, *Casablanca*.

Casablanca was one of the biggest films of 1942. It starred Humphrey Bogart and Ingrid Bergman and interestingly was set during World War Two, facing the audience with the very situation they had gone to the cinema to avoid. It was during the 1940s that Bogart rose to stardom with several hit films such as *High Sierra* and *The Maltese Falcon*. In his 1944 film *To Have And Not Have*, at age forty-five, Bogart met his teenage girlfriend Lauren Bacall. The pair controversially married in 1945.

Swedish actress, Ingrid Bergman, became a household name following her role in *Casablanca* next to the legendary Humphrey Bogart. She was first introduced to American audiences in the English remake of *Intermezzo* in 1939. She brought with her a Nordic vitality and quickly became an American idol, a role model for many US housewives. She went on to appear in three 1940s Alfred Hitchcock movies; *Spellbound* (1945), *Notorious* (1946) and *Under Capricorn* (1949). Other starring roles included *For Whom the Bell Tolls* (1943) based on a novel by Ernest Hemingway.

CHAPTER TWELVE

VICTORY AND THE SLOW RETURN TO NORMALITY

VICTORY AND AFTER

The Allies took the war against Germany into Europe, first from North Africa into Italy and Greece, and then, in June 1944 in the great D-Day landings, from the south of England, which for months had been virtually an armed camp. In the Far East, the war against Japan also moved into a new, even more aggressive phase in 1944, with the Philippines being re-captured by the Americans in October, and Japan's mainland being bombed in November.

But the war was not yet over for Britain, either on the mainland or in the Channel Islands. Even as the Allies, advancing across northern Europe, were crossing the Rhine, Hitler unleashed his V-1 and V-2 weapons against England. It was not until 7 May 1945 that Germany, Hitler having committed suicide in his Berlin bunker, surrendered. The next day, VE Day – Victory in Europe Day – saw cheering and flag-waving crowds throughout Britain – but not in the Channel Islands, which had to wait one more day to be relieved of the German occupation, which had become increasingly harsh.

On 8 May 1945, Winston Churchill, standing on the balcony of the Ministry of Health in London, led the cheering crowd celebrating victory in Europe in a rousing rendition of 'Land of Hope and Glory'. Little did he and the government figures around him know that less than three months later he would be rejected as the nation's leader in Britain's first peacetime general election, in which the Labour Party, led by Clement Attlee, was swept into power.

So it was Clement Attlee, not Winston Churchill, who announced the absolute end of World War Two in August 1945. By the time of VJ Day – Victory over Japan Day – the world had discovered the full, dreadful horror of the Nazi death camps, and British soldiers had burnt one of them, Burgen-Belsen, to the ground in May.

Probably many who had been in that exuberantly joyful crowd outside the Ministry of Health in May were not very surprised by Labour's victory. The way in which the war had been fought by what J. B. Priestley, in one of his hugely popular *Postscripts* radio broadcasts, had called 'the organised militant citizen', had brought about a major revolution in social attitudes and expectations in Britain. Twenty-five million people, including some 1,700,000 servicemen and women, voted in the 1945 General Election, with three votes out of every five being cast against the Conservatives. No one wanted to return to the unemployment, poverty for many and class-dividing social policies of the 1930s.

Britain's working classes had become better off during the war. There had been full employment and good wages, both made possible by the dynamic interventionist policies pursued by the

WINSTON CHURCHILL BREAKS THE GOOD NEWS
The prime minister of Great Britain, Winston Churchill, makes his VE Day broadcast to the world.

government. At the same time, the appalling conditions under which too many working-class people lived, revealed by such things as the poor condition of many of the children evacuated from inner cities to the middle-class suburbs and country towns and villages, emphasised the need for a properly organised and funded welfare system.

Long before the war was over there had been much discussion about the shape that post-war British society should take. In 1941, the Board of Education had begun planning for a new education system, and a committee, chaired by a leading civil servant, William Beveridge, was set up to make a comprehensive study of existing health insurance and other social security schemes and to suggest better ways of providing these. The main concern of the Beveridge Report, which was published in December 1943, was to emphasise the necessity of creating a comprehensive policy of social progress and social security in Britain, in order to overcome the five giants:

Want
Disease

WHY DID CHURCHILL LOSE THE 1945 ELECTION?

Labour's landslide in the 1945 general election will always remain one of the greatest shocks in the history of British politics. How did Winston Churchill, probably the most popular British prime minister of all time, fail to win the election?

At the end of the war in 1954, Churchill's ratings never dropped below 83 per cent. With a few exceptions, everyone – the public and politicians alike – confidently predicted that he would lead the Conservatives to victory. As it turned out, he led them to one of their greatest ever defeats.

Despite having proved himself to be a great leader during the war, many people felt he would be ill-suited to politics during peacetime. If you like, you could say he shot himself in the foot by being a superhuman who had fulfilled an almost impossible task. This in a way had made him redundant as Churchill suddenly found himself without a clear sense of purpose or direction. Conducting the country during the war had been his over-riding passion and military victory was by far the most important of his goals. Party politics, to put it bluntly had come second on his list of priorities and this led to doubts in his ability to lead in times of peace.

Ignorance
Squalor
Idleness

Factors that kept too many people in poverty. The Report was the foundation on which the 1945 Labour government built Britain's new welfare state.

The new Labour government found itself dealing with enormous social problems in a country that many thought would never be prosperous again, so great had been the cost of fighting and winning the war. It was vital that there should be no repeat of the post-Great War failure to make Britain a land 'fit for heroes'. All returning servicemen must have jobs to go to, there must be homes for them and their families to live in, and schools to give their children a proper education.

Returning servicemen and women – brought home in manageable numbers over many months and given the demob suit or clothing to which they were entitled when returning to Civvy Street – found jobs more quickly than their fathers had after 1918. The government, still very much in dynamic directive mode, directed the return to work by dividing workers into two classes, A and B. The B workers – those who had had trades and crafts before the war that could be used again – were given jobs, using the skills they already had: once a plumber, always a plumber in immediate post-war Britain.

For those not in the B group, finding a job was not so easy. Many firms had disappeared altogether and most others needed time to get back into full peacetime production. Even so, the government could feel some satisfaction in the knowledge that by the end of 1945 some 750,000 servicemen and women were back in jobs on Civvy Street.

There were also many resettlement and training schemes, aimed at providing the extra

RETURNING TO CIVVY STREET
A British soldier is photographed after collecting his civilian clothes from the War Office
demobilisation shop at London's Olympia. He received a raincoat, shirt, tie, hat, shoes and two
pairs of socks with which to re-enter 'civvy street'.

800,000 properly trained people the government estimated they would need to get the post-war economy on the move.

One particularly effective training scheme grew out of the wartime recognition that providing Britain's children with a good education was clearly an essential element of welfare state planning: if Ignorance was not defeated, then the giant Idleness, created by unemployment and causing poverty, could not be defeated either. The intensive training scheme for teachers enabled candidates, many of whom did their study while still on army bases, to obtain a teaching diploma in one year.

Britain's schools, whose part in the education of the nation had been dramatically changed and enhanced by the 1944 Education Act, gained some 45,000 men and women teachers through the scheme.

The design of one of the special postage stamps issued to mark VE Day incorporated a dove of peace, a trowel, set square and dividers – an acknowledgement, if any were needed, that reconstruction was going to be the major problem facing the new government. As with social welfare and education, the government had recognised long before the war was over that rebuilding Britain was going to be a very

THE BEVERIDGE REPORT

There was a strong feeling among the British people after the war that they should be rewarded for their sacrifice and resolution. The British government asked Sir William Beveridge to write a report on the best ways of helping people on low incomes.

However, the Beveridge Report proposed nothing less than a revolution, involving cooperation between the state and the individual, in the way social security was provided in Britain.

The welfare state that could be said to have been born in Britain on 5 July 1948, the day when the new National Insurance Scheme and the National Health Service came into operation, developed directly out of the Beveridge Report.

big post-victory task. In 1943, Lord Woolton was moved from the Ministry of Food to head a new Ministry of Reconstruction.

It wasn't just a question of rebuilding the properties destroyed in the war and refurbishing those that had been damaged but were still habitable. It was obvious by September 1944, when official figures were published showing that 200,000 houses had been destroyed in Britain and another 4 million damaged, that it was not going to be simply a matter of replacing them. There had been two million marriages in Britain since the start of the war, and the birth rate was rising. Many more houses would have to be built after the war than had been built in an average year before it.

The government aimed to have the majority of house rebuilding carried out by local authorities. It passed a Housing Act in 1946 that guaranteed subsidies and grants for new housing, setting a target of 240,000 new homes a year. But both manpower and building materials were in very short supply in the immediate post-war years and Labour's target proved unreachable. Various alternative housing stop-gaps were employed, including temporary homes and prefabricating housing. It was not until the Conservatives were back in power – the Labour party losing the 1952 general election largely because they had failed to provide enough new housing – that housing targets were reached.

RATIONING

As for that other great wartime horror – rationing – everyone's hopes that the new government would end it as soon as possible, were quickly dashed. The post-war government had huge bills to pay, not least the one to the United States for the vast wartime Lend-lease programme. It would be some years before people could throw away their ration books and their coupons – some, such as petrol coupons, having been valuable enough to replace sixpenny bits in the wartime Christmas pudding (a surprisingly delicious variation on Lord Woolton's pie, based on carrots, spices and the brown and unlovely National Flour).

Food rationing, which had, in fact, provided many of Britain's poorer people with the first really adequate diet they had ever known, lasted the longest. Butter, margarine and fat rations had to be cut in early 1946. Within months, bread, which had remained unrationed throughout the war, was also rationed, followed by potatoes (also unrationed during the war) in November 1947. These rationings were caused partly by a world-wide food shortage and partly by poor harvests that followed a very cold winter in 1946–47. The stopping of the United State's Lend-Lease programme, two days after VJ Day in August 1945, had not helped the food situation, either, with American dried-egg powder among the ingredients suddenly no longer available.

Women greeted peace in 1945 with a reaction that mixed relief and a certain cynicism. What was there to celebrate in a country heavily damaged by war and marked by austerity and exhaustion? As Nella Last noted in her diary, even the announcement by Stuart Hibbard on the BBC's Home Service that 8 May 1945 would be celebrated as Victory in Europe Day came as something of a damp squib – 'What a FLOP!'. And what were the rosettes and tri-coloured buttonholes in the shop windows all about? But, 'we must celebrate somehow,' thought Mrs Last, so she went into her kitchen, put the kettle on, and looked into the cupboard.

'I'll open this tin of pears.' And she did.

ON THE WAY HOME
Soldiers returning from Europe after D-Day, on a London underground train.

Nella Last was right to be careful about the contents of her kitchen cupboard, even when celebrating victory. Food rationing was to last in Britain for another nine years. For a time, it even became more severe, partly because of a worldwide shortage of basic foods and grains, and partly because the winter of 1946–7 was exceptionally severe and led to poor harvests. The ending of the American Lend-Lease programme after VJ Day in August 1945, by which time there had been a General Election which had swept the Labour Party, led by Clement Attlee, into power, meant that there were no more shipments of such useful foods as dried eggs and dried milk coming into Britain.

The government could not be blamed for bringing Lend-Lease to an end as quickly as possible, as the scheme had to be paid for and was expensive, but its ending did add in the short term to the country's food problems. One way of helping relieve the problems was to keep the Women's Land Army hard at work for another five years. The WLA stood down at the end of 1950, their last duty being a ceremonial parade at Buckingham Palace, where they were reviewed by Queen Elizabeth. The queen let it be known that she felt the parade had been a fitting climax to the notable history of the Women's Land Army. The government did not make any special pension available for Land Girls, however.

Early in 1946 the amounts of the butter, margarine and fat rations had to be reduced. And in the summer, bread, which had remained unrationed (even if of poor quality) throughout the war had to be rationed in July, and was not de-rationed again until 1948. In November 1947, it was the turn of potatoes, which also had not been rationed before, to be added to the still long list of foods for which the house-wife had to find ration coupons. A year later, the food situation took a turn for the better, when the President of the Board of Trade, the future prime minister Harold Wilson, made a root and branch attack on the food controls that had built up since 1940.

Furniture rationing was ended in the summer of 1948, however, it was not until 1953, the year of the new queen's coronation, that the last of the war's furniture restrictions were lifted. In 1946, a continuing lack of materials and workers to make furniture led the government to continue

PLEASE SIR, I WANT SOME MORE!
These children are eager to get their four-ounce allowance of sweets.

POST-WAR RATIONING

GOODS	ALLOWANCE
Bacon and ham	2 oz per person a fortnight
Cheese	1½ oz a week
Butter/margarine	7 oz a week
Cooking fats	2 oz a week
Meat	1s worth a week
Sugar	8 oz a week
Tea	2 oz a week
Chocolates and sweets	4 oz a week
Eggs	No fixed ration
	1 egg for each ration book when available
Liquid milk	3 pints a week
Preserves	4 oz a week
Points–rationed food	4 points per week

Also rationed:
Bread
Soap
Bananas
Potatoes

REGISTER HERE
FOR ALL
RATIONED
FOODS
GOOD STOCKS
AND
Fair Distribution
of Unrationed Articles
ASK
SATISFIED CUSTOMERS

BREAD QUEUES
Queues outside a bakery in Streatham High Street, London, on the last day before bread rationing is introduced.

its restrictions on furniture making. At the same time, the range of Utility furniture made was widened, and the restrictions on its sale were relaxed. Now everyone could buy it, provided they had coupons and points. It was finally phased out, but only after a full-scale debate about it in Parliament. The Conservatives, back in government after the 1951 General Election, had wanted to get rid of this vestige of wartime socialism, but Labour MPs had hoped to retain it. Since Utility furniture had been solid and well-designed, and was exempted from Purchase Tax, its departure from the scene was something of a mixed blessing.

Perhaps of greater interest to all women than the lifting of restrictions on food and furniture was the date for when they could throw away their clothes ration books. Even Queen Elizabeth and her daughters had clothes ration books: when Princess Elizabeth married Prince Philip, Duke of Edinburgh, in November 1947, she had to save coupons to buy the material for her wedding dress.

Women were very tired of their increasingly dreary looking wartime wardrobe, with its pared down fabric content, its few decorative features and its mean use of buttons, pleats and generous lapels. When the French designer Christian

EVEN ROYALTY NEEDED COUPONS
Even Queen Elizabeth II was not exempt from rationing. When she married Prince Philip, Duke of Edinburgh, in November 1947, she had to save coupons to buy the material for her wedding dress.

CHRISTIAN DIOR

Christian Dior, without doubt, was the most influential designer of the late 1940s and dominated the fashion industry after World War Two with his stunning 'New Look'. His name was recognised in all the far corners of the world and his label accounted for half of France's haute couture exports.

At the end of the war his client list included A-list stars such as Ava Gardner and Marlene Dietrich to royalty such as Princess Margaret and the Duchess of Windsor. Despite being desperately shy, Dior was courted by Parisian society.

At the beginning of the war, Dior served as an officer until France surrendered. He temporarily worked for his father and sister on a farm in Provence until he was offered a job in Paris by a leading couturier, Lucien Lelong. Lelong was working with the Germans to try and revive the couture trade, and Dior spent the war years dressing the wives of Nazi officers and French collaborators.

At the end of the war clothes were in short supply, which left Dior with ample opportunities to enter into a new business venture. He convinced everyone that his luxurious new look which showed off a woman's silhouette was the way forward.

Dior sent his New Look clothes down the catwalk in Paris in 1947, British women were astonished and delighted at the length of New Look coats, skirts and dresses, the extravagance of the amount of material used, and the frivolity of its buttons and bows, its hats and its shoes. The Board of Trade was aghast. It could not allow the provision of the materials needed to produce such clothes. British women had to wait another two years for clothes rationing to be ended, in October 1949.

HOW WOMEN ACHIEVED THE NEW LOOK

The New Look gave women back their waists and their own shoulder lines and put them in clothes with long sleeves set in tight armholes and ankle-length skirts requiring yards of fabric. There were rows of buttons, and plenty of decoration in the form of sequins, lace, beads and embroidery. Fashion designer Christian Dior was the answer to women's prayers, and his New Look that was far removed from the utility wear and military uniforms that predominated the war years, dominated the fashion world for about ten years.

Elegantly designed hats were back and shoes had fine, elegant lines and slim, high heels. Still hampered by clothes rationing, women adapted what they had in the wardrobe, or turned, once again, to the precious fabric in old curtains. Skirts were lengthened by adding panels of a contrasting material, often from another, older garment, and, if the skirt was part of a suit, then its jacket – its shoulder pads ripped out – might have had its collars and cuffs covered with the

NEW LOOK DRESSES
A teenager tries on a dress with the new post-war longer length skirt and pinched-in waist, inspired by designer Christian Dior.

THE BUTLER EDUCATION ACT

The Education Act of 1944, usually called the Butler Education Act, after R. A. Butler, president of the Board of Education, raised the school-leaving age to fifteen. It also provided free education for all children, following selection at the age of eleven, in three different types of school – grammar, secondary modern and technical. It was hoped that these choices would accommodate children of all different levels.

The Act also incorporated other benefits established as part of the developing family welfare system. These benefits included free school milk and subsidised school meals service for all children, regardless of their parents' income.

same contrasting material. The waists of dresses were nipped in and old corsets dragged back into use to achieve the tiny, almost Victorian, waist size the style required.

Some servicewomen even re-used the corsets that had, to their horror, been given to them as part of their uniform kit when they first joined the services.

FROM A CHILD'S POINT OF VIEW

The sense among many people that Britain was fighting a losing war, widespread in the first two or three years, gave place to a guarded optimism once the RAF had begun seriously to attack the German industrial heartland and once America, catapulted into the war by the Japanese attack on Pearl Harbor in December 1941, was suddenly 'over here' in large, confident numbers, giving sweets to children, cap badges to boys and shampoo and silk stockings to their older sisters.

Children at play in the counties of southern England soon began to notice how a huge army was taking shape around them. Eight-year-old Janet Foord, playing in the woods round her home in Epsom, Surrey, watched the woods becoming increasingly filled with soldiers, their equipment and the tents in which many of the soldiers lived. The Allies were amassing a great invasion force, hiding it from German surveillance planes in every wood and under every large tree in southern England – or so it seemed to Janet and her friends.

When D-Day eventually came and the invasion of Europe began in June 1944, Janet and everyone else at school thought the war would be over soon. In fact, for children like her, living in the counties surrounding London, the war was to get every bit as dangerous as it had been for years past, as the Germans unleashed their V1 and V2 weapons on Britain. The immediate result of the V-weapons attack was another, albeit quite small, evacuation from the cities in the firing line.

Long before the rocket attacks had ended, those mothers and children who had spent years as evacuees, began to return home in considerable numbers, even to homes that were in cities very much in the V-weapons' line of fire. In many towns, officially organised de-evacuation schemes began in December 1944; soon hundreds of women and children were on the move, in trains organised by local councils, from 1939 Reception Areas back to what had been the Evacuation Areas at the outbreak of war.

In the south of England and in the industrial Midlands, where local councils tried to organise 'official' returns only for those evacuees for whom accommodation was available, de-evacuation plans were complete by March 1945. In London, where the public shelters were closed and the bunks taken out of the Underground in April, as many as eight dispersal points were set up, at which arrivals would be fed and given a great welcome. In the event, most of the de-evacuation trains, organised by the 1500 local authorities who had received telegrams telling them to 'operate London return plans' on 2 May, arrived half-empty because people had already de-evacuated themselves and their children.

Even the Channel Islands, still officially in German hands, began to welcome their children home from late autumn, 1944. More than one

---

VICTORY V CAPS
Children wearing skull caps adorned with the Victory V sign (donated by the British War Relief Society of America) at the Stoughton Nursery School in Guildford.

VICTORY PARTY
Children sit down to a victory party at a V-shaped table which was donated by residents at
Kentwell Close, Brockley, in south London.

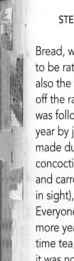

STEPS TO DE-RATIONING

Bread, which was the last food to be rationed in Britain, was also the first food to be taken off the ration, in July 1948. It was followed at the end of the year by jam, marmalade (often made during the War from a concoction based on apples and carrots, with not an orange in sight), syrup and treacle. Everyone had to wait nearly four more years for another food, this time tea, to be de-rationed, and it was not until February 1953 that the food every child, and most adults, had been waiting for, sweets, came off the ration. Photographs of children queuing eagerly outside sweets shops appeared in the newspapers, and there were a few more seven months later when sugar was de-rationed. It was not until July 1954 that ration books could be thrown away, when meat was the last food to be de-rationed.

Channel Islands evacuee returned home with their names written in large letters on their suitcase or bag; their foster parents, seeing how much the child had changed and grown in the five years since leaving home, thoughtfully gave their birth parents a chance of recognising their children, from whom there had been no photographs and very little communication at all since they had waved them off in 1940. For some weeks, returning evacuees to the Channel Islands had to live on Red Cross parcels, so bad was the availability of food in the islands.

Eventually, back in Britain, the rocket attacks stopped, the Allies reached Berlin, and the second world war of the twentieth century was over. The first great celebration came on VE (Victory in Europe) Day, 8 May 1945; then, on 14/15 August 1945, VJ Day celebrated the end of hostilities in Japan and the Far East.

For Britain's children, celebrating the great victory often took the form of street parties, with the children gathered round tables brought out from houses up and down the street. Every mother would either make a dish for the party or provide a precious pot of jam, something from their tea ration or even a pat of butter or fat that could be used to bake cakes, jam or lemon tarts and biscuits. Marguerite Patten recalls being told by children that they ate ice cream for the first time in their lives at a Victory street party.

It was a great shock to many when, once the bells had stopped ringing and the flags and bunting had been taken down after the Victory Celebrations, there was very little relaxation of many of the wartime rules and regulations. Most vexatious of all was the fact that food rationing, so far from being ended, was continued and even increased.

In September 1946, a full year after the war's end, photographs of Aberdeen schoolboy Martin Wagrel's mother filled the front page of the local newspaper, the *Weekly Journal*, photographed as she did her daily shopping, the family's ration books (including Martin's) in her shopping basket. Sited centrally on the page is the inevitable photograph of Mrs Wagrel standing

NOT QUITE OVER!

Huge crowds had gathered outside Buckingham Palace wearing patriotic red, white and blue. As the King, Queen and two young princesses stepped out on to the balcony, a huge cheer could be heard resonating around London.

Earlier tens of thousands of people had listened intently as the King's speech was relayed to people who had gathered in Trafalgar Square and Parliament Square.

Winston Churchill had also made a broadcast to the nation and as only the great man could, informed everyone that the war was finally over. In his speech he paid tribute to the men and women who had lost their lives for their country as well as those who had fought valiantly on land, sea and air.

He said, reminding his people that there was still work to be done, 'We may allow ourselves a brief period of rejoicing; but let us not forget for a moment the toil and efforts that lie ahead ... We must now devote all our strength and resources to the completion of our task, both at home and abroad.'

But people wanted to celebrate, to them it was all over, and they converged on some of London's great monuments which had been specially floodlit for the occasion. There were fireworks and effigies of Hitler burned on bonfires all around the capital.

in a long queue outside a shop. The caption under every other photograph tells whether Mrs Wagrel must use points or coupons to buy the food, whether it is rationed or not and – perhaps most significant, how its price compares with what it was a few years before – badly, of course, with the cost of one day's supply of greens for the family being the same as a week's supply, 'time was'.

While food, its rationing and availability was a long-term, post-war problem, of much more immediate concern to children in the weeks and months after the war was the emotional problems that all too often arose when father returned. Although the government had been planning for demobilisation since late 1942, hoping to avoid the economic and social problems that had bedevilled the country after 1918, it was impossible to plan for the emotional turmoil that could be aroused in a child when a long-absent father came home. As Janet Foord remembers, as an only child she had had her mother's undivided attention during the war. 'I felt very jealous of my father when he came home on leave – and when he came home for good.'

In Janet's case, the jealousy subsided quite quickly – helped a little by the fact that her wartime request for a bicycle, always greeted with the stock reply, 'After the war...', was now answered and she got a new bike. But for many children, less well-circumstanced than Janet's family, or perhaps bombed out from their homes, the reality of their father's return was made worse by the fact that jobs and housing were both in short supply.

LICKING LOLLIPOPS
Three London children enjoy the thrill of purchasing lollipops as the Hackney sweetshop is well stocked with sweets as rationing becomes a thing of the past.

HEADLINE NEWS
British newspapers headline the end of sweet rationing, extra petrol for summer, lights on again in England, off-coupon day in London stores, cheaper railway fares and other welcome news.

BUILDING A NEW BRITAIN

The assertion by the Minister of Labour, Ernest Bevin, at the height of the War in 1943 that the one way to stop moral and social disaster after the War was to build enough houses for every family, could not be acted upon with any speed until the War was over. Planning for the future could start, however, and resulted in 1944 in the passing of the Town and Country Planning Act. The purpose of the Act was two-fold: to replace the housing destroyed in the Blitz and after, and to make the country's towns and cities fine places to live in, with plenty of green, open spaces. The New Towns Act of 1946 brought in the concept of 'New Towns', either completely new or built as satellites of existing towns. The first new town in Britain was Stevenage in Hertfordshire, which got the go-ahead in November 1946.

PREFABRICATED HOUSING

Many a father returned home to be greeted by his family, bombed-out from the house he had left them in, at the door of a 'pre-fab' – a factory-built, pre-fabricated house that was supposed to be replaced within years, if not months, by something more permanent, but which was quite likely to be still lived in for years. Despite committees and mid-war planning, the country returned to peacetime industry very slowly, so that building new houses – and providing the jobs to do the building – took a long time to get going.

Added to the shortage of houses there was a population boom in the 1940s, which meant another two million houses were needed by the end of the decade. The prefab was a answer to this problem, albeit a temporary one. They could be erected in three hours, slotting together prepared walls and roofs made from metal and wood. Some were even built using old aircraft wings. Despite their temporary nature, prefab houses were very popular. Having lost their permanent homes in the war, families were delighted to live somewhere that provided them with running water, inside bathrooms and electric cookers – things which many families had never experienced before the onset of war. Many also had large gardens in which to grow vegetables, especially important as rationing carried on well into the 1950s.

While people lived in relative luxury in their temporary prefabs, the councils were busy building three quarters of a million more traditional brick houses. To make way for these houses many bomb damaged houses had to be demolished as well as several large houses that had not been damaged to make way for the big, new estates. Because of the concern of the number of houses being knocked down, the introduction of 'listing' buildings came about in 1947. This meant that any building that had an

A CAUSE FOR CELEBRATION
Revellers marking the end of World War Two in Europe.

PREFABRICATED HOUSING

Workmen quickly construct a new estate of prefabricated houses in Watford, Hertfordshire, to help alleviate the shortage of homes after the devastation of the war. Opposite, children play happily outside their new prefab home.

interesting architecture of history behind it had to be preserved. At the turn of the century, high rise flats became a common sight on the horizon as land was at a premium. At first, this high-rise style of living was popular, but gradually its popularity dropped particularly when part of a large block – Ronan Point – collapsed in 1968.

Today, to cope with the demand for houses, prefabs are coming back into vogue; but this time they are being built to last. These homes are quick and relatively cheap to build and are of the highest quality. Perhaps the innovation of the war years could well be the homes of the future.

The same issue of Aberdeen's *Weekly Journal* that had followed Martin Wagrel's mother on her shopping expedition in September 1946 also reported on the Town Council's efforts to house the 150 'most necessitous cases' among the many homeless families in Aberdeen. 'They will be moved into Hayton Camp – one of the main war-time training depots in the town – just as soon as the Army moves out.... Electric light, water, cooking and washing facilities are to be laid on, and it is believed that the new homes will be better than what is being occupied in many parts of the city at present.'

While it would be a long time before every family in the country was properly housed, the first steps in the provision of what the Beveridge Report, back in 1942, had called a 'security net' for all, were taken. In June 1945, one of the last acts of the war-time government, now a 'Caretaker' government led by Winston Churchill, brought in the Family Allowances system, starting with the payment to families of five shillings (25 pence) a week for every child after the first one. In the following month, Churchill's Conservative government was defeated by the Labour Party in the first General Election since the war began.

Thus, the creation of Britain's Welfare State, planned in the midst of war, was firmly begun in the first weeks of peace. On the whole, Britain's parents could be justified in hoping for a better world for their children. As for the children of the war years themselves, they can look back on what Janet Foord remembers as the fun and enjoyment of the 1950s. The pretty young princess who had talked to them on the *Children's Hour* programme during the war and had still managed to look lovely both in her ATS uniform as she helped repair Army trucks in 1945 and as she walked down the aisle of Westminster Abbey at her wedding in 1947, was now Queen Elizabeth II.

People were talking about a New Elizabethan Age – there was even a new, glossy magazine for girls called *New Elizabethan*, children had got unrationed sweets back, even if only a couple of months before the new queen's coronation, which took place in June 1953, and there were lots more attractive clothes for children and young people in the shops. There were 'bobby-soxers' in America and quite soon there would be a totally new kind of older children called 'teenagers' everywhere. The war years would soon become just a memory – and not an all bad one.

The contribution of Britain's women to the war effort from 1939 to 1945 and in the immediate post-war years went largely unrecognised for decades. First to get any sort of recognition was the WVS, for which well over a million women had worked during the war. In November 1947, the Home Secretary confirmed that the valuable work the WVS had done throughout the war was still very much needed, and in 1966 it was renamed the Woman's Royal Voluntary Service in acknowledgement of the good work it was doing (and still does), especially in hospitals and among the elderly.

A MEMORIAL TO WOMEN
The Women of World War II memorial in Whitehall, London.

INDEX